William Shakespeare's
Julius Caesar

Shyam S. Agarwalla

ATLANTIC
PUBLISHERS & DISTRIBUTORS (P) LTD

Published by

ATLANTIC

PUBLISHERS & DISTRIBUTORS (P) LTD

7/22, Ansari Road, Darya Ganj,
New Delhi-110002
Phones : +91-11-40775252, 23273880, 23275880, 23280451
Fax : +91-11-23285873
Web : www.atlanticbooks.com
E-mail : orders@atlanticbooks.com

Branch Office
5, Nallathambi Street, Wallajah Road,
Chennai-600002
Phones : +91-44-64611085, 32413319
E-mail : chennai@atlanticbooks.com

Printed in India at Glorious Printers, A-13, D.S.I.D.C.,
Jhilmil Industrial Area, Delhi-110095

PREFACE

Indian students, by and large, are served with half-backed studies of Shakespeare, tempting them to move towards a winding garden-path, which, when reached, turns out to be the wood, mazing and meandering, crossing and criss-crossing, leading to nowhere.

I have tried to leaf through all important editions and criticisms on *Julius Caesar* and to present a maintainable and sustainable account of William Shakespeare in general and *Julius Ceasar* in particular so that Indian students, preparing for their examinations, find it less woody and more leafy. I claim no originality. At best it is a mixture of thorough research and good amalgamation. It will be useful for the students of English literature.

Reasoned disagreement or advice or suggestion is always a source of help that an author can receive. Even when it cannot be accepted immediately, it may, in future, induce further elucidation.

I owe a sense of gratitude to my wife, Satyabhama, to my sons, Pawan and Lalit, and to my daughters, Sunita and Sangita who bore with me patiently.

I thank Dr. K.R. Gupta, Honorary Advisor, Atlantic Publishers & Distributors (P) Ltd. for the interest evinced in publishing this book.

SHYAM S. AGARWALLA

CONTENTS

C. The Characters

D. Discussion of Important Critical Opinions

PART II

PART III

PART I

A. INTRODUCTION

Life and Works of William Shakespeare

William Shakespeare was 'the Warwickshire Wonder', a wonder unsurpassed and unrivalled in the realm of literature. "The Wonder, as we see it now, is simply this : that no writer of any land or age has ever had popularity and renown on such a colossal and astounding scale. There is no civilized, or even faintly civilized, nation which does not read, study, perform, salute (and actually enjoy) the works of William Shakespeare. Even the warmest admirers of 'Sweet Mr. Shakespeare' in his own day could have had no conception whatever of the renown and even worship which their gentle hero was to win" (Ivor Brown, *Shakespeare*, The Reprint Society, London, 1951, p. 14).

This gentle hero, William Shakespeare, was born in Stratford-on-Avon in Warwickshire on 22 or 23 April 1564 and christened on April 26. Except for hearsay and conjecture nothing more is known of this infant until we reach the tangled affair of his wedding in November 1582. Dr. Nirad C. Chaudhuri wrote to his family about modern Stratford: "Stratford is a small town, smaller than Kishorganj (Bangladesh) of my boyhood. But it has all kinds of old and modern China, antiques, old and modern silver, furniture and books. Of course, Stratford flourishes on Shakespeare, and even Englishmen say everything at Stratford is commercialized. But in order to make Shakespeare commercially successful you must have a sufficiently strong interest in him". (Nirad C. Chaudhuri, *A Passage to England*, Orient Paperbacks, New Delhi, pp. 148-149). His father, John Shakespeare, appears to have been a wool merchant and a trusted citizen of the little town. Probably he was a Catholic, and there is a likelihood that his third son William Shakespeare was also trained in the Catholic faith. His mother, Mary Arden, came of a good country family of Saxon and Norman descent.

While it is traditional to say that he received his education at the local grammar school, there are no proofs. The chances are that he did go to school. Where else would he go? His father, though a prominent citizen and reasonably prosperous, at least during Shakespeare's boyhood, would not disdain the free education there offered. There is no reason to think that Shakespeare enjoyed his school days. The lessons were dull, the discipline severe. The journey towards the desk is several times described as slow and sad. 'Creeping like snail unwillingly to school' and 'Toward school with heavy looks' a familiar to all.

In school he may have picked up enough to distinguish one letter from another, and arrange two or more letters in consecutive order to make occasional spelling sense, but he does not seem to have imbibed much of the classics. Latin and Greek were compulsory then, but Shakespeare's unstead walk when alluding to classical sources, myths and stories, stresses the argument that he loved the poetry in a fable more than its authenticity and fidelity to detail.

When he reached the age of eighteen and a half he was again in the records of ecclesiastical information. On November 27, 1582, an entry was made in the episcopal register at Worcester. This set sown the issue of a marriage licence to William Shaxpere and Anne Whateley of Temple Grafton. But a controversy had arisen whether Shakespeare married a Anne Whateley or a Anne Hathaway. But if Hathaway grave-stone in Stratford Parish Church bears a correct inscription we know at least that she was eight years older than her husband. She outlived him by seven years, died on 6 August, and was buried on 8 August 1623, exactly three months before his immortality was assured by the publication of the First Folio of his plays. The statement of her age, 67, is definite.

Two more certain facts are known about William and Anne Shakespeare before the former turns up in London and is mentioned in connexion with playhouse wrangles and the jealousies of the poets in 1592. Of the two hidden years we know this, that a daughter of the couple, Susanna, was baptised on 26 May, 1583, and that twins followed. 'Hamnet and Judeth, sonne and daughter to William Shakespeare', were entered as baptised in Stratford on 2 February, 1585. As there is no record of any subsequent children, one may presume that relations between him and his wife got increasingly cold, and, possibly leaving his wife at Stratford, he decided to walk to London in 1585, in the hope of making more money than was possible in his home town. J.D. Wilson asserts, "In any case — to nail one more slander to the counter — there is no ground whatever for imagining that his married life was an unhappy one, which is not the same thing as saying that he himself was a model husband."

"There is the well-known story of Shakespeare having had to fly away from Stratford because he was too severely prosecuted by Sir Thomas Lucy whose park he had robbed. Several years later when comfortably settled in London, he made a pointless and somewhat unsavoury joke about a dozen 'luces' in Sir Robert Shallow's old coat (*The Merry Wives of Windsor*, I. i. 17-18). The very pointlessness of the joke creates a presumption that the story of the poaching has some foundation in fact" (Dr. S.C. Sengupta, A Shakespeare Manual, O.U. P., p. 23).

It is, however, generally supposed, though without any sure ground, that Shakespeare left Stratford in or about 1596. 'The Queen's Players' paid a visit to Stratford in 1587. It is said by some that this was probably the turning point in Shakespeare's life.

Life in London. Here fancy has vastly enjoyed itself in making Shakespeare school master, lawyer, soldier, sailor, poacher, tippler, theatrical call-boy and holder of horses for the play-going gentry. None of these conjectures about Shakespeare's hidden years need be exclusive. But it is certain that in London Shakespeare quickly got into touch with the rising theatre. Three Warwickshire men, one of them from Stratford, were already prominent among the players. One of these, Richard Burbage, became his special companion. He soon proved a better hand at arranging plays than at acting in them. For strangely enough, Shakespeare never excelled as an actor. He became a member of the Earl of Leicester's company of actors, which on the accession of James I became "the King's Company". Beginning by touching up old plays, he proceeded to put more and more of himself into them and before long he had surpassed all the University Wits as a playwright. His growing popularity led Robert Greene to write *Groatsworth of Wit* in London in 1592. He referred to "an upstart Crow, beautified with our feathers, that with his *Tygers hart wrapt in a Player's hyde*, supposes he is as well able to bombast out a blank verse as the best of you : and beeing an absolute *Johannes fac totum*, is in his own conceit the only Shake-scene in a country." There is little doubt that this refers to Shakespeare, as the parody *Tygers hart wrapt in a Player's hyde* is based on a line in 3 Henry VI, I, iv. At the close of 1592 Henry Chettle, another of the playhouse tribe, apologized in his *Kind-Harts Dreame* for Greene's offensive diatribe on the fraternity of play-makers. Ivon Brown asserts, "From this it is plain that by the end of 1592 Shakespeare was an up-and-coming dramatist and theatre-worker, jealously resented by some for his energy and ability, strongly commended by others (and those of rank) for his integrity of life and for his command of wit and grace in composition . . . The young man was already climbing socially."

Though he had written certainly not less than six plays by 1593, none saw print, and none were recorded or acted. On the 18th of April, the next year, however, his poems *Venus and Adonis* was recorded as one to see print soon. It was the only work of his he saw through the press. It was dedicated to Henry Wriothesly, Earl of Southampton, and there is suspicion that Shakespeare may have had relations with him which society would consider unconventional and even immoral. But the dedication leaves little doubt that Shakespeare had attached and won the court by 1593, and that he was slowly moving in the company of wits and fops and dandies – all of whom he would utilize to great advantage in the plays that were to follow.

The playhouse with which tradition connects him was called "The Theatre", and was built by a player and joiner, James Burbage, in 1577, in the fields outside the City Walls, on the west of Bishopsgate Street, in Shoreditch. In 1598, it was pulled down and in 1599 rebuilt as "The Globe," on Bankside, Southwalk. In 1596 his son Hamnet died, and it was in this year that his father John Shakespeare, who had been financially at a loose end, applied, obviously with the poet's assistance, for a coat of arms.

His publications. There are three factors governing the development of Shakespeare's work. "The first is economic, the second is professional, the third is personal. He wrote for himself, as a professional theatre-worker with an eye to a competence, in friendship and finance, from first to last: and he wrote as a man of feeling, intensely susceptible to beauty, to passion and to nature, easily and overwhelmingly horrified by the bestiality of man, and yet easily restored to calm and happiness by 'a fancy from a flower-bell'. If we bear these three traits and conditions in mind, we shall better understand the various ages of men" (Ivor Brown, *Ibid.*, pp. 169-170).

Seven Ages of the Man

(After Ivor Brown, Shakespeare, 1951)

Age one:

Henry VI, Parts 1, 2, 3.

Titus Andronicus

The Comedy of Errors

Richard III

The Two Gentlemen of Verona

Age Two: 1592-3 to 1596

Venus and Adonis

Lucrece

The Early Sonnets

Love's Labour's Lost

Romeo and Juliet

A Midsummer Night's Dream

The Merchant of Venice

Age Three : 1596 to 1599 (Historical Plays)

King John

Richard II

Henry IV, Parts 1, 2

Henry V

Age Four : 1598-1600

Much Ado About Nothing

The Merry Wives of Windsor

As You Like It

Twelfth Night

Shakespeare was only thirty-six when all this was accomplished. Then, with the turn of the century, there was a turn of temper too. So we pass from the fourth Age of High-fantastical to the Fifth Age, that of Bitter Comedy. They are :

All's Well that Ends Well

Troilus and Cressida

Measure for Measure

The Sixth Age of Shakespeare records the Dark Vision amid which comedy at last becomes impossible and only the blackest tragedy will suffice for his beating mind. This Age of the Dark Vision lasted nearly ten years.

The pieces of this Age are :

Julius Caesar
Hamlet
Othello
Macbeth
King Lear
Timon of Athens
Antony and Cleopatra

Now we reach the last phase of all, which may be described as Fancy Free. It yielded from 1608-13,

Pericles
Cymbeline
The Winter's Tale
The Tempest
Henry VIII.

Last Years of Shakespeare

In London he passed through his many moods of infatuation, passion, ecstasy, humiliation, despair, and calm. But all the time he was a man of property. By 1596 Shakespeare was in a position to press for both status and estate. In 1597 he paid William Underhill £ 60 for the principal house in Stratford, New Place, built by Sir Hugh Clopton more than a century before. To this august house Shakespeare returned later in life; it remained in the family until the death of his grand daughter, Lady Barnard, in 1670. Then, a letter from Abraham Sturley, Chamberlain of Stratford, mentioned that in the opinion of Quiney's father their countryman, Master Shakespeare, was 'willing to disburse some money upon some odd yard-land or other at Shottery or near about us'. In the Stratford Corporation records it is also set down that William Shakespeare was the holder of ten quarters of corn in Chapel Street Ward, in which lies New Place.

Shakespeare was by now regarded in Stratford as the man to whom to turn for a little capital. So much for Stratford. Shakespeare's London property was for a long time in theatrical shares. He never set up house there. Apart from his shares in theatres Shakespeare's only investment in London was the purchase in 1613 from Henry Walker of the Gatehouse, Blackfriars, near the playhouse in which he was then much interested.

Whether Shakespeare had affairs or not, he was a family man at Stratford and a thrifty man in London. He loved his garden and he loved his acres. Had he, in the company of his 'steady', quoted the happy words of his own Sly in the last months at Stratford :

> Come, madam wife, sit by my side and let the world slip,
> We shall ne'er be younger.

He died on 23 April, 1616 after a short illness, brought on, it is said, by his too liberal entertainment of his friend and rival Ben Jonson and another visitor.

Critical Estimate of William Shakespeare as a Poet and a Dramatist

Dr. S.C. Sengupta writes, "Today Shakespeare's is possibly the most formidable name all over the world. You may call yourself a Newton or a Napoleon but not a Shakespeare, at least not a William Shakespeare, except at your own peril. There is a story that a gentleman one day arrived at a hotel, and when asking for accommodation, gave his name as William Shakespeare. The officials looked puzzled, detained him and informed the police, and when he insisted on saying that his name was, indeed, William Shakespeare, a wag retorted, 'Well, if you are William Shakespeare, then I am Queen Elizabeth!' I cannot say if the story is authentic, but it is true in the sense that it gives a fair idea of Shakespeare's hold on people's minds" (Dr. S.C. Sengupta, *A Shakespeare Manual*, Oxford University Press, 1982, p. 1).

S.T. Coleridge sums up Shakespeare's art, "Shakespeare first studied patiently, meditated deeply, understood minutely, till knowledge, became habitual and intuitive, wedded itself to his habitual feelings, and at length gave birth to that stupendous power, by which he stands alone, with no equal or second in his own class" (S.T. Coleridge, *Biographia Literaria*, Ch. 15).

Myriad-minded Shakespeare's plays are bountiful. "Green fields and sunshine and purling brooks; men and women of every class; fairies, spirits, and strange monsters; crowded cities and storm-tossed seas — all are there. We drink in nature as we read his words; his characters are our intimate acquaintances; we quote Shakespeare without knowing it, so thoroughly have his wise and witty sayings become part of our language" (Haynes).

In modern age, lawyers have claimed that he was of their tribe; whereas the large number of medical terms in his works have led people to hazard the guess that he might have been a doctor. It has been said both as a merit and as a effect that Shakespeare had no philosophy and yet one after another all the philosophies have been discovered in him. Bernard Shaw complained of the lack of religion in his plays, and yet he is the greatest product of the Protestant Reformation and the Tudor religious settlement. But Catholics have claimed him as one of their fold and their claim is based on the semi-authoritative assertion of the Rev Richard Davies that he 'dyed a Papist'.

Matthew Arnold describes him, "Others abide our questions, Thou art free". Shakespeare created a Hamlet, a man of indecision and also created a Macbeth, a man of decision. Shakespeare, unlike Valmiki and Tulsidas, believed that no man is complete in himself. His characters, therefore, are reflections of strengths and weaknesses of a full man. This was possible because Shakespeare was the product of the English Renaissance. This Renaissance showed that a man is neither wholly good nor wholly bad. Circumstances make him either good or bad. In the light of this Renaissance, man had come to know that he was less wise, more feelingful.

In the light of the above-mentioned observations, we can evaluate Shakespeare critically as a playwright and a poet.

We shall proceed first to examine Shakespeare as a poet, for it has been rightly observed that "he was a poet before he was a dramatist". His plays are remarkable for their genuinely poetical qualities, a fact which can be at once realized by comparing a Shakespearean play with any play of a modernist, say, Bernard Shaw. His ideal of poetry has been admirably set forth in the well-known lines of *A Mid-Summer Night's Dream*:

> "The poet's eye, in a fine frenzy rolling,
> Doth glance from heaven to earth, from earth to heaven;
> And as imagination bodies forth
> The forms of things unknown, the poet's pen
> Turns them to shapes and gives to airy nothing
> A local habitation and a name."

Shakespeare's own works are a beautiful commentary on these lines. He wrote on endlessly varied topics; but throughout the whole range of his writings breathe forth the ideals created by his own imagination. The men and women which people his dramatic world are ideal types of humanity that work towards the uplift and elevation of mankind. Shakespeare the man presents a contrast to Shakespeare the poet. In the ordinary walk of life he was a plain man, with an imperfect education — "Small Latin and less Greek'' (as Ben Jonson has characterized it in his malice) who wrote copiously for the stage, accumulated a fortune, bought an estate and was ambitious of founding a family and died in prosperity and honour. But the poet Shakespeare, the author of *Hamlet, Othello, Macbeth, King Lear* etc., is a being of far different order. Not all the books in the British Museum could make him a wiser man. Srichandra Sen writes, "Once I compiled a list of flora and fauna in Wordsworth and great was my surprise to discover the paucity of his references. He mentions far too few trees and flowers by name and his fauna is too meagre .... Compared with Wordsworth, Shakespeare is a veritable encyclopaedia of knowledge in this sphere. He seems to know every tree, plant and flower — he knows their shape, form and smell. And his songs make the landscape of flowers and forest trees alive and breathing. How miraculously he invests these with voice and personality, how miraculously they sing their songs! He gives a picture of Merry England which not a thousand volumes can rival'' (Srichandra Sen, *Arnold on Shakespeare*, University of Calcutta, 1981, p. 13).

As far the social life at the highest level or the lowest, his insight is everywhere unerring. He seems to speak as if he had known and seen everything at first hand. Here is Theseus talking about his hounds in '*A Mid-Summer Night's Dream*' :

> My hounds are bred out of Spartan kind
> So flaw'd so sanded; and their heads are hung
> With ears that sweep away the morning dew;
> Crook-knee'd and dew-lapp'd nice Thessalian bulls,
> Each under each — A cry more tuneable
> Was never hola'd to, nor cheer'd with horn,
> In Crete, in Sparta, nor in Thessaly. (IV.1.116)

This is a piece of astonishing knowledge, it is reinforced by his understanding of the dog's features and voice, which earn special credit.

His songs are surpassing in their beauty of sound and meaning and their evocative power.

''Who is Silvia?'' (*Two Gentlemen of Verona*) was set to music by a continental master ''O, take those lips away'' (*Measure for Measure*), the songs of Ariel, and Autolycus (*The Winter's Tale*). '' When daisies pied and violets blue'' (*Love's Labour's Lost*) reincarnate Nature's soul at the advent of spring. They are a homage to the English landscape which has found no pen as eloquent as Shakespeare's to exalt it by a plain and faithful rendering joined to a lover's delight. They enrich and extend the scope of music, not by technique but by unlocking the heart and its delight. Added to these are his wonderful knowledge of human nature, his inimitable gift of humour and wit which plays on his subjects like sunshine on ripples, and the rich ethical tone that he maintains throughout all his plays. All these have contributed to the genuinely poetic character of his plays.

The manner of his poetry blends harmoniously with the matter. Here, beauty comes out of the perfection of style and versification, the aptness and variety of the images and the charm of the rhythm.

The style of Shakespeare is superb. It translates thought into visible images. His magic of words, richness of imagery and excellence of similes have never been bettered. Besides, the style is as varied as life itself, being adapted admirably to the mood and characters of the speakers. When the subject is grand and the emotional pitch of the speaker's mind is high, the style is grand and sonorous. Witness Macbeth's speech:

> "...Out, Out, brief candle.
> Life's but a walking shadow, a poor player,
> That struts and frets his hour upon the stage,
> And then is heard no more; it is a tale
> Told by an idiot, full of sound and funy,
> Signifying nothing."

When the matter is more plain, the style in which it is couched becomes direct, simple and colloquial:

> "This fellow's of exceeding honesty,
> And knows all qualities, with a learn'd spirit,
> of human dealing" (*Othello*, III, iii, 269-270)

When a character narrates an event, he does so in a curiously modern and journalistic style. Witness Casca's ironical description of the offer of the crown to Caesar and his refusal to accept it:

> "I saw Mark Antony offer him a crown; yet
> it was not a crown neither, it was one of these
> coronets; and, as I told you, he put it by once; but
> for all that, to my thinking, he would
> fain have had it." (*Julius Caesar* I, ii, 232-234)

The blank verse of Shakespeare is a revelation of the highest musical possibility of the English language. No purely lyrical poetry in English weds words and metaphors more triumphantly to ideas or contains more varied, richer and more delicate sonorities than what Shakespeare produces in the blank verse of his plays.

As a Dramatist

> Let us repeat Matthew Arnold's words :
> "Self-school'd, self-scann'd, self-honour'd, self-secure
> Didst walk on Earth unguess'd at."

Arnold declares in these words that the poet was absolutely independent and alone in his creative world and that he scarcely belonged to our Earth, where he walked 'unguess'd at' like a visitor from another planet. This leads us to draw a conclusion that Shakespeare's mind and imagination were a veritable mountain-stream, which cannot be contained within fixed bounds. Surprising as it may seem, he saw and heard everything in his luminous mind. This is the gift of a saint or seer. Shakespeare, too, seemed to possess this super-natural power of achieving immediate knowledge. From the crowned king to the cobbler, he seemed to see everybody by this direct medium. He heard them speak in words appropriate to the occasion and the station of their life and there was therefore no need for him to burden himself with tablets in his pocket as aid to his memory. If we now go in to ask ourselves in what visual context this world figure impresses itself upon us, then we see again the most varied and contrasting scenes: ceremonies of state alongside tavern drinking-bouts and rough brawls, tender love-scenes alongside court festivities, marching armies and solemn coronations, masquerades and village fetes, assassination and pensive soliloquies, merry dances and dumb shows, songs and the melancholy music of the lute. There is similar variety in the language, for we hear stylized speeches as well as rapid prose dialogue, rich and formal Elizabethan verse alongside coarse jokes, witty repartee of high comedy and the slang of everyday speech, melodramatic rhetoric in the scenes of grand passion, and simple, terse utterances in moments of distress.

Similarly, the form of Shakespeare's play was not strictly fixed or laid down. When he began to write, there was on the one hand the neo-classical rhetorical drama in the Senecan tradition, and on the other the crude popular play. There were Lyly's courtly comedies with their refined wit and polished dialogue, and Marlowe's powerful tragedies; the mystery plays and moralities were still performed. This varied abundance proved to be exactly the right soil, in which his dramatic art was able to take root and flourish. *Richard II*, with its lyrical and reflective richness and its comparative lack of sensational stage action, follows the utterly different history of *Richard III*. How different is *A Mid Summer Night's Dream* with its inter-weaving of the world of the fairies, the mechanicals' sub-plot, and the entanglements of the Athenian lovers! And there is nothing in the whole field of satiric drama which can be compared with *Troilus and Cressida* — the strangest, boldest, most provoking and therefore the most difficult comedy Shakespeare ever wrote. This means that Shakespeare does not feel himself limited by any rules, any three unities or superimposed sense of decorum.

It is also well known that Shakespeare did not, as a rule, invent the plots of his plays, but borrowed most of his subject-matter from others. He could be called a plagiarist, but he was an amalgator as well. This gift of assimilation is most evident when Shakespeare combines opposite and diverse material in order to form a new unity. The contrast between the world of Falstaff and the world of the king is among other things a contrast of comedy and tragedy. As Dr. Johnson observed,

> "Shakespeare's plays are not in the rigorous and critical sense either tragedies or comedies, but compositions of a distinct kind; exhibiting the real state of sublunary nature, which partakes of good and evil, joy and sorrow, mingled with endless variety of proportion and innumerable modes of combination; and expressing the course of the world, in which the loss of one is the gain of another; in which, at the same time, the reveller is hasting to his wine, and the mourner burying his friend; in which the malignity of one is sometimes defeated by the frolick of another; and many mischiefs and many benefits are done and hindered without design."

> The German writer Herder said in 1773 that Shakespeare had 'created a miraculous unity out of the most heterogeneous materials by virtue of his creative spirit.' This holds good in many plays, for instance, in *The Merchant of Venice, Cymbeline. The Winter's Tale, All's Well That Ends Well.*

The third characteristic of his work is his practical sense of the theatre with the poetic genius. Hamlet's advice in his speech to the players — to suit the action to the word, the word to the action — was followed by Shakespeare himself in the composition of each play. The result is the uniquely fortunate case of poetic language which is of great complexity and expressiveness, but which always gives us the impression that we are listening to the speaking voice of the actor. This combination has never been achieved by any dramatist so successfully.

The fourth characteristic of his work is the presence of different levels of significance and of effects. For, it not only contains on the plane of action one or two sub-plots which vary and comment upon the main plot, but it also combines several layers of meaning. Under the surface of the external action it is possible to trace a complex network of images and concepts. These express and vary the themes of the play in a manner comparable to musical counterpoint.

The fifth characteristic feature of Shakespeare's dramatic plays is that they were written for an extremely mixed audience in which all classes of society and degrees of education were represented, and they were capable of meeting the varied expectations and demands of this mixed audience. His range of appeal is so great that he achieves a synthesis of crude and refined effects, of simple and subtle devices. This particular balance was never regained by later dramatist, for either they were coarser and more limited, without Shakespeare's breath and subtlety, or they were altogether more literary, and wrote without Shakespeare's uninhibited vitality for a primarily middle-class audience. Brutus and Antony speaking over Caesar's body, Hamlet and the ghost on the platform, Lear with his three daughters and the map of his kingdom and Othello at Desdemona's deathbed, all these tableaux compress the essense of a figure, and sometimes of a whole play, into a single visual image. These symbolic moments on the stage are often more eloquent than many speeches because of their simplicity, for they can make the meaning vivid to every spectator.

The sixth characteristic feature of his play is : this is a drama of inner balance, and consequently displays the greatest possible objectivity of characterization. Inner balance means that every play contains both light and shade, both good and evil, even if these two halves are not always of exactly equal weight. Everywhere we find that one attitude is corrected by the other, the opposites serve to counterbalance and clarify each other. Romeo's emotional enthusiasm is accompanied in the first part of the play by Mercutio's wit and mockery. Hamlet has the neutral voice of Horatio at his side.

We are not aware of the absence of any philosophical or religious bias in Shakespeare's play as opposed to the French, German and Spanish drama of his age. Hotspur lost his laurels to his rival, Prince Hal. The fact distressed him even more than the agony of death —- he could scarcely endure the thought that the Prince should add a feather to his cap at his cost. But in a moment he overcame the jealousy and a light broke out in upon him in which he beheld things in their cosmic aspect:

> "And thoughts, the slaves of life, and life, time's fool
> And time, that takes survey of all the world,
> Must have a stop. (*I Henry IV.* V. iv. 81)

These lines are significant in our understanding of philosophy, embedded in the major plays. Macbeth paved and reinforced it so that it could serve the need of a high road. Timon was better even in his death, unforgiving in spite of a noble mind.

In 'Shakespeare and Religion', an essay which Aldous Huxley concluded with his last breath, he describes Prospero's farewell aspect as being permeated by the conception of Maya. Hotspur recognized religion as a path to achieve eternity. Lear has no interest in thought of liberation as a conscious aim till he achieves it and breaks the fetters that bound him.

To Sum Up : We quote Arnold's Sonnet:

> "All weakness that impairs, all griefs that bow,
> Find their sole voice in that victorious brow."

Arnold is obviously thinking of the great tragedies but the praise he gives here is even more stupendous than the transcendental elevation he discovers in the poet. What are to think when he goes on to tell that Shakespeare's is the sole voice for "All weakness that impairs, all griefs that bow". It is an exaggeration of an exaggeration, it is fantastic. For what did Homer, Euripides and Aeschylus who are the founts of the Western Tradition or Valmiki and Kalidas of the Eastern Tradition wrote on the same subject. Are their performances to be pushed aside so that the pride of place may be given to the English Poet and Playwright?

If Arnold's attitude is carefully followed, the conclusion will seem inevitable. All the poets who wrote before, wrote from experience and imagination, never abandoning their role as fellow-sufferer. Shakespeare alone was different. He was transcendental and saw everything from an elevation inaccessible to others. They could achieve fragmentary views, deal with individual cases and limited areas. Shakespeare alone saw the soul, the cause of mundane suffering — which lay in pride, ambition, jealousy and ingratitude. His work on the surface of it concerns itself with individual characters but deep down is the bitter flood at which no one had looked but the Poet Shakespeare. His work therefore is a series of symbols for the human situation — as valid as the Cross where the Son of Man was condemned by the envious mob.

The Evolution of the English Drama upto the Days of Shakespeare

The excellence of Shakespeare's dramatic works owed as much to the mental preparation of the time as to the dramatic's individual powers. W.H. Hudson writes, "If it was the strength of his genius that lifted him to the top of the heap, it was also the greatness of the heap that enabled him to reach and maintain that elevation"; and this heap was composed of the accumulated matter left by Shakespeare's predecessors in the English drama and some of his senior contemporaries.

The first heap was revived by the clergy. It arose out of a perception that what we see with our eyes makes a greater impression upon us than what we merely hear with our ears. It was seen that many events in the life of Christ, as well as in the history of the Christian Church, would easily admit of being dramatized, and thus brought home, as it were, to the feelings and conscience of men more effectually than by sermons. The early plays which thus arose were called '*Miracles*', or *Miracle Plays*, because miraculous narratives, taken from Scripture or the lives of the saints, formed their chief subject.

The earliest known specimens of these miracle plays were composed in Latin by one Hilarius, an English monk, and a disciple of the famous Abelard, in the early part of the twelfth century. Similar compositions in French date from the thirteenth century; but Mr. Wright does not believe that any were composed in English before the fourteenth. A passage in Chaucer spoken by the Wife of Bath says:

> "Therefore I made my visitaciouns,
> To vigilies and to processiouns,
> To preching eek and to thise pilgrimages,
> To pleyes of miracles and mariages."
>
> (Chaucer, *Canterbury Tales*, Wife of Bath's Prol. 555)

The Coventry Mysteries were performed in Easter week. The Towneley Mysteries belonged to the old Catholic family of 'Towneley of Towneley' in Lancashire, might perhaps with more propriety be named the Wakefield Mysteries, as having been written for the guilds of the town.

The second heap was the product of mediaeval philosophy. This philosophy dealt much in abstract terms, and delighted in definitions and logical distinctions. Debarred, partly by external hindrances, partly by its own inexperience, from profitable inquiry into nature and her laws, the mind was thrown back upon itself, its own powers, and immediate instruments; and the fruits were, an indefinite number of metaphysical cobwebs, logical subtleties, and quips on plays upon words. The mediaeval playwrights refined away the scriptural personages into mere moral abstractions. Thus, instead of the Jonathan and Satan of the mystery, we come to the Friendship and the Vice of the moral play, or morality, – a dramatic form which seems to have become popular about the middle of the fifteenth century.

Down to the end of the sixteenth century these moral plays were continually appearing on the stage. Moral plays are frequently described by their authors as interludes. But there was difference. Whereas in a Moral play the characters are personified qualities (Felicity, False semblance, Youth, etc.), in an Interlude they are true persons, but not yet individuals; they are the representatives of classes. Thus, in Heywood's clever Interlude of *The Four P's* the leading characters are, the Pedlar, the Palmer, the Pardoner, and the Poticary.

Fortunately this type of drama was cut short by the revival of ancient learning. The plays of Terence, Sophocles and even those of Seneca began to be known widely. The result is the earliest known English comedy, *Ralph Roister Doister*. Its author was Nicolas Udall, probably written in 1551. It is written in jingling rime, the lines being usually of twelve syllables, though frequently shorter. It is divided into acts and scenes, like those plays of Plautus and Terence of which it is a professed limitation. *Gammer Gurton's Needle* and *Misogenus*, both probably composed before 1560, are comedies of the same kind, but of still ruder workmanship. No comedies worthy of note after these mentioned appeared for more than twenty years — not till the time of Greene, Peele, and Marlowe, the immediate predecessors and contemporaries of Shakespeare.

The earliest known tragedy was brought upon the stage in 1562, under the title of *Gorbodue*, or *Ferrex* and *Porrex*. It was jointly composed by Sackville, afterwards Lord Buckhurst, and Thoman Norton, a Puritan lawyer. It is the first English drama of any kind written in blank verse. In form the play follows the model of Seneca's tragedies, and is provided with a chorus.

The fondness for seeing the past history of the nation exhibited in dramatic show, conduced, more than any other single cause, to that constant neglect of the dramatic 'unities' for which English playwrights are conspicuous. Marlowe, in his historical tragedy of Edward II and Shakespeare, in his ten historical plays, proceed upon this principle.

Shakespeare's Predecessors. Christopher Marlowe, who for his rare gift of expression might fitly be called the Keats of the sixteenth century, was born at Canterbury in 1564. The appearance of his tragedy of *Tamburlaine the Great* in 1586 Marks an epoch in the history of the English Drama. Blank verse is used in it with so much force and ingenuity that from that time the adoption of this as the regular dramatic measure was a settled question. The gorgeous language, the rants, the bombast, the Asiatic pomp, which deck this dramatic presentation of the Tartar conqueror, though they provoked Shakespeare to good-natured satire (*Henry IV*. Part II. Act II. Scene 4), did not prevent the play from making an extraordinary impression.

Marlowe's greatest work, *The Tragedy of Dr. Faustus* (1588), has attracted much attention owing to the celebrity with which Goethe's great work has invested the old story. This character may be considered as a personification of the pride of will and eagerness of curiosity sublimed beyond the reach of fear and remorse.

Robert Greene, who ran through his life and used up his genius as quickly as Marlowe, is the acknowledged author of several plays. These are, *Orlando Furioso*, *A Looking-glass for London and England*, *Friar Bacon and Friar Bungay* and some other plays. Greene's influence on Shakespeare was based up the nostalgic charm of the next county (Suffolk for Greene, Gloucestershire for Shakespeare); the woodland setting and idyllic atmosphere, where evil though present in its blackest form, is easily dispelled, the capable and high spirited heroine, fond of disguising herself as a boy; Oberon and his fairies as factors in a human love story; and the melancholy, worldly humorist (Bohan Jacques) as a commentator on Utopia.

John Lyly carried the enormous vogue of *Euphues* into the drama in a series of seven comedies, beginning with *Compaspe* about 1581 and closing with *Mother Bombie* about 1590, in prose. His Euphuistic style consisted of various constituents; mock natural history, classical mythology, fable and anecdote, alliteration, antithesis and the like.

George Peele, a Christ Church man, was an intimate friend of Greene, Nash, and Lodge. *His Arraignment of Paris*, though classically divided, had in general no idea of structure, no common sense or reserve. Reason, order and consistency simply were not his; but he had in very rare degree some immortal gifts. One was the power of drawing an unearthly beauty out of words, a power that makes him as belonging to a class of poets different from Lyly, Greene, or Kyd; to the class, that is, in which we naturally place Marlowe and Shakespeare. Other gifts are more peculiarly dramatic. His three great plays have an intensity of fancy that enables him to transcend the logic, and they are filled with a kind of dramatic intuition that is the strangest thing about Peele.

Thomas Lodge is the author of *Marius and Sylla*, a rather fine tragedy in blank verse, written to illustrate and enforce the countless miseries of civil war.

Thomas Kyd is the author of the famous tragedy *Jeronymo*, acted in 1588, and of its sequel, *The Spanish Tragedy*. They are ranting plays, full of sensational incident; half of *Jeronymo* is in rhyme.

The Elizabethan Theatre

The Elizabethan theatres were of three varieties : (*a*) public play houses, (*b*) private playhouses, and (*c*) Court theatres in which some royal hall would be converted into a playhouse.

So far as the public theatre is concerned, the question is best answered by De Witt sketch of the Swan. In spite of Dover Wilson's unprovoked and ill-tempered gibe (Shakespeare Survey, Vol. I, p. 21), this sketch corresponds on many important points to the description of the frame, the galleries, the stage, and the tiring-house given in the contracts of the Fortune and the Hope on the Swan, this rough handiwork of two Dutchmen may, with modifications suggested by other indubitable evidence, be accepted as a reliable replica of an Elizabethan stage. It shows a building of three tiers, with a stage jutting from a wall into the yard or centre of the building. The tiers are roofed, and part of the stage is covered by a roof that projects from the rear and is supported at its front on two posts, but the groundlings, who paid a penny to stand in front of the stage, were exposed to the sky. (Performance in such a playhouse was held only in the day time; artificial illumination was not used.) At the rear of the stage are two doors; above the stage is a gallery. Taking the measurements of the Fortune contract, the yard is 55 feet square (55 x 55), and the platform would be about 27½ feet long and 43 feet broad. For patrons willing to pay more than the general admission of the groundlings, there were to be three galleries provided with seats. From the third chief source, stage directions, one learns that entrance to the stage was by doors, presumably spaced widely apart at the rear, and that in addition to the platform stage there was occasionally some sort of curtained booth and alcove allowing for "discovery" scenes, and some sort of playing space "aloft" or "above" to represent the top of a city's walls or a room above the street. The stage, protected by a "shadow" or "heavens" or roof, is entered by two doors; behind the doors is the "tiring house" in which the actors robed. The upper storeys of the tiring house could be used as a balcony, or an upper storey of a house, according to the needs of the stage. It was from the balcony that Juliet talked to Romeo who was below, or Jesiccapoured bags of gold for Lorenzo to carry. Sometimes the tiring house was used in a play to represent an inner chamber. Some evidence suggests that a throne can be lowered into the platform stage, perhaps from the "shadow", certainly characters can descend from the stage through a trap or traps into the cellar or "hell". Sometimes this space beneath the platform accommodates a sound-effects man or musician (in *Antony and Cleopatra* "music of the hautboys is under the stage") or an actor (in *Hamlet* the "Ghost cries under the stage"). Most characters simply walk on and off, but because there is no curtain in front of the platform, corpses will have to be carried off, or will have to fall at the rear, when the curtain on the alcove or booth can be drawn to conceal them.

Women's parts were played by boys. John Masefield elaborates, "The plays were played straight through, without waits. The only waits necessary in a theatre are (*a*) those which rest the actors; and (*b*) those which give variety to the moods of the spectators. The double construction of Shakespeare's plays provided a sub-plot which held or amused the audience while the actors of the main plot rested."

Costumes were costly and beautiful and extravagantly magnificent, but they were not designed to secure an accurate reproduction of the costumes of the period in which the play was set. Lamborn and Harrison observe, " Costume was a means of indicating rank and office more than time and place; and it was meant to reveal the character than the setting of the story."

There was little or no scenery to most plays. The properties, that is, chairs, beds, etc., were not many. The Elizabethan actor spoke to his audience, unlike the modern actor who pretends to be unaware of it. Hence there was nothing incongruous in the use of soliloquy. Shakespeare made up for "the deficiency of the scenery by his wonderful description of landscapes, castles and wild moors. All that poetry would have been lost had he had painted scenery at his disposal" (Jusserand).

So much have been called the so-called "public theatre". The private theatre was basically a large room, entirely roofed and therefore artificially illuminated, with a stage at one end. In 1576 one such theatre was established in Blackfriars. All the actors were boys about eight to thirteen (in the public theatres similar boys played female parts; A boy lady Macbeth played to a man Macbeth). This private theatre had a precarious existence, and ceased operations in 1584. In 1596 James Burbage, who had already made theatrical history by building the theatre, began to construct a second Blackfriars theatre. He died in 1597, and for several years this second Blackfriars theatre was used by a troupe of boys, but in 1608 two of Burbage's sons and five other actors (including Shakespeare) became joint operators of the theatre, using it in the winter when the open-air Globe was unsuitable.

The Elizabethan World Picture

One can say dogmatically that the Elizabethan world picture was solidly theocentric, and it was a simplified version of a much more complicated medieval picture. Though the general medieval picture of the world survived in outline into the Elizabethan age, its existence was by then precarious. There had been Machiavelli, to whom the idea of a universe divinely ordered throughout was repugnant, and in the seventeenth century men began to understand and heed and not merely to travesty and abuse him. Recent research has shown that the educated Elizabethan had plenty of text books in the vernacular instructing him in the Copernican astronomy, yet he was loth to upset the old order by applying his knowledge. The new commercialism was hostile to medieval stability. In the words of Tillyard, "The greatness of the Elizabethan age was that it contained so much of new without bursting the noble form of the old order ... Somehow the Tudors had inserted themselves into the constitution of the medieval universe ... It was a serious matter not a mere fancy if an Elizabethan writer compared Elizabeth to the primum mobile, the master-sphere of the physical universe" (E.M.W Tillyard, *The Elizabethan World Picture*, Penguin Books, p. 17).

The World picture was ruled by a general conception of order, for at first sight that drama is anything but orderly. One of the clearest expositions of order (and close to Shakespeare's though a good deal earlier in date) is Elyot's in the first chapter of the *Governor*:

> "Hath not God set degrees and estates in all his glorious works? First in his heavenly ministers, whom he hath constituted in divers degrees called hierarchies. Behold the

> four elements, whereof the body of man is comport, how they be set in their places called spheres, higher or lower according to the sovereignty of their natures. Behold also the order that God hath put generally in all his creatures ...."

Hooker's version is of course avowedly theological and it is more explicit, but the order it describes is Elyot's and Shakespeare's. His name for it is law; law in its general sense, at once the inherent tendency of things and a principle of regulation: 'that which doth assign unto each thing the kind, that which doth moderate the force and power, that which doth appoint the form and measure, of working, the same we term a Law.' Divine and natural and man-made laws are thus ranged in the same definition. Elsewhere, Hooker adds that the law of Nature is 'an infallible knowledge imprinted' in the mind; the need to maintain a regulated order, then, is dictated by man's place in the universe.

And the Renaissance gave new force to the notion of order in the stress it laid on such urban terms as 'civil' and 'civility'. A dialogue on *Civil and Uncivil Life* (1579), urging gentlemen to leave the country and settle in town, indicate the direction of the current. Renaissance theorists held that art was, should be, a construction of human reason, continuing and completing the work of Nature; and so too with their views of organized society.

Besides theological lore, it has been the pattern St. Paul imposed on the Christian material and it persisted in spite of all disputes and eruptions as a great formative force in men's lives, until with scientific revolution of the seventeenth century it slowly receded into this and that citadel. The orthodox scheme of salvation was pervasive in the Elizabethan age. Atheism not agnosticism was the rule. Though there are so few references to the Pauline scheme of redemption in the sonneteers and dramatists, their scarcity is a sign of familiarity to the Elizabethan world picture. But in Spenser's *Hymns* the scheme of salvation is given a principal place :

> 'Could man amends to God for man's misguide,
> But only man himself, who self did slide.'

Yet disorder or chaos, the product of sin, is perpetually striving to come again. And if by tradition, the way to salvation is through God's grace and Christ's atonement, there is also the way, paired with it through the contemplation of the divine order of the created universe.

The Elizabethan world picture is also, in the words of Pope in the

Essay on Man, 'the vast chain of being.' The chain stretched from the foot of God's throne to the meanest of inanimate objects. One of the finest short accounts is by Sir John Fortescure, the fifteenth century jurist, in his Latin work on the law of nature:

> "In this order hot things are in harmony with cold, dry with moist, heavy with light, great with little, high with low ... So that there is nothing which the bond of order does not embrace."

But this chain of being is still a means of spiritual ascent : but only in an ideal interpretation. But, in reality, in Shakespeare's *Tempest*, man is distanced into a more generally cosmic setting. The heavens are actively alive. It was by Providence divine that Prospero and Miranda survived in the boat. Ariel and the other angelic powers, elves and demi-puppets, are all, according to W.C. Curry, in the orthodox tradition of the Renaissance Neo-platonists, who were the great exponents of the chain of being. Prospero is at the apex of humanity while Trinculo and Stephano are low in the scale of humanity. Caliban is largely bestial. Nor are the beasts forgotten. Prospero tells Ariel that his groans from the pine-tree prison

> 'Did make wolves howl and penetrate the breasts
> of every hungry bears.'

The world order so far dealt with was vertical: that of a chain beginning on high with the noblest and descending to the meanest things of creation. But the second picture of the same world was largely horizontal. It consisted of a number of planes, arranged one below another in order of dignity but connected by an immense net of correspondences. The different planes were the divine and angelic, the universe or macrocosm, the commonwealth or body politic, man or the microcosm, and the lower creation.

Shakespeare Criticism through the Ages

The first significant criticism of Shakespeare was made in the prefatory matter appended to the First folio in 1623, and for about three centuries-and-a-half there has been no end of writing about him. There is scarcely any aspect of his life or work that has not been thoroughly explored and yet we feel that he is inexhaustible. Criticism of Shakespeare seems to fall into three well-marked stages. Seventeenth and eighteenth century criticism may be described as neoclassical, nineteenth century criticism was romantic, and twentieth century criticism is objective or impersonal.

Neoclassical criticism is dominated by the concepts of imitation in content and shapeliness in form. Drama is the imitation of nature, in whatever way we may interpret 'imitation'. And it is primarily the narration of a story, the unfolding of the Fable or Plot. If the play is to be well-made, there must be unity of action so that attention may not be confused or diverted, and there must be gradual evolution from the beginning to the middle and from the middle to the end. These standards may not be very appropriately applied to Shakespearean drama. That is why there is an undertone of discomfort in even the best neoclassic criticism of Shakespeare, such as that made by Dryden and Dr. Samuel Johnson. Ben Jonson said that Shakespeare wanted art; Dryden praised Shakespeare for his largeness and comprehensiveness but seemed also to be disturbed by his inability to write a regular play. He would praise Shakespeare one day only to denigrate him the next, and his adaptations of Shakespeare's dramas are an indication of his imperfect appreciation of Shakespeare's genius.

After Dryden, Johnson is the greatest neoclassic critic of Shakespeare. Johnson's principal virtue as a critic is common sense, but common sense is a weapon that is sharpened only at one end. With his common sense he sees through the folly of imposing the law of the unities of time and place on Shakespearean drama or on any kind of drama, because drama is based on stage illusion, and the mixture of comedy and tragedy is justified with reference to life in which joy and sorrow are inextricably intermingled. But Johnson is fettered by the neoclassic superstition that poetry is the imitation and mirror of life, a faithful representation of general nature and that its aim should be primarily to instruct men by distributing rewards and punishments justly. The aesthetic side of drama is thus tagged on to the moral and literature becomes lay scriptures. For Johnson drama is partly a game of skill and partly a moral class-book. He praises Shakespeare for accurate observation and for representation of general human nature but blames him on account of the looseness of his plots and for violation of the laws of poetic justice. Johnsonian common sense could not soar to the empyrean heights of Shakespearean poetry.

Neoclassic criticism is sober and commonsensible. But it has three basic limitations. First, following Aristotle, it emphasizes the movement of the plot as more important than the other elements in Shakespearean drama. Secondly, the aesthetic aspect is subordinated to the realistic and the moral. It is forgotten that poetry transports us into a loftier world where we feel that life imitates art as much as art imitates life. If truth to nature were a test of art, Shakespeare's sources would be more 'probable' than Shakespeare's dramas. And whatever morals there may be in poetry are only an emanation from the poetic world which Indian aesthetics calls *alaukika*, rather than something attached to or super-imposed upon it. As Chesterton says, the bad fable *has* a moral, and the good fable *is* a moral. The third limitation of neoclassic criticism is that it tries to judge poetry and drama by certain rules which are looked upon as absolutes and which all kinds of art must conform to. Here the upholders of reason become unreasonable, because they lose sight of the fact that most of the ancient rules were derived not from the nature of drama but from the conventions of the ancient stage.

III

From these limitations romantic criticism is free. As its greatest exponent Coleridge points out, genius dictates its own form, and Shakespeare's judgment is equal to his genius. Formal rules did not worry the Romantics or their immediate successors. According to them, it should be the business of criticism to recapture the magic of the original, to enter the enchanted world created by the poet. Criticism thus becomes a recreation of or a substitute for drama rather than an evaluation of it, and imaginative apprehension rather than judgment by reason is set as the aim of the critic. There is an analogous change in the attitude to the relationship between art and morality. Art on this view teaches by expanding the range of sympathy rather than by restricting it through the imposition of realistic or didactic standards which are foreign to it. Art may imitate nature but it also transcends nature. That is why in Shakespeare, the greatest of artists, we find a reconciliation of opposites which are irreconciliable in life. Dr. Johnson was attracted by Falstaff's perpetual gaiety but finds nothing estimable in his character and is undisturbed by the rejection at the end of 2 *Henry IV*. Not so Maurice Morgann, the pioneer of romantic criticism. He, too, finds nothing wrong with the final rejection, but the sympathetic picture of Falstaff which emerges from his marvellous analysis is one that Johnson could not dream of. For Maurice Morgann, Falstaff has a complex personality, made up of an external and an internal character. He is a liar and a cheat and a coward and a debauchee, but behind these vices, which, like his corpulence, are no part of his essential nature, there is his inner character of which we have secret impressions that are fitful but compelling and vital.

The reference to Maurice Morgann takes us to the heart of romantic criticism which focuses attention on characterization as the distinctive feature of Shakespeare's dramatic art. It is Shakespeare's characters who live again in the pages of Morgann, Coleridge, Hazlitt, and most of all, in Bradley. Shakespeare's plots, his ideas and his language are important only in so far as they help project his characters, all of whom from the Prince of Denmark to the First Lord and the Third Murderer are supposed to be endowed with distinctive personalities such as we expect from men and women in real life. That is why we piece together isolated actions and try to extract the total character of persons who strut and fret on the stage for a few minutes. We have to visualize these personages when they are off the stage and Bradley speculates where Hamlet was when his father died and when Duncan's murder was first plotted. Criticism has its ironies like every other field of human activity. Neoclassic criticism strove to be realistic but it created an artificial world governed by conventions that had little connexion with real life. Romantic criticism starts on the assumption that the poet creates an autonomous world where the Imagination reigns supreme and then applies to the denizens of this fantastic world the same standards by which we judge men and women in real life. Thus romantic criticism contradicts its own premise. It poses a fanciful world and then peoples it with human beings who might be called imitations of reality.

Apart from this basic self-contradiction, romantic criticism of Shakespeare is open to some grave objections. First of all, by focusing attention on one element in a complex form of art it fails to assess properly the importance of plot, ideas and language. Sometimes, as in the analysis of Macbeth and Othello, it credits characters with the command of poetical language which distinguishes Shakespeare rather than the puppets through whom Shakespeare speaks to his audience or readers. Then, secondly, by assuming that these puppets are as much alive as real men and women, it draws conclusions that are unwarranted by the dramas which Shakespeare wrote, and it claims to know characters in their totality, although Shakespeare presents them only isolated episodes. Was Othello temperamentally jealous? If so, not only does he cease to be a heroic figure but the play also much of its significance, particularly in the first two Acts and the last. If he was not originally jealous, we have to accept the absurd hypothesis that he becomes so in the course of less than half an hour, before Iago has given any proof in support of what are little more than hints and innuendoes.

Then, again, what right have critics to imagine what the *dramatis personae* do when they are away from the stage? A waggin undergraduate is reported to have retorted on Bradley and Bradleyites, saying that it would be as relevant to speculate when Hamlet was at the time of his father's death — the play starts same time after the event — as to inquire where he was when the lights went off! As these romantic critics proceed on an unwarranted assumption and by that assumption are led to irrelevant digressions, they recreate characters that have little similarity with the men and women in Shakespeare. It has rightly been pointed out that Coleridge's Hamlet is more like Coleridge than like the Prince of Denmark whom Burbage impersonated at Globe Theatre. Romantic criticism is too personified and subjective and reflects more the aesthetic hedonism of Pater or the Hegelianism of Bradley and Croce than Shakespeare's dramatic craftsmanship.

As a reaction against this subjectivity twentieth century criticism is objective and impersonal. The immense critical literature which has been produced during the last half a century may be grouped under four principal heads : textual, theatrical, historical (including biographical) and symbolist. But there is one common point; all these approaches are objective. A good deal of research has been made to find out how much of Shakespeare's work is Shakespeare's own and what exactly he wrote and when. A large body of bibliographical literature has been produced on the subject, into the details of which it is not possible for me to enter here. Suffice it to say that the tendency in this field is to restore Shakespeare rather than to amend him. The same tendency to objectivity is traceable in modern theatrical criticism which looks upon Shakespeare not as a philosopher or a poet but as a practical playwright writing for the stage. He was a popular rather than a scholarly dramatist, even if he was not probably as unlearned as was thought previously. He was a master of the stage, whose art is to be investigated with reference to the peculiarities of his theatre and the demands of this audience. The Elizabethan stage has vanished beyond recall, but even now he must be understood as primarily a theatrical craftsman who grips our attention when his dramas are properly presented.

From theatrical criticism to historical criticism it is but one step. If

Shakespeare was a practical playwright producing plays for an Elizabethan audience under certain conditions prescribed by his age, he can best be understood with reference to the ideology and conventions of his own times, and the methods by which the work of a nineteenth or twentieth century novelist is analysed are inapplicable to his dramas. Although some critics have tried to psycho-analyse Shakespeare or some of his characters, it is claimed by these historical critics that Shakespeare was no psychologist but a playwright presenting certain Elizabethan themes and creating a dramatic illusion for an Elizabethan audience. If there is any substance to be discovered in these 'shadows', it is only a commentary on the stirring themes of the days of Elizabeth, such as the question of succession or the Essex rebellion. It is not merely popular themes or dramatic conventions which would give us a key to Shakespeare's meaning but embedded in his dramas are the dominant ideas of the Elizabethan world, and Shakespeare has to be interpreted with inquiry into Elizabethan ideology and dramaturgy has revealed new aspects in Shakespeare's work and even old strata which have hitherto been hidden from view. It has been discovered that the Renaissance was less revolutionary than we thought and medieval ideology and medieval dramatic conventions are the bedrock on which the Elizabethans built. Shakespearean drama, on this view, harks back to the Miracles and Moralities, to Boccaccio and Lydgate, even beyond Boccaccio and Lydgate to St. Augustine, and the great Falstaff has been presented as a variation on the medieval Vice tempting mankind.

There are two other aspects of historical criticism on which a word should be said here. The inquiry into the historical milieu of Shakespeare the dramatist has been accompanied by investigation into the facts of Shakespeare's life. We cannot say that such an investigation is at all new, for Shakespearean biography is as old as Nicholas Rowe. But there is a distinction between the old approach and the new, particularly between the nineteenth century and the twentieth. We may compare the works of Dowden and Chambers in this field to realize this difference. Dowden's famous work on Shakespeare's mind and art seeks to relate Shakespeare's dramatic work to his life and traces Shakespeare's development as an artist to the mental growth of Shakespeare the man. That was one of the most characteristic products of the nineteenth century attitude to Shakespeare's work. Chambers in the twentieth century is more impersonal; he only studies facts and problems. There are some modern writers, such as, notably, Frank Harris and Wyndham Lewis, who have tried to explain poetical and dramatic problems biographically, but such adventures in criticism are looked upon as whimsical and amateurish; they belong more to exciting journalism than to sober scholarship.

The other branch of Shakespearean criticism referred to in the above paragraph is about Shakespeare's sources. Just as some critics explain Shakespeare through a study of the conditions and conventions of the Elizabethan stage for which he produced his works, others think that Shakespeare's meaning can be adequately understood if we examine the materials that lay ready to his hand. A single example will throw light on the claims advanced by these critics. The so-called problem comedies have posed an aesthetic problem for critics who have not examined their sources. They seem to be too problematical and 'dark' to be comedies and yet they are not also tragedies. But such puzzles are only invented by critics unacquainted with the sources used by Shakespeare. W.W. Lawrence has shown that the bed trick employed by Helena and Mariana is a part of the traditions of medieval folklore. We should not transfer our sensitiveness and squeamishness to Shakespeare who was anxious 'to fit his artistic conception to the plot as he found it, rather than to remake the plot to fit a preconceived effect of his own'. This tendency is noticeable in every branch of modern Shakespearean criticism. Shakespeare's Histories, for example, are often looked upon as embodiments of the Tudor historical myth as propounded by Polydore Vergil, Hall, Holinshed or the authors of *The Mirror for Magistrates* rather than as artistic creations emerging fully developed from Shakespeare's head as Minerva out of Jove's.

The defect of historical criticism is that it submerges Shakespeare's work in a flood of extraneous details and gives a very imperfect account of his originality. It helps an understanding of Shakespeare but does not enable us to appraise and appreciate him properly. I have elsewhere tried to show that Shakespeare's originality lies not, as Stoll and other historical critics would lead us to believe, in producing an illusion of life but in giving us a direct and penetrating vision of reality presented through development of plot and character and their impact on each other. The defect of historical criticism everywhere is that it gives primacy to factors that are only of incidental importance. It is, indeed, true that Shakespeare was influenced by Elizabethan or medieval traditions, but so were his innumerable contemporaries in poetry and drama. It is not these traditions that made Shakespeare what he is; the important point for consideration is what Shakespeare made of these traditions. The poet's fine frenzy does not create out of airy nothing but transforms the materials and conventions lying ready to his hand; it is this transforming power which the tools of historical criticism can never measure and often distort.

Criticism which I have described as symbolical — it is also sometimes called the 'new' criticism — does not generally care for historical factors or sources or even Shakespeare's intentions. It explores the significance of words, images, metaphors and finds in them patterns of meaning below the level of plot and character. I should draw the reader's attention to the word 'pattern', because it occurs frequently in the writings of these critics and gives the clue to their approach. For them Shakespeare is primarily a poet and they try to find out the poetic patterns woven by words and images. These critics, too, are severely objective. Their starting point is T.S. Eliot's dictum that poetry is not the expression of personality but an escape from personality; for them "the poet has not a 'personality' to express, but a particular medium, which is only a medium and not a personality, in which impressions and experiences combine in peculiar and unexpected ways". It is these unexpected combinations and correspondences which the modern critic seeks to trace in Shakespeare's characterization, his manipulation of materials, but most of all in his words and images. These are symbols or 'objective correlatives' behind which the critic senses the basic idea or emotion of which the drama as a whole is the expression. The idea or emotion — royalty or order or honour — may not be very striking when viewed in itself, but in the plays it is presented through a complex web of symbols, and it is the intensity or richness of their fusion that constitutes the greatness of Shakespearean drama. Such criticism is impersonal or objective, but it may be taken as an elaboration of Keats's famous dictum : 'Shakespeare led a life of allegory : his works are the comments on it.'

I have referred to the persistent irony which one may detect in the history of Shakespearean criticism. The realists built a world of unreal conventions which are inapplicable to Shakespearean drama. The romantics believed in the existence of a world of Fancy, a kind of Shakespearean super-Nature and then proceeded to examine Shakespeare's characters as if they were men and women in real life. The 'new' criticism starts with the notion of a world of 'objective correlatives' detached from the personality of the dramatist, but it constantly reads its own meaning into these symbols. This meaning is not only obviously unconnected with whatever intentions Shakespeare may have had but also distorts the symbols and does violence to the average reader's playgoer's (if such a person exists) impressions of them. Claudius becomes a 'kindly uncle', and Shylock the submerged self of Antonio. It is also suggested that it is Petruchio who is tamed, not Katharina and that of the two daughters of Baptista Minola, it is Bianca and not Katharina who is the real shrew! Every critic finds his own private symbols, and it seems that poetry only escapes from the personality of the poet to be an expression of the critic's personality. Lost in the mazes of meaning propounded by the 'new' critics, we realize the truth of Cicero's remarks in *Julius Caesar* :

> ... men may construe things after their fashion,
> Clean from the purpose of the things themselves.

In trying to find out patterns of meaning in Shakespeare these critics display ingenuity but they also do injustice to the dramatic quality of Shakespeare's work. Even if we take a drama as a pattern — a theory on which I shall have to say something presently — it must be remembered that in a pattern everything is in its place, and nothing should be taken out of its setting. But this is a liberty which modern interpreters are constantly indulging in. As an example, we may take Ulysses' great speech on 'degree', which is presented as standing for Shakespeare's own philosophy of order. But in its dramatic context it is only an argument advanced by Ulysses to explain the temporary eclipse of the Greek army in the Trojan war. And we may remember, further, that Henry V, who is looked upon as Shakespeare's ideal king, scoffs at 'degree' as a part of idle Ceremony:

> O ceremony, show me but thy worth!
> What is thy soul of adoration?
> Art thou aught but place, *degree,* and form,
> Creating awe and fear in other men?
>
> (*Henry V.* IV. i. 264-7)

If images and episodes are taken away from their context, the plays will yield any 'total' significance the interpreter chooses to read into them.

The very concept of a 'pattern' has something undramatic or un-Shakespearean about it. A pattern is an artistic design which suggests that everything is in its place and at rest. This presents before us a static, stable world, and interpretation of this world must admittedly be 'spatial'. But movement is of the essence of drama and Shakespeare creates a world which is in continual flux. If it is to be described by means of an analogue, it may be likened to a flowing stream which retains its individual form in the midst of variations rather than to a fixed mould or a static design. And the movement of drama is primarily a movement of story and character so that any attempt at finding meanings below this level is bound to be misleading. The modern hunters after patterns of meaning remind us in one respect of eighteenth century criticism; for both these schools Shakespearean drama is a game of skill and Shakespeare's achievement lies in the adroitness with which he has played this game.

(Adapted mainly from Dr. S.C. Sengupta's *A Shakespeare Manual*)

Characteristics of a Shakespearean Tragedy

The most distinctive feature of a Shakespearean tragedy is the volume and depth of human suffering that the dramatist exhibits.

A tragedy is the story of human suffering. The nature of suffering and its intensity determine the quality of tragedy. And the nature of suffering and its intensity depend on the character of the sufferer and his social situation.

The sufferer is usually one person, the 'hero' or at most of two, the 'hero' and the 'heroine', though it brings before us a considerable number of other persons. The story depicts the troubled part of the hero's life which preceds and leads to his death. As to the hero of a Shakesperean tragedy, he is a person of 'high estate', a king or a prince. As King Lear or Hamlet, or a leader of state like Brutus and Coriolanus. This is the cardinal difference between a Shakespearean and a modern tragedy, where the hero is generally a person of ordinary rank. The reason why Shakespeare elevates the rank of his tragic hero is that his fate affects the welfare of a whole nation or empire and when he falls from the height of prosperity, the spectacle produces in us a sense of the powerlessness of man and omnipotence of fate, which no tale of private life can possibly produce. Calpurnia says this in *Julius Caesar:*

> "When beggars die, there are no comets seen;
> The heavens themselves blaze forth the death of princes."
>
> (Act II, Scene ii, lines : 30-31)

The high degree is not all. He is an exceptional being, raised above the level of average humanity and commands respect from all. His passions, desires and will assume a terrible force. But he has a tragic flaw. He is generally good but he has some fatal weakness because of which he suffers. This is the Bradleyean line of thinking. If Shakespeare had followed this theory it would have led him to the creation of some sort of anaemic neoclassical drama and not his tragedies exhibiting the very complexity of human life. In a general way no man is perfect and hence the flaw is not peculiar to the hero. Further, why speak of the tragic flaw of the hero only? Why not speak of the tragic flaw of the villain also? Brutus is a noble man but he is also a great egoist. He has the capacity to suffer but he does not suffer intensely and for long. It may not have a rational explanation but it should be convincing as Hamlet's is. Cassius is an intriguer. He dupes Brutus for the satisfaction of his own personal ends. But he is nobler than Antony. He dies nobly and his stoicism and death are like Gloucester's suffering in *King Lear* adding to the total impression of heroic struggle in the play.

A Shakespearean tragedy moves on two planes simultaneously; one is the social-moral plane of the external world and the other is the subjective plane of human consciousness. The conflict spreads to both the planes. Hamlet finds himself in contradiction with the world of Polonius, Claudius and Gertrude. This is the world of social relations based on greed, lust and selfishness. Brutus, a good man, is duped by Cassius to join the conspiracy against Caesar. He is moved by noble motives but he does not understand the people around him. The meaning of both plays lies in our increased awareness of the sordidness of the world which Hamlet hated or Brutus felt disgust in our increased sympathy for the good that is represented by Hamlet and Brutus. And the meaning of the tragedy also lies in our experience of human suffering revealed in all its magnitude unknown to us before.

On the subjective plane he reveals to us the intricacy of human motives. We have glimpses of the unfathomed world of powerful and often contradictory human impulses. He brings to the surface the under-currents of human consciousness, designated today as the Unconscious. This knowledge of the human mind coupled with deep sympathy for all who suffer should give a meaning to the tragedies of Shakespeare.

Shakespearean tragedy is both romantic and realistic. Romanticism provides a kind of enveloping atmosphere for the inner realistic kernel. Shakespeare used the rich material of native folklore for the purpose. The witches and the ghosts have a good deal of specific English colouring. In *Julius Caesar* we are told about the unnatural events that took place at the time of Ceasar's fall. We hear or see about these extraordinary events. The theory seems to be that natural and human society together form such an entity that the disturbance in one is a harbinger of a similar disturbance in the other. In *Julius Caesar* the unnatural event could be only the murder of Caesar. And yet we are made to sympathise with Brutus.

Shakesperean tragedy is made of both prose and verse. That itself is symbolic of its dual romantic-realistic nature. In the words of Dr. R.B. Sharma, "It is just to compare Shakespearean tragedy with Gothic Cathedrals. The Gothic architectonic lies not simply in the massiveness, the decorative effects, the repetition of patterns, the variety of incident and character, it also lies in the rich emotional mosaic, the interweaving of mighty passions, the fusion of opposite impulses, the blending of the tragic, cosmic and other elements with unprecedented skill and audacity."

Bradley pointed out the abnormality of the heroes of Shakespeare. We find in them abnormal conditions of the mind, insanity, somnambulism, hallucinations, etc. Of the four heroes, Macbeth is the one who has hallucinations. The hesitation of Brutus before the deed is elaborated into the brilliant picture of the fears and hallucinations of Macbeth. But the delusions of grandeur and persecution characteristic of the paranoid personality are found to be absent in the tragic heroes of Shakespeare.

There is an element of poetic justice in the tragedies of Shakespeare. Virtue may or may not triumph but vice is never seen victorious. Goneril, Regan, Edmund, Iago, Claudius, Laertes, all are destroyed or are promised sure destruction in the end. The romanticism underlying his concept of poetic justice is an essential component of Shakespeare's humanism. He believes in the ultimate destruction of evil. Good will survive even though reduced in a very large measure. This concept of poetic justice is also a subtle artistic device for saving a tragedy from a totally pessimistic conclusion and for making it bearable to the spectators.

Supernatural elements like ghosts, witches do not take direct part in the action of a play but serve only to intensify or illuminate some human action. The hailing of Macbeth by the witches arouses the latent ambitions of Macbeth and he hesitates not for the tiniest fraction of a second. In *Julius Caesar*, the appearance of the ghost of Caesar before Brutus illuminates the state of Brutus's mind by giving a confirmation to the sense of failure that was already in him. It is Brutus's evil spirit.

Shakesperean tragedy is essentially a drama of dissent. It expresses dissent not only with conventional morality and the general norms of social behaviour but also with traditional faith concerning sin, redemption, damnation and God and the human soul. It is remarkable how little speculation there is in his tragedies about the next world. Lear suffers greatly. Men surrounding him often talk about God and his justice. But what consolation is there for Lear? What answer is there to his questions : Why should Cordelia die? Why should Portia die? Is it because she is concerned for the welfare of her husband? She swallowed fire and died.

Shakespeare seems to feel how good religion is. He seems to admire the beauty of the illusions created by human faith as an aid to survival. But in the end he rejects these illusions. There is no heaven, no hell, no immortal soul, everything would pass away.

> And, like the baseless fabric of this vision,
> The cloud-capp'd towers, the gorgeous palaces,
> The solemn temples, the great globe itself,
> Yea, all which it inherit, shall dissolve.

For Prospero, for Lear, there is no vision of an enduring God.

With traditional faith and its pessimistic negation is woven the thread of another philosophical strain, — Stoicism. The ideal man is Horatio,

> ''... for thou hast been
> As one in suffering all that suffers nothing,
> A man that Fortune's buffets and rewards
> Has ta'en with equal thanks ...''
>
> (*Hamlet*, Act 3, Scene 2, lines : 63-66).

''That man is free'', says Epictetus, ''who lives as he wishes, who is proof against compulsion and hindrance and violence, whose impulses are untrammelled, who gets what he wills to get and avoids what he wills to avoid.'' This is the ideal which Horatio and Edgar uphold. But the tragic heroes are unable to overcome the disturbance caused by their emotions. Stoicism remains an ideal for them. Stoicism and passion form the two poles of the axis on which the action of Shakespearean tragedy revolves.

Stoicism also determines for Shakespeare the nature of a certain type of heroism in the tragedies. Surrounded by unnatural pain on all sides the hero defies death, dies fighting or even commits suicide. Epictetus quotes with approval the saying of Diogenes, ''A quiet death is the one sure means of freedom.'' Brutus, Othello, Antony, Cleopatra, Eros all die in the same stoic way. But a kind of perverted stoicism may lead to the creation of monster like Iago. Hence for Shakespeare love and compassion modify the stoic doctrine.

B. THE PLAY

Shakespeare's Treatment of the Source

"William Shakespeare took his material from three of Plutarch's *Lives*, those of Marcus Brutus, Julius Caesar and Marcus Antonius. From three separate accounts of the events leading to and resulting from the assassination of Caesar, presented with different emphasis and some differences in detail, he put together a plot which supremely well proportioned in its distribution of interest and wholly consistent in its development of character, and which seems inevitable in its chain of cause and effect" (T.S. Dorsch, *Julius Caesar*, Metheun and Co., p. xiii).

It has often been pointed out that Shakespeare, while accepting Plutarch's portrait of Caesar as a basis, lays more stress on his physical weakness. He adds a deafness in one ear and makes more of the falling sickness. Plutarch, indeed, who has no love for Caesar, comments on the way he overcame his physical disabilities. His soldiers admired him 'that he always continued all labour and hardness'. He

> 'yielded not to the disease of his body, to make it a cloak to cherish him withal, but, contrarily, took the pains of war a medicine to cure his sick body, fighting always with his disease, travelling continually, living soberly, and commonly lying abroad in the field' (*Lives*, vii, p.141).

He refuses the crown offered him by Antony so as to demonstrate that he did not wish to be a king; he postpones the reading of Artemidorous's warning that his personal interest are of less importance than those of the state; as Brutus admits, he has never let passion usurp the place of reason. But some of his utterances like: 'Cowards die many times before their deaths', 'Dange knows full well', are the manifestations of pride, of the 'self-approving self-dramatisation' of which Dr. F.R. Leavis accused Othello in *The Common Pursuit.*

It was argued by Schucking that Shakespeare had no intention of depicting Caesar as a braggart ... he is informing the audience that Caesar is godlike, not implying that the character is making excessive claims for himself. But Mr. J.I.M. Stewart argues that Shakespeare is leading the judicious members of his audience to discern that the 'public Caesar is the creation of an inflexible well'. But Caesar, as depicted by Shakespeare, has little in common with Hitler or Stalin. Nor do the conspirators themselves accuse him of anything except ambition. Caesar is the victim, not the hero. Thrice has Caesar refused a crown — however reluctantly — so that conspirators and Brutus have little justifi-cation that Caesar would change his nature. Brutus himself admits, that Caesar has not disjoined remorse from power, or allowed himself to be governed by his passion. What is even more absurd — as Coleridge pointed out in *Shakespearean Criticism* I, p.14 — is that Caesar was already an absolute ruler.

There was a case for the assassination of Caesar, as Shakespeare was aware; but in his soliloquy (Act II, Scene i, p. 10-34) Brutus has not given a single valid argument. But it seems likely that the soliloquy was carefully designed to reveal the flaw in the mind of the hero, Brutus. He is completely blind to the realities of the situation, Caesar's absolute power.

Brutus is essentially Plutarch's Brutus in Shakespeare. Yet, even here, for all that makes him a dramatic character as distinct from a copy-book hero, his divided mind, his self-deception, his final tragic disillusion, Shakespeare received the hints from Plutarch. Shakespeare depicts Brutus as a bad judge of character, but as by no means devoid of political shrewdness and practical wisdom. For instance, in Plutarch it is Antony who suggests that Caesar's body should be honourably buried, and not in hugger-mugger, lest the people might thereby take occasion to be worse offended in they did otherwise'. Shakespeare transfers the argument to Brutus in Act III, Scene i, 239-43.

"The 'hugger-mugger' suggests," says Ernest Schanzer, "that Shakespeare had that very passage from Plutarch at the back of his mind when writing these lines, a striking example of how North's more vivid idioms were garnered up in the poet's memory, to be brought out when some similarity of situation recalled them."

The characters of both Cassius and Antony are shown in the play in a nobler light than in Plutarch. Plutarch's Cassius was choleric, cruel, prone to injustice and selfish game. But in Shakespeare he is out and out a patriot, though jealous of Caesar's greatness, having a number of great qualities — worldly wisdom, keen insight, military experience, etc.

Plutarch's Antony is a mixture of the base and the great, capable of both good and evil. In Shakespeare Antony is a sensualist, given to pleasure, who suddenly blazes forth as an eloquent orator, a successful diplomat and a warm friend of Caesar and becomes the chief instrument in the avenging of the murder of Caesar.

Plutarch also provided the basis for the portraits of Portia, Calphurnia and Cicero. Shakespeare made the most of the few words he found in Plutarch about, for instance, the sick Ligarius's faith in Brutus, Metellus Cimber's petition to Caesar, and the poet Cinna's treatment in the hands of the mob; but it is his own touches that gives a lively reality to these men for the few moments that they are before us. Dowden has pointed how profoundly true to Roman life and character Shakespeare manages to seem; he also observes that he "was aware that his personages must be men before they are Romans"; and certainly the personages of Julius Caesar minor as well as major, come to life as real human beings.

The historical period covered by the incidents may be said to extend over three years, beginning with Caesar's entry into Rome, 45 B.C., and ending with the battle of Philippi, 42 B.C. though the Lupercalian festival described in I, ii takes us forward from 45 B.C. to February 44 B.C. Shakespeare compresses the events of these years to a matter of six stage days, employing the same devices which he used in the English Chronicle plays, only more softly and with greater dramatic effectiveness. In I, ii, Cassius says that he will this night throw writings at Brutus's window, urging him to join their conspiracy, and in I, iii, Cinna is asked to carry out this programme. Yet in II, i, which seems to follow without an interval, Brutus says that he has for a long time received these instigations, and there are other indications to show that the events of the first Act have been left behind. Secondly, in the third Act, the interval between Caesar's murder and Antony's incitement of the mob has been reduced to a minimum so that the contrast between Brutus's speech and Antony's may be fully effective. Then, again, in history there is a lengthy interval between the events of Act III and those of Act IV, occupied mostly by the jealousies and intrigues of Antony and Octavius, but in the drama it seems to be slurred over. The many adventures and wanderings of Brutus and Cassius since their flight from Rome are also more or less ignored. There are other instances of compression but all these do not interfere with the impression of the lapse of long periods of time, which alone can give credibility to the tremendous upheavals portrayed in the drama. Shakespeare's purpose in these deviations from historical facts, was to give greater artistic unity to the drama. The essential conception of characters have been changed to make the play more dramatic. His object is to enlist our sympathy with the republican leaders, and for this he has underrated Caesar and magnified Brutus and Cassius. Moreover, by ennobling the conspirators he has added to the interest of the play as a tragedy of character. We experience alternations of emotions, "Out feelings being balanced between admiration of the character of Brutus and pity for the injury done to Caesar". Antony is ennobled, for it was fitting that the work of avenging Caesar's death and the triumph of Caesarism should be performed by no mean instrument.

Besides Plutarch, other sources of Shakespeare's play have been pointed — (1) A Latin play, called *Epilogus Caesaris Interfecti,* the work of Dr. P. Edes, performed at Oxford in 1582. (2) An anonymous English play on *The Tragedy of Caesar and Pompey* performed at Whitehall in 1562 and published in an edition in 1594. But it may be safely asserted now that Shakespeare's indebtedness to these is slight. Some suggestion for Antony's famous oration may have been furnished by Appian's history, *The Civil Wars;* translated in 1578.

Date of Composition

On 21 September, 1599, a Swiss doctor travelling in England, who was much taken with the London playhouses and their elegant entertainments, went across the river at about two o'clock in the afternoon to the 'house with the thatched roof' in order to see a play about Julius Caesar. He recorded afterwards in his journal that it was very well acted by 'about fifteen persons', 'and there was a most elegant and curious dance' at the end. What he had seen was almost certainly a performance of Shakespeare's play during its first run at any theatre. It is rare for us to be able to date a performance at an Elizabethan public playhouse so exactly; the interest on this occasion is enormously increased because the theatre concerned was to be the most famous in modern Europe — the first Globe (1599-1613) of Shakespeare's company, the King's or Lord Chamberlain's Men, which had just that autumn opened its doors.

Weaver's *The Mirror of Martyrs,* a work published in 1601, contains certain lines, which clearly allude to Brutus's and Antony's funeral orations :

"The many-headed multitude were drawne
By Brutus speach, that Caesar was ambitious,

When eloquent Mark Antonie had showne
His vertues, who but Brutus then was vicious?

But T.S. Dorsch thinks differently, "*The Mirror of Martyrs* was printed in 1601, but a passage in the Dedication to William Couell says that it 'some years ago was made fit for the Print' whence it has been inferred that it was written as early as 1599. But Weever's statement was not true" (T.S. Dorsch, *Julius Caesar*, the Arden Shakespeare, London, p. viii). According to Charles Crawford, "*The Mirror of Martyrs* is literally packed from beginning to end with oddments stolen from Fairfax's Godfrey of Bulloigne, which was unknown before 1600" (Charles Crawford, *Englands Parnassus,* Clar. Press, 1613, p. 388). The poem cannot therefore have been lying in corner of Weever's study for two years, as he claims, in anything like complete form. His allusions to the speeches of Brutus and Antony is interesting as a comparatively early reference to the play, but does not help us to date it with any accuracy.

Julius Caesar is not mentioned in Francis Mere's *Palladis Tamia: Wits Treasury,* a book published in 1598 containing a list of Shakespeare's plays up to that time. Hence it may be presumed that the play was produced after 1598.

Another passage which bears upon the date is a stanza of Drayton's poem, *The Baron's War (1603)*:

"Such one he was, of him we boldly say,
In whose rich soul all sovereign powers did suit
In whom in peace the elements all lay
So mixt, as none could sovereignty impute."

These lines resemble Antony's last speech over the dead body of Brutus and are evidently a borrowing from Shakespeare:

"His life was gentle, and the elements
So mix'd in him that Nature might stand up
And say to all the world 'This was a man!' "

Caesar's story was fresh in Shakespeare's mind when he wrote *Hamlet*. There is a distinct reference when Polonius says: "I did enact Julius Caesar. I was killed i' th' Capitol, Brutus killed me" (Act III, Scene ii, lines 100-101). *Hamlet* was published in 1601 and this proves that Julius Caesar must have preceded it. Thus from these evidences it is clear that *Julius Caesar* was not produced earlier than 1598 and later than 1601.

In tone of thought, in style and versification. *Julius Caesar* closely resembles *Hamlet* and other plays of the same period. The characteristics of the plays of this period is an even balance between thought and expression, which is also the characteristic of *Julius Caesar*. The metrical test also points to the same date. Rhyme has largely disappeared. The feminine or double endings reveal a marked increase upon the percentage registered in, say, *Twelfth Night* coming to the 'end-stopped' and 'run-on' lines we note a very slight increase in the former but a material increase in the latter. Puns, conceits, superficial, over-wrought rhetoric, — the characteristics of the style of youthful plays — have almost wholly disappeared from *Julius Caesar*.

The Story of the Play

Julius Caesar, successful in a civil war, has returned in triumph to Rome. In the first scene the two tribunes of the people reprove some workmen for not being at work and for celebrating Caesar's triumph, which they themselves deplore, as his victory was against fellow-Romans, the two sons of the great Pompey. They fear the rise of Caesar to this great position and popularity. Two others who are similarly apprehensive are Brutus and Cassius, and when they hear offstage great shouts from the crowd they instantly assume great honours are being heaped on Caesar. They learn from Casca that Mark Antony has three times offered Caesar the crown, which the victor has three times, but with increasing reluctance, refused. Cassius secretly plans to arrange for a number of letters, apparently from different people, to be thrown through Brutus's windows that night, to convince him that many are fearful of Caesar's ambition and think of Brutus as a potential natural leader of the opposition. That night there is a fierce thunderstorm and strange and unnatural happenings are reported (for example, a slave's hand flamed and burned 'like twenty torches' without getting scorched, and Casca encountered a lion near the Capitol which 'glaz'd upon me, and went surely by, /Without annoying me'). Such frightening omens are seen by Cassius as 'instruments of fear and warning' from heaven, aghast at the ambitions of Caesar. Quickly Cassius begins to form a conspiracy.

Meanwhile Brutus, sleepless and anguished debates with himself, torn between his honourable nature, his liking for Caesar and his fear of Caesar's possible tyranny. He has come to the conclusion that for Rome's sake Caesar must die,when the conspirators arrive. Although Cassius has formed the conspiracy, all look to Brutus as the natural leader. Brutus disagrees with Cassius, and has his way, in two matters. He does not think it necessary for them to swear an oath to bind themselves to perform the deed ('what need we any spur but our own cause'), and he refuses to countenance the murder of Mark antony as well. He urges that they should 'be sacrificers, but not butchers',that they should kill 'boldly, but not wrathfully', and that Antony, who 'is given/ To sports, to wildness, and much company' can 'do no more than Caesar's arm/ When Caesar's head is off'. When the conspirators have gone, Brutus's wife Portia comes to him, sadly aware that something is troubling him and wanting to share it with him.

Then we see Caesar, also sleepless in this troubled night of storm. His wife Calpurnia has dreamed of Caesar being murdered and begs him not to go to the Capitol. His servant reports that the priests he has been sent to consult urge Caesar not to stir forth that day. Caesar scorns these fears but gives way to her entreaty. At this point Decius Brutus comes to escort him to the Capitol, and persuades him to go, because he will be thought to be afraid if he does not and because he is to be offered the crown that day. The other conspirators all come to accompany Caesar to the Capitol. We briefly observe Artemidorus, reading aloud a letter he has written to Caesar warning him of the conspiracy and naming the conspirators, which he intends to give to Caesar as he passes. Portia agitatedly sends the servant Lucius to the Capitol, and a soothsayer who earlier warned Caesar to 'Beware the Ides of March' (15 March), which it now is, passes on his way to warn Caesar again.

Caesar comes to the Capitol, brushing aside the soothsayer and Artemidorus with their warnings. In the Senate House, one of the conspirators Trebonius lures Antony away, and Caesar rejects an appeal by Metellus Cimber on behalf of his banished brother. The conspirators gather round as if to plead the banished man's cause and stab Caesar to death one by one, Brutus giving the final blow. Brutus reassures the senators and others present: no one else is in danger now that 'ambition's debt is paid' with the death of Caesar. Cassius calls for 'Liberty, freedom and enfranchisement' to be cried out in the streets. Trebonius returns, reporting that Antony has fled to his house appalled; soon Antony's servant comes to say that his master will 'not love Caesar dead/ So well as Brutus living' if he can be 'resolv'd/How Caesar hath deserv'd to lie in death', and is sent to fetch him. When Antony comes, he grieves over 'mighty Caesar' laid so low, 'finds no hour so fit/As Caesar's death's hour' for his own death, and calls on the conspirators, if they intend to execute him, to kill him straightaway. Reassured of their amity he shakes each bloody hand, at the same time asking dead Caesar's forgiveness. He asks permission to take Caesar's dead body to the market-place to speak at his funeral. The generous spirited Brutus immediately agrees, though Cassius sees danger in this. When the conspirators withdraw, Antony in a soliloquy asks pardon of dead Caesar 'that I am meek and gentle with these butchers' and grimly prophesies bloodshed and civil strife.

In the forum (market-place) Brutus tells the crowd that despite his love for Caesar he loved Rome more, and that is why, 'as he was ambitious, I slew him'. Then Mark Antony enters with Caesar's body, and in a famous speech contrives to move from temperate praise of Brutus gradually to questioning his motives and action, and then, despite continual references to his 'honourable' nature, to incriminate him and the conspirators. He stirs the crowd to lament Caesar's death, pointing out that he had three times declined the offer of the crown, and holding up the torn and blood-stained mantle. Finally, he tells them that in his will Caesar had left his gardens to Rome and a sum of money to every citizen, thus inflaming them to mutiny and to seek revenge. After the people have carried off Caesar's body, news is brought to Antony that young Octavius Caesar has arrived in Rome, and that Brutus and Cassius have abruptly left the city. The first victim of the inflamed mob is Cinna the Poet, mistaken for Cinna the conspirator.

Antony, Octavius and Lepidus form the 'triumvirate' (rule of three men). They decide on who is to be executed, and when Lepidus is sent to fetch Caesar's will — Antony intending to meddle with its provisions and lessen the outgoing payments — Antony shows his real ruthlessness further in scornful denigration of Lepidus. In camp near Sardis we witness an angry quarrel between Brutus and Cassius, in which finally Brutus is placatory and Cassius quickly then responds. Brutus now reveals that he is 'sick of many griefs', the chief of them being the news he has received of his wife Portia's dreadful suicide. News is brought that Mark Antony and Octavius are advancing with their army to Philippi. Brutus proposes an immediate march and attack, but Cassius prefers to let the enemy seek them. Brutus dominates in this, claiming that their own forces are now 'at the height, ready to decline', and they should seize the initiative: 'There is a tide in the affairs of man, /Which, taken at the flood, leads on to fortune', and it is so agreed. That night, his boy Lucius having fallen asleep while playing and singing to him in his tent, Brutus is briefly visited by the ghost of Caesar, come as 'they evil spirit, Brutus' to warn him that they will meet again at Philippi. On the plains of Philippi Octavius observes with satisfaction that the enemy forces have come down off the hills. Brutus and Cassius confront Antony and Octavius in an angry exchange. Cassius, whose birthday it is, confides in Messala that it was against his will and advice that the decision has been taken to fight here, and refers to ill omens — ravens, crows and kites flying in the sky above their army. He and Brutus then part, before taking up their separate positions in the battle array : 'If we do meet again, why, we shall smile;/ If not, why then this parting was well made'. In the battle Cassius's men flee, and, believing that Brutus's force has been surrounded and that the day is lost. Cassius calls on his servant to kill him, and dies. But in fact Brutus has overthrown Octavius. The victorious Brutus, learning of Cassius's voluntary death, feels that the spirit of Caesar (which had again appeared to him at night) 'walks abroad, and turns our swords/ In our own proper entrails'. He sadly salutes his dead companion, and continues the fight, but there has been a reverse and Brutus, saddened by loss, death and ill omens, feels his hour has come and asks his friend Volumnius to kill him, which he refuses to do. But another, Strato, agrees to hold the sword while Brutus runs on to it. The victors Antony and Octavius enter, and Antony pays tribute to Brutus, 'the noblest Roman of them all./ All the conspirators save only he/ Did that they did in envy of great Caesar;/ He only, in general honest thought,/ And common good to all..'

The Supernatural in Julius Caesar

The Elizabethan people believed in supernatural appearances and powers, in witches, ghosts and fairies. Though the English Renaissance forged a new spirit in the sixteenth century England, yet the old belief in ghosts, witches, prophecy and magic did not subside immediately. Not only the groundlings, but even learned persons like James I believed in their powers. Hence, it is not surprising that Shakespeare, whether he believed in ghosts or not, has introduced them in his works. This is especially so, because the introduction of the supernatural adds an element of mystery and deeper moral significance to the drama. It symbolizes the mysterious connexion of men with the unseen world.

The supernatural machinery plays an important role in *Hamlet, Macbeth* and *Julius Caesar.* Unnatural phenomena of weather, such as quakes, storms or fire, which occur in *Julius Caesar,* were recognizable both by their presence and by the remarks on them as omens that unnatural events in the world would occur. To Elizabethans, to whom the explanations of physical science was veiled events pertaining to weather and climate still retained some of the magical. Shakespeare drew on this traditional concept of the storm before the Ides of March. In Act I, Scene iii, Casca appears on the street, carrying an unsheathed sword. He tells Cicero :

> "... O Cicero,
> I have seen tempests, when the scolding winds
> Have riv'd the knoty Oaks; and I have seen
> Th' ambitious ocean swell and rage and foam,
> To be exalted with the threat'ning clouds:"

He further says :

> A common slave, you know him well by sight,
> Held up his left hand, which did flame and burn
> Who glaz'd upon me, and went surly by,
>
> ... ...
>
> ... When these prodigies
> Do so conjointly meet, let not men say,
> "These are their reasons, they are natural".

Clouds drop fire instead of rain, graves are giving up their dead. What do all these mean? Do not these presage some alternation in human life? Thus a bond of connexion has been established between the natural and human worlds. The commotion in nature is accompanied by commotion in the human world.

Thus do these supernatural signs illuminate the course of coming events, but they do not mould or determine them. An instance of the supernatural agency intensifying human action is to be found in *Macbeth* also. The witches in *Macbeth* do not originate a course of action but merely quicken an impulse which is already in the mind of Macbeth.

Similarly, prophecy is part and parcel of Roman superstition. The Soothsayer warns Caesar:

"Beware the Ides of March". But Caesar dismisses him by saying: "He is a dreamer. Let us leave him. Pass. "The whole Act II, Scene iii is taken by Artemidorus, reading a paper, forewarning Caesar:

"Caesar, beware of Brutus; take heed of Cassius; come not near Casca, have an eye to Cinna; trust not Trebonius; mark well Metellus Cimber; Decius Brutus loves thee not; thou hast wrong'd Caius Ligarius. There is but one mind in all these men, and it is bent against Caesar. If thou beest not immortal, look about you: security gives way to conspiracy. The mighty gods defend thee! Thy lover."

But Caesar dismisses him by saying :

"What, is the fellow mad" (Act III, Scene i)

E.M. Forster says : "The first of these explosions is of course the murder itself. The preparation of this is masterly — the growth of the conspiracy, omens, storms, apparitions, Portia's forebodings, Calpurna's dream, the tempting of Caesar to the Senate House, the failure of Artemidorus to save him, the luring away of Antony: and then the dead" (E.M. Forster, *Two Cheers for Democracy).*

When Cassius went to Philippi, some birds also followed him. First of all, his forces were accompanied by birds of good omen, then these fled and carrion birds, of the worst possible omen, flew with them. The birds of ill-omen, appearing when they did, telegraphed a message to Shakespeare's audience, familiar with the convention, indeed the tradition, of meaning through birds.

Most significant is the appearance of the ghost of Caesar. At Sardis the ghost of Julius Caesar appears before Brutus and promises to do so again in Philippi. At the appearance of the ghost the hair of Brutus stands and his blood runs cold. When the ghost vanishes at Sardis, Brutus says : "Now I have taken heart thou vanishest" (Act IV, Scene iii). Commenting on this utterance of Brutus, Hudson observes: "Thus strongly, though quietly, marks the ghost as subjective: as soon as Brutus recovers his firmness, the illusion is broken. The order of things is highly judicious here, in bringing the 'horrible vision' upon Brutus just after he has heard of Portia's shocking death. With that sorrow weighing upon him, he might well see ghost." But this theory of subjectivity cannot explain away all the ghosts in Shakespeare. The ghost in Hamlet is seen not only by the prince, but by Marcellus and Bernardo, the unimaginative soldiers, and what is more, by the sceptical Horatio who had declared a moment ago that " 't will not appear". The ghost of Caesar gives a definite shape to and intensifies some movement already present in the mind of Brutus. It intensifies the "sense of failure" already present there and urges him to step forward towards his doom.

The ghost of Caesar fulfils also another purpose in *Julius Caesar,* namely, it "serves as a kind of visible symbol of the vast posthumous power of the Dictator's" (Dowden) and thus gives unity to the drama. The living Caesar dominates the first part, and his angry spirit controls the second. Again the ghost represents the 'spirit of history' and indicates that Caesar, the being of flesh and blood, may be struck down by the conspirators, but the trends originated by him are not thus to perish.

Shakespeare's presentation of the ghost shows him as an artist of the highest order. The ghosts in the hands of minor poets have something of the gross and ridiculous in them. They appear too palpably and are loquacious. But Shakespeare skilfully prepares his audience for receiving these apparitions. He excites the imagination of the audience by some previous event, gives a wildness to the scene, lulls the critical faculty, and only after that brings in the ghost, so that we give willing credit to it. Thus in *Julius Caesar* the ghost appears to Brutus when the mind of the audience has been prepared for such supernatural manifestation by the recently received news of the shocking death of Portia, by the gloom and silence of the night, by the dreamy music of Lucius, by the flickering of the taper. The appearance is brief and the spirit does not utter too many words and vanishes soon. It is this artistic handling of the ghost that makes it so impressive.

Julius Caesar – A Political Play

Stopford Brooke remarks: "The Play (*Julius Caesar)* is a political play and of kind different from that of any other in his works." The situation presented in the first scene is distinctly a political situation; and it is accordingly against a background of politics that the action is cast. The figure of Julius Caesar stands out, brilliant. From the start he is idealized in point of power, general respect, glory. He is endured dramatically with strength, importance, almost divinity. He is a sublime figure-head:

> "Why, man, he doth bestride the narrow world
> Like a Colossus ..." (I, ii. 135)

The Caesar-idea is accompanied by all the usual Shakespearean suggestions of world-glory and life-beauty. Here they are raised to a high pitch. The men of Rome put on their best 'attire' (I, i, 53) for his triumph, 'strew flowers in his way' (I, i, 55). His images are robed and decked with his 'trophies' and 'ceremonies' (I, i, 69-74). Everyone's attention hangs on his words:

> "Peace, ho ! Caesar speaks." (i. ii. 1)

His entry is accompanied with music. He is associated with images of infinity, the North Star and Olympus (III, 1, 60, 74). He is conscious of his own triumphant destiny:

> "...danger knows full well
> That Caesar is more dangerous than he:
> We are two lions litter'd in one day,
> And I the elder and more terrible". (II, ii, 44).

The idea of Caesar is far greater than Caesar the man. This is Caesarism. It is also significant that he often speaks of himself in the third person.

> "Caesar is turn'd to hear..."
> "Yet Caesar shall go forth..."
> "Shall Caesar send a lie?"

When he warns Antony of Cassius, he adds:

> "I rather tell thee what is to be fear'd
> Than what I fear; for always I am Caesar."

Martin Buber, in his great book, *I and Thou,* has made us familiar with an important distinction between the world of 'thou' (the world of relationship) and the world of 'it' (the world where things, and even people, are treated simply as objects, and manipulated accordingly).

But the strange thing is this that there is no sign that the people of Rome, unlike the plebeian in *Coriolanus,* have any grievance against him. They seem to be quite happy, and fairly prosperous; only eager, like the good fellows they are, 'to get themselves into more work'. There is no sign that they feel themselves to be victims of any sort of oppression, and evidently the notion that there is anything unworthy in acquiescence in a rule that is merely righteous (we have Brutus's testimony that it is righteous) is a political conception far beyond them. Comparisons of the relative merits of good government and self-government would be meaningless to them. But it has been argued that an Elizabethan audience would know the way to distinguish a good ruler from a tyrant and since Caesar surrounds himself with flatterers and yes-men, and rules by caprice rather than by reason, they would certainly have regarded him as a tyrant. Mr. Bernard Breyer concludes :

> "In short he shows himself the very picture of a tyrant above his fellow men, above the law, above reason itself. No Elizabethan in the theatre could doubt that here was a man ripe for the knife. And none, I believe, could have viewed his ensuing slaughter with anything but complete satisfaction, or could have blamed Brutus for his part in the deed" (Bernard Beyer, 'A New Look at *Julius Caesar' in Essays in Honour of Walter Clyde Curry,* 1954, p. 177).

In the opening scene, Marullus rebukes the Cobbler :

> "You blocks, you stones, you worse than senseless things !
> O you hard hearts, you cruel men of Rome,
> Knew you not Pompey?" (I, 1.35-37)

Marullus and Flavius in this scene are represented as two republican oligarchs and politicians, enemies of Caesar. They do not appear again in the play; there is later just one brief mention of them; but they serve their turn, and their words and actions make clear the kind of political principles which form the entire stock-in-trade of the lesser members of the aristocratic conspiracy, and even of the nobler protagonists, Brutus and Cassius. When Marullus and Flavius are left to themselves :

> "These growing feathers pluck'd from Caesar's wing
> Will make him fly an ordinary pitch,
> Who else would soar above their view of men
> And keep us all servile fearfulness." (I. i, 72-75)

There it is; just repudiation of the principle of the rule of the single person, Caesarism. Cassius cries:

> "Now is it Rome indeed, and room enough,
> When there is in it but one only man.
> O you and I have heard our fathers say,
> There was a Brutus once that would have brook'd
> The eternal devil to keep his state in Rome
> As easily as a king. " (I. ii. 154-159)

Some ten years later than the composition of *Julius Caesar,* Shakespeare, in *Antony and Cleopatra,* put the same political doctrine into a speech of the younger Pompey:

> "What was't
> That moved pale Cassius to conspire And what
> Made all-honoured, honest, Roman Brutus,
> With the arm'd rest, courtiers of beauteous freedom,
> To drench the Capitol — but that they would
> Have one man but a man?" (II. iv. 15-19)

Brutus, at one point, was against the symbol of royal rule rather than the actual kingship. The strange soliloquy of Brutus 'in his orchard' has puzzled commentators. 'What character', asked Coleridge, 'did Shakespeare mean his Brutus to be? ' The puzzle ceases, however, when we recognize that the Brutus of Shakespeare is, for all his studious habits, no profound or subtle thinker, that he has no coherent political philosophy, and is not the 'ideal Republican' Swinburne imagined him to be. Shakespeare unlike the modern playwrights wrote essentially personal drama — drama based on the actions of living and real men, not symbols. In a modern play like Galsworthy's *Strife* the two leaders only symbolise the classes to which they belong – the real conflict is between the labouring class and the masters. Shakespeare, perhaps, was not much interested in 'ideal Republicans', but he was greatly interested in a nobly-natured mistaken man, such as he pictured a man who, in Dowden's phrase, was 'studious of self-perfection', but who, just because his motives were so unblemished and his reasons so confused, was terribly liable to go astray. 'It must be by his death,' Brutus begins. That, by Cassius's persuasion, seems settled; and Brutus goes on to find justification for the deed which he now feels to be a duty laid on him. He has 'no personal cause to spurn at' Caesar, and the absence of personal grievance seems to go some way to warrant the act. One must murder on principle and 'for the general'; that is to say, for commoners like the carpenter and the shoemaker. Brutus, however, makes an attempt to be honest with himself.

> "Th' abuse of greatness is when it disjoins
> Remorse from power." (II. i. 18-19)

It is to be noted that it is the abuse and not the greatness itself, that Brutus boggles at, but the Cobbler and his fellows so far have not suffered from the abuse; for then follows a tribute, the highest that could well be paid, to the calm wisdom and impartial justice of Caesar's rule —

"...and, to stark truth of Caesar, I have not known when his affections sway'd more than his reason..."

'The quarrel', he confesses, 'Will bear no colour for the thing he is', 'that is, on its merits there is no case; but we may 'Fashion it thus'. Caesar wishes to be crowned (though, to be sure, that is just Casca's suspicion about him); and that might 'change his nature'; and so to avoid a hypothetic disaster, let us —

> "... Think him as a serpent's egg,
> Which, hatch'd, would, as his kind, grow mischievous,
> And kill him in the shell." (II. i. 32-34)

Such, in Shakespeare's, is Brutus the politician.

All others stand against Caesar because of their grudges. The cause for which they avoidedly stand is that of Republicanism. Rome has a Republican form of Government. The Romans hate the system of monarchy. Caesar threatens this form of government. The Republicans, therefore, murder him in order to avoid this danger. But Shakespeare seems to assert that forms of government are never to be looked upon in the abstract. They arise out of the crying needs of a nation. Imperialism was the crying need of the nation. The citizens who, with strange irony, would have in Brutus a new Caesar, were voicing the sentiments of the age itself.

The play, in the words of Stopford Brooke, ''puts in an artistic form, the two reasons why these revolutions which are in the right do not always succeed against forms of government which are in the wrong; why a struggle for freedom fails against tyranny, or if it should succeed for a time, as in the French Revolution, why it falls again under the power of despotism.'' These two reasons are — that the revolutionaries are mostly — actuated by ''personal motives'' and that the leaders of the revolutions, ''have no settled form of government ready to replace that which they have overthrown.'' In *Julius Caesar,* the so-called Republican ardour of the conspirators fails. Caesarism survives in the person of Octavius. This is evident from the dying remarks of Brutus —

> ''O Julius Caesar, thou art mighty yet''

The fact is evident that Caesarism or imperialism is an indestructible force. It is independent of persons. It is permanent constitutional factor and Shakespeare in the play has emphasised it. This has led many critics to agree with Walt Whitman who says, ''Shakespeare is incarnated, uncompromising feudalism in literature.''

Role of Irony in *Julius Caesar*

Jacqueline Pearson says, ''What is perhaps most striking about the play (*Julius Caesar)* is its range of ironic devices, including deflation, parallelism and contrast, and even ironic manipulation of sources : no important character is presented simply or from only one viewpoint'' (Jacqueline Pearson, ''Romans and Barbarians'' *in Shakespearean Tragedy).*

To take the last point first, to Flavius and Marullus Caesar is a usurper who has come 'in triumph over Pompey's blood' (I. i. 51). Immediately after this, we see a Caesar with royal charisma, not only kingly but godlike, and, in the words of Antony: ''When Caesar says, 'Do this, it is perform'd' (I. ii. 10). To Cassius his personal weakness renders ludicrous his political strength. To Brutus he is a moderate man never previously swayed by his passions, but who is a ''serpent's egg'' (II. i. 32) which may hatch out a venomous snake. To both he is a usurper. To Antony on the contrary he is the murdered king, ''royal'' (III. i. 127), ''most noble'' (III. i. 156), ''the noblest man'' (III. i. 256) whose ''sacred blood'' (III. ii. 135) has been shed so that destructive civil war must result. None of these views, though, is to be seen as having absolute validity.

Caesar the hero is repeatedly deflated by our glimpses of Caesar the man. At his first appearance his perfect control of the situation and Antony's assertion of his godlike power are undermined by our progressive discoveries that he is childless, deaf in one ear, and epileptic. Sometimes the Tamburlainean self-assertions are more ludicrous than impressive: "Danger knows full well/That Caesar is more dangerous than he" (II. ii. 44-5).

He denies that he is one of the mass of "ordinary man" (III. i. 37) but is rather as "constant as the northern star" (II. i. 60). This claim to superhuman stability is shockingly, and at once, disproved by his murder. The man who is more dangerous than danger, who is constant as the northern star, is actually all too ordinary and all too mortal. One of Shakespeare's most powerful ironic device in the play is this juxtaposition of starkly contrasting details, like the northern star and the bloody corpse.

Antony is similarly presented in terms of contrast. His Forum speech is an emotional masterpiece, but there are clearly moments when the rhetoric masks an inner dishonesty : there is no way he can know, for instance, which dagger made which hole in Caesar's mantle. Moreover, the speech contains a passionate attack on murder as a political weapon, and culminates in the reading of Caesar's will. However, in one of the play's revealing juxtapositions, when we next see him he is himself using murder as a political weapon by agreeing to the proscriptions (IV. i .I), and is himself trying to devise a way to circumvent the terms of Caesar's will.

In the case of Brutus, his idealism, his concern for the public good, his personal suffering, and his dislike for the means he must use lead him fatally to misjudge Antony's nature. He is often guilty of misunderstanding the situation or of muddled thinking. On the field of Philippi he gives the word too early (V. iii. 5), just as Cassius' too hasty suicide finally loses the battle. In his quarrel with Cassius he repeatedly fails to recognize his own muddled thinking. Throughout the play Shakespeare uses juxtaposition and deflation remorselessly to expose the human flaws behind the facade of Brutus, Caesar or Antony.

There is an even ironic manipulation of source — Plutarch. When Cassius tries to draw Brutus into the conspiracy, he launches a bitter personal attack on Caesar. He once lost a swimming match with Cassius, who then had to rescue him like Aeneas saving the elderly Anchises. But this vivid speech contradicts Plutarch. His Caesar is a famous swimmer who once, attacked in Egypt, "leaping into the sea, with great hazard saved himself by swimming". Even Cassius's identification of himself with Aeneas is Janus-faced. Cassius implies that legitimate rule of the state founded by Aeneas lies with himself and the democratic party, and not with Aeneas' usurping blood-descendant Caesar. At the same time, however, Renaissance writers were as likely to be aware of the non-Virgilian tradition that Aeneas at Troy was not a hero but a traitor. Does Cassius represent legitimate government or treason?

Similarly, we find ironies of parallel scenes and speeches. Antony's Forum speech contrasts with Brutus's, the quarrel between Brutus and Cassius with that between Octavius and Antony. Brutus, who murders Caesar for the common good, is offered Caesarship by the uncomprehending plebeians (III. ii. 52). In the quarrel scene his self-righteousness actually leads him to echo Caesar. His "wrong I mine enemies?/And if not so, how should I wrong a brother?" (IV. ii. 38-9) comes disturbingly close to "Caesar doth not wrong" (III. i. 47). Shakespeare presents political life in all its shabbiness and compromises.

Another aspect of irony is a tendency for different interpretations to be offered for the same event. This is obvious in the case of the central events — for Brutus the murder of Caesar is an extreme act of public-spiritedness, for Antony "bloody treason" (III. ii. 194). Cassius, walking through the storm on the eve of Caesar's murder, suggests two different meanings for this "monstrous state" (I. iii. 71). First of all, he sees discord in the heavens reflecting disorder on earth, a disorder whose cause is Caesar's usurpation (I. iii. 72-8). A moment later, though, he sees the storm prefiguring the murder of Caesar, an act at once necessary and horrifying, "most bloody, fiery and most terrible" (I. iii. 130). Simple good and evil do not exist in the world of the play. Every character, every event, offers a number of possible interpretations.

Destiny in Julius Caesar

The entire play, *Julius Caesar*, is dominated by the idea,

> "There's a divinity that shapes our ends,
> Rough-hew them how we will."

Men are but playthings in the hands of this divinity, and even the greatest is not immune from a fate which overhangs him and which is decreed by some invisible power. In *Julius Caesar*, Shakespeare paints two characters of different hues. On the one hand is Caesar, 'the noblest man that ever lived in the tide of times,' the man who 'doth bestride the narrow world like a colossus', the supreme example of a man of action. On the other hand is Brutus, the man whose life was most disinterested and unselfish, 'the noblest Roman of them all', in whom the elements are so mix'd in him, that Nature might standup/And say to all the world, "This was a man!" Yet neither the man of action nor the man of idea and intellect is able to withstand the onslaughts of the invisible hand of Destiny. They and the rest of the characters are mere pawns on the chessboard whose movements and actions are directed by Fate.

At every stage in the play we find the truth of this statement. Caesar is so much "the foremost man of all this world" – to borrow Brutus's description – that his greatness and nobility do not need to be emphasized. Yet this brave and shrewd general is frightened in his heart when he hears his wife's dreams in which she cried out' "Help, ho! They murther Caesar!", and consoles himself with the thought:

> "What can be avoided
> Whose end is purpos'd by the mighty gods?"

A blind fate seems to be leading him to his destined fate. Therefore, all the entreaties of his wife, which had slightly shaken him and which had made him to decide to abandon his visit to the senate, prove of no avail before the sweet and carefully designed words of Decius. Only if at that moment Antony had come, whom Caesar expected and through whom he wanted to send word of his not attending the senate, he would have escaped death. Again, if he had listened to the warning of the Soothsayer and not merely dismissed him as a dreamer things would have been well. Similarly, even if at the last moment he had not brushed aside the written warning which Artemidorus had thrust in his hand with the remarks that which concerned him personally would be last attended to, he would still have escaped. Above all, the whole supernatural machinery is utilized to further this same effect. The owl hooting in the market place is simply a reminder that the ultimate control of things is beyond calculation or human management.

It is the same with Brutus. He is driven from the seclusion of his study to perform a task which is not congenial to him. Again, despite Cassius's pleading he spares Antony's life and even allows him to address at Caesar's funeral. He could very well have demolished the effects of Antony's speech on his audience if he had employed Cicero, a matchless orator, greater than Antony. He again, on the field of battle lightly treats the suggestion of Cassius not to stake the entire fortune of the battle on one single fight, and gives the word for the battle too soon. Though a wise man, he is robbed of his sound judgments by the cruel and unseen fate and which ultimately leads him to suffer and his suffering is strangely out of proportion to what he does. And as the supernatural portents indicated the impending doom of Caesar, so also the ghost of Caesar appearing before Brutus undermined his great faith in the Stoic philosophy, and made him believe that his end was near, and he says: "I know my hour is come. (v. v. 19)

The same is true of Cassius. One of the most clear-sighted and shrewd statesmen of Rome, he easily surrenders his clear and sound judgment to the hazy wishes of Brutus. On the field of battle a nameless fear seizes him. He too like Brutus was a philosopher and did not believe in omens. And yet he recalls fearfully :

> "This is my birth-day; as this very day
> Was Cassius born,". (V. i. 72-73)

He tells Messala that against his will "am I compell'd set/Upon one battle of all our liberties", he also reminds him that there was a time when he strongly believed in the Epicurean doctrine which is against a belief in supernatural happenings. Now he says

> " . . . now I change my mind,
> And partly credit things that do presage." (V. i.)

He then relates the story of two eagles, how they were with their ensign till they reached Philippi, and then they fled away and instead

> " . . . do ravens, crows, and kites
> Fly o'er our heads, and downward look on us,
> As we were sickly prey." (V. i. 85-87)

Fates again intervene when mistaking Titinius being captured by the enemy, Cassius puts an end to his life with the same sword with which he had stabbed Caesar. This is the time when victory seems to go to Brutus and Cassius.

If destiny is unkind to Caesar, Brutus, Cassius and the conspirators, it is kind to Antony and Octavius. By a sheer fluke Antony is prevented from being present in the Senate when Caesar was murdered, for if present he would have rushed to save Caesar and then done to death by the conspirators. Octavious comes when his visit is most opportune to the interests of both in Rome, and above all at a time when they were in grave danger on account of their weak position at Philippi, as Brutus and Cassius occupied the hills and upper regions where they could not be attacked successfully. Brutus foolishly orders his forces to come down to the plains, as it were guided by an unseen power, and brings about his own destruction. Thus the general atmosphere of the play is surcharged with the idea of all-pervasive divinity. Perhaps Shakespeare with the consciousness that he was writing a Roman play kept close to Plutarch in whom also the same idea is found emphasised. Perhaps he so designed the play in order to heighten its tragic effect.

Though there is a certain sense of doom before Caesar's murder which makes one feel that his death is inevitable, it would be wrong to suggest that Caesar is in the grip of a relentless destiny which cannot be avoided. In this respect, the application of "Character is Destiny" in Shakespeare is equally powerful and effective. It means the man plays the same part in building his future as the Destiny in the Classical drama did in controlling 'the fortunes of the heroes and heroines'. In other words :

> "The fault, dear Brutus, is not in our stars,
> But in ourselves, that we are underlings." (I. ii. 138-139)

He becomes prosperous or miserable according as he acts, and plucks for himself the fruits of his own deed.

In *Julius Caesar*, the dictum "Character is Destiny" is an exaggeration and misleading one, but nevertheless it is the exaggeration of a vital truth. When the tragedy advances to its close we feel that the calamities and catastrophes follow inevitably from the deeds of men and not from external forces, which may be called Fate or Destiny. Thus Caesar provokes Nemesis by his action to revive the title of king and seizes all political power. Snider says, "He could not tame his wild ambition, a fault which history might have pointed out. But he heeded her not. He wished and attempted what was not ripe for it. By his self-committed error, by his haughty ambition, he precipitated his fate." Brutus and Cassius too work out their own fate. "They erred in thinking that Rome could be saved by re-establishing the republic; as if the prosperity of a state depended on its form, as if a few individuals could bring about the moral regeneration of a nation by the magic of words." Besides, while Brutus was guided by a purity of motive, the other conspirators were jealous of Caesar's powers. Thus they brought about their doom. Thus far characters in this play may be called destiny.

This dictum summarises the personal accountability insisted upon by the Christian tradition and accepted by Iago when he tells Roderigo that " 'tis in ourselves that we are thus or thus ... the power and corrigible authority or this lies in our wills'' (*Othello*, I. iii. 332). The latter phrase also sums up a commonplace idea which Calvin expresses when he declares that ''all sin results from our own will and inclination'' (Quoted in Wilhelm Niesel, *The Theology of Calvin*), while Edmund's ridicule of the notion that ''we were villain on necessity, fools by heavenly compulsion'' or ''by a divine thrusting on'' similarly recalls a member of the logical expressions. Shakespeare combines Plutarch and the Christian tradition in *Julius Caesar*.

The Funeral Orations

The funeral orations of Brutus and Antony revealing fully the characters of the speakers, are designed to present strong contrasts. Brutus is a Stoic philosopher, having a cold and rational temperament, and in him emotion or passion is sternly repressed. His speech ''to the citizens approaches the Baconian ideal of establishing a just relationship between the mind and things : ''it is a pithy appeal to look at the facts'' (M.M. Mahood, *Shakespeare's Wordplay*, 1957). But this is one side of the coin. The other side, in the words of Antony :

> ''. . . . But were I Brutus
> And Brutus Antony, there were an Antony
> Would ruffle up your spirits, and put a tongue
> In every wound of Caesar that should move
> The stones of Rome to rise and mutiny.'' (II. ii. 228-231)

It means that Brutus was well-known for his eloquence. Plutarch also states that when Brutus's mind was ''moved to follow any matter, he used a kind of vehement and forcible persuasion that calmed not till he had obtained his desire.'' But Brutus was eloquent when he had to denounce tyranny or oppression; when he had to defend himself, as in the funeral oration, his eloquence dried up. It is noticeable, for example, how he abandons the old, logical prose of his funeral oration and speaks in verse in order to get a hearing for Antony.

Brutus, speaking first as he thought best to do, makes what he thinks will be the definitive statement on the assassination. He gives a reasonable exposition of the motives for the act. He delivers a sober, quiet statement in simple prose, though not without the balanced and periodic sentences characteristic of Roman rhetoric.

He displays his lack of insight into human character. Forthright and simple, he nevertheless uses a superficial catch-phrase to rally his defence:

> "Not that I love Caesar less, but that I loved Rome more." (III. ii. 22-23)

He gives a reason ("his ambition") for his part in assassination. Yet he leaves the motive unexplored in depth. The mob understand it even less, but they want to make him Caesar instead. He offers his own life in expiation and this wins him temporary acclaim from the mob. He rallies them in temporary enthusiasm for freedom with his rhetorical questions:

> "Who is here so base, that would be a bondman? If any, speak; for him have I offended. Who is here so vile, that will not love his country? If any, speak; for him have I offended." (III. ii. 30-34)

This exercise in dialectics with its rational arguments was not likely to create lasting impression on the crowd. They applaude him even though they do not understand him, because they feel honoured that a public character like Brutus should account for his conduct to them, and appeal to their wisdom. Hence as Brutus steps down from the rostrum, he is greeted by the cry, annihilatory in its unconscious irony, "Let him be Caesar." There cannot be a more eloquent comment on the effect of the speech on the audience than this cry which shows that they want to make him exactly that idol, Caesar, whom he has so long laboured to throw into disrepute and whose murder he has sought to justify.

In sharp contrast with Brutus, Antony was a demagogue and a master of mob psychology. He did not start with the advantage of Brutus's reputation as a man of character. He was known to be a reveller and a pleasure-seeker. He found the mob siding with Brutus when he appears in the Forum he hears the cries of the mob shouting 'Live, Brutus! live! live!, A lesser man than Antony would have lost his nerve and not ascended the rostrum. Yet he dares to face the hostile crowd , confident that he would be able to turn their hostility to him into a hostility against the conspirators.

Antony addressed the mob in verse. "To the modulation of flawless verse it unites the lucidity and breadth of ideal platform oratory and the tactical and adroitness of a first-rate debating speech." The first part of the oration is spoken as by a humble pleader and it is his humble attitude:

> "Here, under leaves of Brutus and the rest."

Coupled with a humble reiteration of respect for the one who gave him permission :

> "And Brutus is an honourable man."

Note how, in contrast to Brutus's address "Romans, countrymen and lovers!" he speaks — "Friends, Romans and countrymen."

Another devices that he adopts is to fathom the feelings of his mob by throwing word like 'If' into their sea of consciousness :

> "The noble Brutus
> Hath told you Caesar was ambitious,
> If it were so, it was a grievous fault."

Finding no response from the mob, he uses word 'honourable' eight times, till by constant repetition he makes it a term of sarcasm, and mixing it with facts and arguments he so

> "Plays upon the nerves of the citizens who, themselves, begin to feel its irrelevance, till at last upon Antony's supreme stroke : "I fear I wrong the honourable men/ whose daggers have stabb'd Caesar." (III. ii. 153-154)

One of them cries out in savage repudiation : 'They are traitors, Honourable men!'. The knowledge of this success heartens him up and he now proceeds to play with them as a skilful musician plays on the key-board. Then by means of another clever device he excites them to mutiny, by urging them not to mutiny. For it is a well-known principle of rhetoric that if you urge a man not to do a thing, you thereby excite his curiosity to do that very thing. After thus exciting the feelings of the crowd, he introduces a new topic — Caesar's will — and hints at its provisions. The greed of the mob has been roused, they form a ring around him. They clamour for the will be read, but he defers it. Instead he constructs the whole scene of Caesar's murder. He reveals the rents in Caesar's garments by the conspirators. This way he rouses emotions of the audience through the eye as well as the ear. Then as tears begin to flow from the beholders, he plays the trump-card by removing the mantle and displaying the body of Caesar to the gaze of the audience. The citizens are now thoroughly roused; they forget the will; they are only conscious of the bleeding body lying before them. The shouts of the crowd, "O traitors! villains!" "We will be revenged", "Burn! — Fire! — Kill! — Slay! — Let not a traitor live", are an eloquent tribute to Antony's supreme skill. Then comes the most subtle devices of rhetorical art – namely, an affectation of bluntness and straightforwardness, which is quite in accordance with the principle that the orator should depreciate his own power of persuasion, — "since whatever is attributed to the eloquence of the speaker is so much deducted from the s'rength of his cause":

"I am no orator, as Brutus is".

And at the very moment when the crowd is about to set out to fire the houses of the conspirators, he holds them back. He knows that the crowd is fickle, and that just as he has undone the work of Brutus, some other speaker might undo his work. Therefore, to make sure that the crowd will not desert his cause, he produces the will which the crowd had forgotten. His last and supreme appeal is to their self-interest — the one motive which can bind them all together. Caesar has left, he tells them, to every Roman citizen 75 drachmas, his orchards and private arbours for common use. 'Here was Caesar! when comes such another?' — these concluding words of Antony add fuel to the fire.

Antony thus sets in motion by a bit of calculated demogoguery, expressed in stirring verse, and delineated with cleverness, sophistry; sarcasm, cynicism and knowledge of mob-psychology, the fury which will bring about his prophecy made earlier over Caesar's body:

"A curse shall light upon the limbs of men;
Domestic fury and fierce civil strife
Shall cumber all the parts of Italy." (III. i . 263-265)

The speech is called by Granville Barker as a "triumph in histrionics."

The Quarrel Scene between Brutus and Cassius

The quarrel scene between Brutus and Cassius reveals the highest powers of Shakespeare and has been popular from Shakespeare's own days. The occasion of the quarrel is Brutus's condemnation of Lucius Pella, an agent of Cassius, for taking bribes and Cassius's refusal to Brutus of certain sums of money which he had desired for the payment of his legions.

As soon as Cassius meets Brutus he starts the quarrel in the presence of his own and Brutus's troops; but at the suggestion of Brutus they retire into the tent, where the quarrel is conducted in right earnest. Cassius is upset because his letters in defence of Lucius Pella, accused of taking bribes, have been disregarded. Brutus believes that Cassius demeaned himself in intervening on behalf of a bribe-taker, but Cassius contends that in the troubled times they are now enduring, it is inadvisable to ensure every little offence. Brutus, whose uncompromising hatred for anything like corruption pays no regard to time and person, now charges Cassius, too, having "an itching palm", that is, to take graft; only Cassius's high office has allowed him to escape punishment for it. Brutus reminds Cassius in the interests of justice and that therefore they, above all men, must act with perfect righteousness. Cassius, furious at being criticised, says to his friends that he has no right to "hedge me in," that is, no right to correct or reprover him. Brutus enrages him yet further by waving him off as a frivolous, trivial person, saying, "Away, slight man." Cassius says that even Caesar would not have dared provoke him in like manner and asks Brutus not to presume too much on his love. Brutus now brings in another charge; he cannot understand how Cassius could have refused him the money which he had desired to pay to his legions with. Cassius denies having sent a refusal and explains that the misunderstanding was due to the fool who brought his answer back to Brutus. He cries that he is "hated by one he loves," meaning that he has lost Brutus's friendship and, after the dramatic offer of his dagger so that Brutus may kill him, he is spent. Brutus is softened, and the friends begin to be reconciled.

There are many interpretations to this scene, some sharp and revealing; others vague and half-truth. For instance, Coleridge remarks: "I know no part of Shakespeare that more impresses on me the belief of his genius being superhuman than this scene between Brutus and Cassius."

This scene undoubtedly became popular even in Shakespeare's own day and provoked imitation. Beaumont and Fletcher had imitated it in *The Maid's Tragedy and* Dryden in his *All For Love*. R. G. Moulton remarks : "The Quarrel scene shows how low the tone of Cassius has fallen since he has dealt with assassination as a political weapon; and even Brutus's moderation has hardened into unpleasing harshness. There is at this point plenty of relief to such unpleasing effects : there is the exhibition of the tender side of Brutus's character as shown in his relations with his page, and the display of friendship maintained between Brutus and Cassius amid falling fortunes." This scene thus shows us the two leading conspirators brought down from a political to a human plane. It thus wins for them a measure of sympathy which is retained right to the very end despite their failure in their enterprise. Then, according to A.C. Bradley, "Shakespeare often appeals to an emotion different from any of those excited in the first half of the play, and so provides novelty and generally relief. As a rule this new emotion is pathetic; and the pathos is not terrible or lacerating, but, even if painful, is accompanied by the scene of beauty and by an outflow of admiration or affection, which come with an inexpressible sweetness after the tension of the crisis." But Bradley is not quite right in relegating to it a secondary place in the play. Its effect on the mind of the spectators and readers is profound. Johnson, not an enthusiastic admirer of the play, nevertheless, confessed that "the contention and reconcilement of Brutus and Cassius is universally accepted." John Dryden observes : "The occasion which Shakespeare, Euripides and Fletcher have all taken is the same, grounded upon friendship; and the quarrel of two virtuous men, raised by natural degrees to the extremity of passion, is conducted in all three to the declination of the same passion, and concludes with a warm renewing of their friendship. But the particular groundwork which Shakespeare has taken is incomparably the best" (John Dryden, Preface to *Troilus and Cressida*, 1679). Leonard Digges, one of the earliest eulogists of Shakespeare makes reference to the popularity of this scene :

> "So have I seene, when Caesar would appeare,
> And on the Stage at halfe-sword Parley were,
> Brutus and Cassius: oh how the Audience, Were ravish'd."
> (Leonard Digges, From Commendatory verses to Shakespeare's Poems, 1640)

Brandes has described it as "significant, profound and brilliantly constructed." It is a significant scene in that it throws a flood of light on the characters of the combatants and gives us a glimpse of the real cause of the weakness of the republican party. It shows how Brutus, the unpractical dreamer, has an influence over the experienced soldier, and it is to this that the failure of the conspiracy is due. It is profound because it goes beneath the surface of thing and shows us the intimate personal relation between the two conspirators. It is brilliantly constructed because although it is a mere episode in the drama, it has all the vividness of a play complete in itself. In the whole scene it is Brutus who is more provoking, more unreasonable and more quarrelsome, while Cassius is tolerant, sympathetic and passive. Our sympathy goes to Cassius and we lose faith in Brutus. Brutus is intolerably ironical and bitter, grounded as he is on great self-confidence as an incorruptible and infallible purist. Cassius vents his passion more naturally and is sooner appeased because his anger is of the nature of wounded love. Therefore, the contention of Rymer that it presents "two drunken Hectors huffing and swaggering for a two-penny reckoning" is totally unwarranted.

Another great importance of the scene lies in the fact that it illustrates the overpowering presence of Caesar's spirit. Caesar is mentioned three times in the course of the quarrel. As Stopford Brooke has noted, "Did not great Julius bleed for justice' sake?", Brutus cries in the midst of the quarrel with Cassius. 'When Caesar live'd', cries Cassius, 'he durst not thus have mov'd me! Strike, as thou didst at Caesar', he cries again, when he bares his breast to Brutus. "The dead man is an overshadowing third in that interview". Thus the scene not only reveals the characters of the drama but also bears reference to the dominant note of the tragedy, namely, the power of Caesarism.

Julius Caesar and *Hamlet*

Both *Julius Caesar* and *Hamlet* were produced almost at the same time, there being only an interval of six months between the two. Naturally they reveal some common characteristics in tone of thought, mood of mind and style.

A.C. Bradley writes, "Hence the name 'tragedy of thought', which Schlegel gave to *Hamlet,* may be given also, as in effect it has been by Professor Dowden, to *Julius Caesar.* The later heroes, on the other hand, Othello, Lear, Timon, Macbeth, Antony, Coriolanus, have, one and all, passionate natures, and, speaking roughly, we may attribute the tragic failure in each of these cases to passion. Partly for this reason, the later plays are wilder and stormier than the first two" (A.C. Bradley, *Shakespearean Tragedy,* 1904). J.C. Maxwell observes, "But one Shakespearean theme which becomes predominant in *Hamlet* certainly makes its first notable appearance in the presentation of Brutus in *Julius Caesar* : the notion of a disparity between the man and what he does. This notion still seems somewhat intrusive : the play is not built around it as *Hamlet* is. The result in (to exaggerate a little) that where Hamlet is a mystery Brutus is a puzzle." Brutus is presented by Shakespeare as a doctrinaire intellectual, and one whose doctrine (classical republicanism) is one with which he has no spontaneous imaginative sympathy. Yet he is surprisingly successful in making somewhat positive out of his limitations. The best example is Brutus's soliloquy in II.i. Shakespeare seems here to be whittling away the whole meaning of theoretic republicanism, and it is not an adequate answer to point to the monarchical assumptions of Shakespeare's day. Brutus in this soliloquy is and is not a republican, and the obscurities in the speech, though in part the result of Shakespeare's lack of sympathy with the ideas involved, also convey "the instinct of a man over the threshold of whose awareness a terrible doubt perpetually threatens to lap" (J.I.M. Stewart, *Character and Motive in Shakespeare*, 1949, p. 52). Ultimately, he is prevailed upon to take the lead under the compulsion of the idea that it was his duty to do so :

> "Brutus had rather be a villager
> Than to repute himself a son of Rome
> Under these hard conditions as this time
> Is like to lay upon us."

On the other hand, Hamlet deliberates and is unable to act even though he is convinced of his duty to do so :

> "The time is out of joint : O, curs'd spite
> That ever I was born to set it right."

Brutus, though he errs, nevertheless does not lose our esteem or our sympathy; we, on the other hand, are irritated by the indecision of Hamlet.

Moral evil is not so intently scrutinised or so fully displayed in them as in the succeeding tragedies of Shakespeare. In *Julius Caesar*, we may almost say, everybody means well. In *Hamlet*, though we have a villain, he is a small one. The murder which gives rise to the action lies outside the play, and the centre of attention within the play lies in hero's efforts to do his duty.

Revenge, destiny, the mystery of life and death, superstitions and religions are dealt with in both ways. That *Julius Caesar* was occupying the mind of Shakespeare when he composed *Hamlet* is also borne out by the close resemblance of the scene of prodigies and portents described in the Roman play to the following lines in *Hamlet* :

> "In the most high and palmy state of Rome,
> A little ere the mightiest Julius fell,
> The graves stood tenantless, and the sheeted dead
> Did squeak and gibber in the Roman streets" : (I. i. 113)

As the life of Brutus draws to a close and he broachs on the issues of the coming battle, he says:

> "O ! that a man might know
> The end of this day's business ere it come;
> But it sufficeth that the day will end, And then the end is known."

Grenvill-Barker observes, "That is the voice, they are all but the very words of Hamlet. Shakespeare is to run the gamut of the mood of helpless doubt — the mood which has kept Hamlet our close kin through three disintegrating — to more if not to better purpose." Reference to fate or destiny are almost identical. Compare, "There is a tide in the affairs of men", of Brutus with "There's a divinity that rough-hews our end," etc. of Hamlet.

Brutus's melancholy is developed into a fascinating study in *Hamlet*. Instead of quick action there is delay which is linked with the melancholy feelings of the hero. This melancholy is overcome giving *Hamlet* deeper meaning than *Julius Caesar* possesses. Portia dies grief-stricken. In *Hamlet* Ophelia is distracted like Portia but she does not swallow fire; she does more poetically in the midst of flowers. Caesar's ghost wanders thirsty for revenge and he plays an important role in deciding the fate of Brutus. When alive Caesar is ludicrous; since his death is not shown as a crime, there is little in his desire for revenge. In *Hamlet* the ghost is majestic; it becomes pitiable but not ludicrous. It sets the ball rolling and then the conflict develops among living men who alone ultimately resolve it.

Compare also the close resemblance between the eulogy of Antony on Brutus :

> "This was the noblest Roman of them all.
> ....
> His life was gentle, and the elements
> So mix'd in him, that Nature might stand up
> And say to all the world, 'This was a man!' "
>
> (V. v. 68-75)

and Ophelia's description of Hamlet :

> "O, what a noble mind is here o'erthrown!
> The courtier's, soldier's, scholar's, eye, tongue, sword,
> Th' expectancy and rose of the fair state,
> The glass of fashion, and the mould of form,
> Th' observed of all observers..."
>
> (III .i. 153-157)

Lastly, both the plays purge our heart of the tragic emotions of pity and fear and leave "a calm of mind, all passions spent", by bringing in a vision of the new order of things. Octavius in *Julius Caesar* establishes a stable and peaceful reign after the ruin of the conspirators and their victim; Fortinbras, the prince of Norway, ushers in a better and peaceful time after the contending persons in *Hamlet* have perished.

*

C. THE CHARACTERS

1. Julius Caesar

Nearly a century and a three-fourth ago Hazlitt wrote of the play *Julius Caesar:*

"It . . . is remarkable for the profound knowledge of character, in which Shakespeare could scarcely fail. If there is any exception to this remark, it is in the hero of the piece himself. We do not much admire the representation here given of Julius Caesar, nor do we think it answers to the portrait given of him in his commentaries. He makes several vapouring and rather pedantic speeches, and does nothing" (Williams Hazlitt, *Characters of Shakespeare's Plays,* 1805).

The view that Shakespeare has drawn his Caesar merely as "a grand, strutting piece of puff-paste, . . a glorious vapourer and braggart, full of lofty airs and mock-thunder," has, with a few dissentient voices, persisted to the present day. Dr. Dover Wilson carries it further thus : "A Roman Tamburlaine of illimitable ambition and ruthless irresistible genius; a monstrous tyrant who destroyed his country and ruined 'the mightiest and most flourishing commonwealth that the world will ever see' – one feature remained to add before the sixteenth century stage figure of the great dictator was complete, that of a braggart, of the 'thrasonical Caesar,' to whom Shakespeare refers more than once" (Dover Wilson, Introduction to N.C.S. *Julius Caesar,* p. xxv). According to some other critics, Shakespeare has painted Caesar as a great person and not an invalid, and his greatness is shown less in his own person than in the enormous influence he exercised upon his environments. There are truth and justice in both these views, and it is by combining these two that we may arrive at a correct view of Caesar.

Caesar's greatness is assumed throughout the play. It fills the mind of the dramatist and is communicated to his audience in phrases that fall from his pen whenever Caesar is mentioned, even by his enemies. This Caesar has got the start of the majestic world. He bestrides it like a Colossus. His fall is heralded by a strange impatience of the heavens' and by portentous things which shake the minds of the stoutest of the Romans.

Cassius, meeting Casca in the storm, names to him a man 'most like this dreadful right, prodigious grown and fearful'. Caesar is about to die and 'all the sway of earth shakes like a thing infirm'.

The essential greatness of Caesar being thus assumed, Shakespeare is free to exhibit in him human weaknesses apparently inconsistent with it. There are many advantages in this method of presentation. It give reality to Caesar, the man; it suggests that Caesar's spirit is mightier than his person, a suggestion which is essential to the unity of the play. John Palmer has rightly remarked : "It enables the dramatist to present him in flesh and blood without reducing in stature the men who murder him; finally, it permits the audience to sympathise with Brutus just sufficiently to give poignancy to the disaster which overtook him ... The play could not easily have risen to the level of tragedy if Caesar had been portrayed consistently in full majesty" (John Palmer, *Political Characters of Shakespeare,* 1945). Secondly, Shakespeare is concerned with the last phase of Caesar's life and character. We learn from Plutarch that Caesar in old age had shown evident signs of deterioration both in mind and body. Hence historical accuracy, too, demanded that Shakespeare should give us an imperfect picture of the Caesar who was on the verge of death. This is exactly what Shakespeare has done.

The greatness of Caesar is evident from the very first scene of the play. He comes upon the stage, a great crowd following. He calls Calpurnia to his side. Casca commands silence with the words :

> "Peace, hol Caesar speaks."

The crowd is hushed to silence and awaits the oracle. Caesar is a born ruler of men, a King and Commander, every inch of him. When he somewhat superstitiously bids Antony touch Calpurnia in his holy chase, Antony replies,

> "When Caesar says, 'Do this', it is perform'd."

All Rome is bent to hear this Caesar. Cassius speaks of his eyes "whose bend doth awe the world" and shows how far removed Caesar is from common humanity by the comparison —

> "Why, man, he doth bestride the narrow world
> like a Colossus."

Not only the common people, but the senators regard him with reverential awe. "The angry spot doth glow on Caesar's brow/And all the rest look like a chidden train." We should notice how they rise as Caesar enters the Senate and one of them addresses him as —

> "Most high, most mighty, and most puissant Caesar."

Lastly, there is a subtle touch in the words with which the mob greets Brutus, as he descends from the rosturm —"Let him be Caesar." This shows that Caesar had developed into "permanent constitutional factor, indestructible by the cancelling of an individual life."

Allied to this greatness, are certain physical infirmities. In the words of Palmer, "They are in part historical and in part derived from Plutarch's delight in the foibles of great men .... Caesar, like any other men of destiny, is superstitious. Caesar, like other exalted personages, refers to himself in the third person. Caesar, like other men whose position requires them to assume superhuman qualities, claims to be impervious to fear or argument and determined to enforce his will, even though he knows himself to be in the wrong. These are traits common to all dictators" (John Palmer, *Political Characters of Shakespeare,* 1945). But Caesar, as depicted by Shakespeare, has little in common with Hitler or Stalin. He is concerned for his wife's barrenness, he faints when he is offered the crown, he 'had a sickness when he was in Spain,' he listens to Calpurnia's dreams and fears. This representation of Caesar painfully reminds us of the Homeric heroes in *Troilus and Cressida.*

The pride and arrogance of Caesar have been fully emphasised in the play. Pampered by base flattery and servile respect, he has become proud and arrogant. It is the conceiled, vain-glorious Caesar that speaks :

> ". . . . Danger knows full well
> That Caesar is more dangerous than he."

This speech has the imperial tone of a Sultan, whose lightest word is law, and he constantly speaks of himself in the third person as "Caesar's turned to hear," "Caesar shall forth", "Caesar doth not wrong," and so on. The Senate is "his Senate", and when he chooses to stay at home, he will not even send them a courteous message.

By comparing himself to the North Star and to Olympus, Caesar is projecting a god-like image of himself. We must note the contemptuous manner in which he rejects Metellus' pleadings as "Low-crooked courtesies, and base spaniel fawning". But his vaingloriousness has been defended by such an eminent critic as J.I.M. Stewart : "Shakespeare's is not a modern technique, and we must regard the self-characterization of Caesar as being more naive dramatically than has hitherto been supposed by his critics.... and there is no intention of charging Shakespeare with the odium of vanity or vainglory because he says these things'' (J.I.M. Stewart, *Character and Motive in Shakespeare,* 1949).

Then as to Caesar's superstition, there is reason for holding divided opinions. He believes that if Calpurnia is touched by Antony during the ''holy chase'' she may be cured of her barrenness. But this was a belief common to all the Roman of his day, and his subscription to it has no significance in a consideration of his character. Shakespeare took it from Plutarch. When the Soothsayer bids Caesar beware the Ides of March, he brushes him aside as a ''dreamer''. A really superstitious man would have taken the warning seriously; but Caesar will not regard a threat to his personal safety, even if it comes from a soothayer. Cassius notes how superstitions now affect Caesar:

> ''For he is superstitious grown of late,
> Quite from the main opinion he held once
> Of fantasy, of dreams, and ceremonies.'' (II. i. 195)

In the words of G. Wilson Knight, ''This is not surprising : it is a normal correlative to his superstitious respect for his idealized self. Nor, in this world, in superstition a fault: it is fully justified'' (G. Wilson Knight, *The Imperial Theme,* 1985, p. 66).

Then again, old age had not impaired some of his good qualities. In his reception of the conspirators when they come to his house on the fateful morning, he manifests the courtesy and urbanity for which he was famous. His insight into human nature has not been obscured by the base flattery of men. He rightly characterizes Antony as a frivolous being who is given to mirth and revels. He shrewdly remarks of Cassius as having ''a lean and hungry look; He thinks too much: such men are dangerous.'' And the subsequent course of events fully justify Caesar's analysis of the character. The domestic scene in which Calpurnia tries to dissuade Caesar from going to the Capitol, presents him as a natural man. Caesar has had a bad night. Nor heaven nor earth has been at peace. Calpurnia has thrice cried out in her sleep. Caesar is thoroughly and humanly upset. He sends a servant off to the priests, ordering them to do present sacrifice and report on their success. There is a touch of the sublime in his declaration, ''What touches us ourself shall be last serv'd'', when Artemidorus presses upon him his petition regarding Caesar himself. It will not be too much to say that his noble spirit of self-denial contributed to his undoing. Had Caesar been a little more selfish, he would have read the paper and thus averted his fate. It is not a tyrant, but a ruler anxious to follow the principles of justice and benevolence, who opens the meeting of the Senate by inviting appeals for redress of anything that has been done amiss. It is the heroic man who speakes out "Cowards die many times before death".

Moulton says, "The force and strength of his character is seen in the impression he makes upon forceful and strong men" (R.G. Moulton, *Shakespeare as a Dramatic Artist,* 1885, p. 176). As far as the presentation of Caesar by Antony is concerned, we are reminded in Antony's speech of his "conquests, glories, triumphs, spoils"; we are told that he was the "heart" of the world (III. i. 208), and is now.

> "...the ruins of the noblest man
> That ever lived in the tide of times;"

Brutus exclaims :

> "O Julius Caesar, thou art mighty yet !
> Thy spirit walks abroad, and turns our swords
> In our own proper entrails." (V. iii. 94-6)

The ghost of Caesar, as Dowden says, "serves as a kind of visible symbol of the vast posthumous power of the dictator" (Dowden, *Shakespeare : His Mind and Art,* 1875, p. 288). Both Brutus and Cassius die with Caesar's name on their lips. Cassius turns upon himself the sword that ran through Caesar's bowels, with the words,

> "Caesar, thou art reveng'd
> Even with the sword that killed thee."

Brutus dies with the full realization of his failure. He apostrophizes Caesar's spirit as he runs upon his sword :

> "...Caesar, now he still;
> I kill'd not thee with half so good a will."

T.S. Dorsch says, "Caesar has some weaknesses, of course.

He has ambition, if that be a weakness, and not rather an essential accompaniment of greatness; his was not the uncontrolled and wicked ambition of Macbeth. He has pride and vanity, but these are qualities that not infrequently fall to the share of the great. He has one or two physical disabilities, but these do not prevent us from remembering that he was one of the mightiest conquerors in the world's history — and we are reminded in the play that he was so....Shakespeare has also made the almost legendary figure of Caesar himself come convincing to life."

2. **Marcus Brutus**

Virgil K. Whitaker says, "Brutus is the first of Shakespeare's superb tragic figures who fails through moral choice'' (Virgil K. Whitaker, *Shakespeare's Use of Learning,* 1953). Farnham remarks, ''Before Brutus there had been no tragic hero on the English stage whose character had combined noble grandeur with fatal imperfection'' (William Farnham, *Shakespeare's Tragic Frontier,* 1950). Schanzer observes, ''Shakespeare depicts Brutus as a bad judge of character, but as by no means devoid of political shrewdness and practical wisdom'' (Ernest Schanzer, *Shakespeare's Problem Plays,* 1963). Palmer remarks, ''The reflective idealist, living in imagination, is more impressed by the idea or symbol of power than by the thing itself'' (John Palmer, *The Problem Plays of Shakespeare,* 1963). All these comments aptly sum up the character of Brutus. Brutus has many things in common with Shakespeare's tragic heroes. In nobility of character he is most like Hamlet. He is a scholar like him. He is courageous and a stoic in his outlook like many heroes of Shakespeare. He loves the name of honour more than he fears death. Like Hamlet he gazes upon his Ophelia with ''ungentle looks''. What is surprising is that like Hamlet he too walks ''unbraced''. He is filled with maddening rage at moments like Lear and Hamlet; otherwise he is gentle like a lamb.

> ''O Cassius, you are yoked with a lamb
> That carries anger as the flint bears fire,
> Who much enforced, shows a hasty spark,
> And straight is cold again.''

Such a man could easily apologize to Laertes and when older, to Cordelia. He is impatient like Othello, and Portia, wiser than Desdemona, does not do anything to increase his impatience. Like Othello he tries to keep his agony to himself and tells lies to his wife.

''I am not well in health, and that is all.'' The most striking and also very instructive resemblance is with Macbeth when Brutus talks of the death of his wife. He keeps the news to himself even as he quarrels with Cassius. When they become friends again he speaks most laconically about her death. When Cassius wishes to linger a little more on the theme he shuts him up with;

> ''Speak no more of her.''

When Messala informs him of the same fact he says briefly,

> ''Why, farewell, Portia. We must die, Messala.
> With meditating that she must die once,
> I have the patience to endure it now.''

These brief statements do not mean that he did not love her. He speaks about dead Cassius in the same way,

"....Friends, I owe more tears
To this dead man than you shall see me pay.
I shall find time, Cassius, I shall find time."

When Macbeth says about his wife's death,

"There would have been a time for such a word." — he means exactly what Brutus means. They are both stoics in their own different ways and the brief remarks about the objects of their love do not indicate absence of deep sorrow.

Brutus is a man who wants to be guided by motives of right reason, by deliberate moral choice, but he finds at every step how difficult it is to accommodate abstract reason to the concrete realities of life. This realization which wearies him spiritually is forced upon him by gradual stages and is more corrosive than defeat on the battlefield. When we meet him first (I. ii), he is already in the grip of a spiritual conflict between his republicanism and his personal loyalty to Julius Caesar. But he does not think of doing any injury to Caesar. Only he wishes that he "had rather be a villager/Than to repute himself a son of Rome" (I. ii. 171-2), But Cassius's malicious zeal is so infectious that half unknown to himself, Brutus has been influenced. He now extends an invitation to Cassius that they will meet, and when we see Cassius in the next scene, he proudly claims that three parts of Brutus are theirs already. We have to wait till the second Act for the fourth part to be yielded.

But the spiritual conflict has revealed a new aspect of Brutus's character. His reason has been persuaded but his unconscious self asserts itself through the forces of imagination which the mental struggle has unleashed. The interim between the acting of the dreadful thing and the first motion is like a phantasm, a hideous dream, and his state is like so little kingdom in insurrection (II. i. 61-64). The thunder and lighting described in the previous scene (I. iii) may be interpreted as an external symbol of the turmoil in Brutus's soul. But his reason is clear; he has no doubt about the nobility of the enterprise. Soon, however, he finds that it is difficult to harmonize deliberate moral choice with the necessities of practical life, for expediency requires that Antony and Caesar fall together, but then their course will seem too bloody and a ritual sacrifice will be indistinguishable from an ordinary murder. The sparing of Antony is a tactical blunder, but Brutus does not correctly view the situation, because he is obsessed by a notion of the even virtue of his enterprise.

In Brutus, Shakespeare discovered the noble hero with a tragic flaw. Though Marlowe's Tamburlaine had achieved grandeur, it was of a kind not to be called noble, and he had achieved it by being free from any fatal imperfection except a moral nature and thus by being a dubious tragic hero.

The heroes of *Julius Caesar, Hamlet, Othello* and *King Lear* are blood brothers in their nobility. If good and evil are mighty opposites in the finite universe, as Shakespeare often makes them in his tragedies, then Brutus, Hamlet, Othello, and Lear can be placed on the side of good. Because these heroes are incorruptible, their tragic flaws do not reach into the centres of their characters. The flaws of Hamlet and Brutus do not lead either hero to the doing of evil. The high-minded Brutus tries dutifully to do right, even by means of assassination, which for him is a form of judicial execution, and comes to ruin because of fatal mistakes in judgment growing out of faulty wisdom. Shakespeare, therefore, does not put Brutus in a class with Judas and make him worthy of a place in deepest Hell for treacherous betrayal of a master, as Dante does.

Schanzer contends soundly that Brutus was not a 'political naivete'. The oration of Brutus over the dead Caesar is extremely shrewd political step. How does he achieve it? He begins by subtly, unobtrusively, flattering his audience. Then comes the assertion that only a superior love of his country made him slay his dearest friend. Still no charge has been brought against Caesar. Then suddenly the question is sprung on him: "Had you rather Caesar were living, and die all slaves, than that Caesar were dead, to live all free men?" Caesar was ambitious, an accusation vaguely hurled at him. And at once, before they have time to ask for evidence, there follows the series of rhetorical questions which so ingeniously forestall any objection from the audience:

"Who is here so base, that would be a bond man?" Nothing could be more skilful. The whole speech is as shrewdly contrived and, as the response of the people shows, quite as effective as Antony's.

At other times, too, in the play Brutus does not show himself devoid of practical wisdom. The reasons for marching to Philippi may be mistaken, but they certainly show no lack of an eye for the expedient and politic. A host of critics like Brents Stirling in *Unity in Shakespearean Tragedy;* Adrien Bonjour in *The Structure of Julius Caesar;* and above all Maria Wickert are unanimous that Brutus's oration is not deficient in skill.

Brutus, of course, is not a deliberate villain as Macbeth is; but like Macbeth he is presented as losing his way in a nightmare world — 'like a phantasma', something both horrible and unreal, 'or a hideous dream'. In other words, Brutus's wrong choice not only leads to wrong action, it delivers him to a world of unreality. As soon as *Julius Caesar* falls, Cinna cries out :

> "Liberty! Freedom! Tyranny is dead !"

And Cassius :

> "Liberty, freedom, and enfranchisement !"

Brutus cries :

> "Let's all cry, 'Peace, freedom, and liberty!"

This cry of Brutus is against the imperialism of Caesar but the irony is that the mob wants him to be a Caesar. Long before the assassination he tells Cassius that they murdered "but for supporting robbers" — Caesar, as Brutus admits, has not disjoined remorse from power, or allowed himself to be governed by his passions. What is even more absurd — as Coleridge has pointed out — is that Caesar was already an absolute ruler. He had crossed the Rubicon, entered Rome as a conqueror, and destroyed the power of the Senate. Brutus does not mention these things and is worried only by the fear that Caesar, if he is crowned, will undergo a transformation. Brutus's soliloquy was carefully designed to reveal his blindness to the realities of the situation, Caesar's absolute power. He is concerned only with the title of King and the fact that his ancestor and namesake had driven out the Tarquins. It is not that he is unintelligent: he substitutes ideas for realities. He was a reflective idealist.

The Stoicism of Brutus is worthy of note. He was trained up in the Stoic school of Philosophy, founded by Zeno. He receives the news of Portia's death with a stoical resignation and the incident extorts from him nothing but a brief exclamation. In the quarrel-scene he gives way to passion, for the time being, but very soon he recovers his mental composure. "Brutus is a Stoic by profession and in reality the reverse-acting deeds against his nature by the strong force of principle and will." In his relations with the domestic he shows a rare sensibility. An exquisite little event brings out Brutus's sweetness of demeanour. There is almost a touch of womanly tenderness in his action when noticing how the boy Lucious, wearied out and fallen asleep, is lying in a position to injure his instrument, he rises and disengages it without waking him. His case of suicide is the very negation of his Stoic philosophy. He is also a loving and affectionate husband.

Antony speaks a noble eulogy over his body. Octavius will have it "order'd honourably" (V. v. 79). He is the noblest Roman of all. G. Wilson Knight says, "He suffers, and makes others suffer, for his virtue : but such virtue is not enough.... He thus fails in life and dies sadly, pathetically searching at the end someone 'honourable' enough to slay him." His earnest pursuit of virtue amounts to a refined kind of egoism. He is ambitious, not of political power, but of personal honour, the honour to be derived from living a consistently virtuous life. He might, therefore, say, like Henry V :

> "If it be a sin to covet honour,
> I am the most offending soul alive."

Critics on Brutus : "This is the noblest Roman of them all. This is the impression that Brutus leaves with us. He leaves us with the feeling, too, that the play, though it rightly bears Caesar's name, is rather "The Death and Revenge of Julius Caesar" than "The Tragedy of Julius Caesar", for its tragedy is the tragedy of Marcus Brutus." — T.S. Dorsch.

"Shakespeare's Brutus has nobility and great beauty — but Dante would have found that no figure in all the dramas commits a darker crime. How came Brutus to join the conspirators? There is an element of unresolved mystery here, strongly underlined in that groping soliloquy in the orchard upon which so much commentator's ink has been spilt. It is clear that he is concerned for his disinterestedness" — J.I.M. Stewart in *Character and Motive in Shakespeare*.

3. **Mark Antony**

Mac Callum writes: "Shakespeare conceives him as a man of genius and feeling but not of principle, resourceful and daring, ambitious of honour and power, but unscrupulous in his methods and a voluptuary in his life" (Mac Callum, *Shakespeare's Roman Plays*, pp. 289-90). Antony's character belongs largely to the last three acts. In the first two he is an unimportant figure, and appears little more than "a limb of Caesar". Up to the time when he faces the triumphant conspirators he speaks just thirty-three words. He is so far a dark horse. The only hints we have of his potential greatness are the fact that Caesar has singled him out for his special regard, and the opinion of Cassius that he is a "shrewd contriver" who, with the means at his command, may well prove a danger if he is allowed to outlive Caesar.

In the first two acts we are told that he is something of a voluptuary, which is not the same thing as saying that he is dissolute. We learn from Brutus and Cassius that Antony is a reckless libertine, given to pleasure, wildness and much company, a "gamesome man", a "masker and a reveller". Even Caesar, to whom he is so ardently devoted, refers to his midnight revels, and love of plays. This voluptuousness and self-indulgence of Antony are found to be fully developed in *Antony and Cleopatra,* but even in this play Shakespeare, with no uncertain touch, points to these moral defects which later on proved his ruin, thus justifying Brutus's judgment on the ultimate issues of his character.

The crisis produced by the murder of Caesar calls into play all the latent power of Antony's mind. He develops altogether new sides of his character after that tragic event, of which we get no hint earlier in the play. Antony loves passionately and ardently. He feels real grief for Caesar but is, so to speak, effortlessly separate from the grief when he feels it. In the words of A.D. Nuttall, "We therefore have something which is psychologically more disquieting than the ordinary machiavel, who pretends emotion while he coldly intrigues for power. Antony feels his emotion and then rides them, controls them, moderating their force as need arises" (A.D. Nuttall, *A New Mimesis,* p. 110).

In Antony's words only we see the Caesar of history:

"O mighty Caesar ! dost thou lie so low ?
Are all conquests, glories, triumphs, spoils,
Shrunk to this little measure ?" (III. i. 148)

His speech is full of feelings for his dead mentor, Caesar. To him, the conspirators' swords are "rich with the most noble blood of all this world" (III. i. 155). Again,

"Thou art the ruins of the hoblest man
That ever lived in the tide of times,
Woe to the hand that shed this costly blood!". (III. i. 256)

He sees him as a man he loved; also as a supremely noble man; and still further, as a symbol of government and peace. Now that he is rashly slain, forces of disorder will rage unchecked :

"Domestic fury and fierce civil strife
Shall cumber all the parts of Italy." (III. i. 263)

To Antony Caesar is Rome's lover. Caesar hath 'wept' for the poor of Rome. "He was my friend, faithful and just to me" (III. ii. 90). Then Caesar is shown as general lover :

> "And dying, mention it within their wills,
> Bequeathing it as a rich legacy
> Unto their issue." (III. ii. 137)

Even Casesar's mantle is suffused with emotions, almost sentimentality :

> "If you have tears, prepare to shed them now.
> You all do know this mantle." (III. ii. 173)

Then Antony shows them Caesar's body itself :

> "Kind souls, what ! weep you when you but behold
> Our Caesar's vesture wounded?" (III. ii. 199)

Antony is a political genius unlike Brutus. Consider the behaviour of Antony, first, when he moves into the circle of assassins as they stand around the body of the newly-slain Caesar (III. i). Antony moves, with great circumspection but also with extraordinary 'verve' within sword's length of men who may at any moment turn on him. He is their greatest potential danger, but the potentiality (as with Caesar) is fraught with doubt. These are the reasonings of a Brutus and it is on them that Antony counts. The conscientiousness of Brutus is for him a weakness to be exploited. Antony knows just how much of his grief for Caesar it is safe to express. He shakes hand with the murderers and is left alone on the stage, to plot the ruin of Rome. Naturally it is Brutus who is the man of the past, the doomed order of things, and Antony who is the man of the future.

More recently Price has said: "Antony is the least Roman of the Romans. Where they are steadfast, he is liable; where they keep their emotions under lock and key, he will coin his heart for whatever gold it will bring him; where they are virtuous, he is dissolute, where they are straightforward in language, he loves to play with words, to tease and deceive by double meanings, and he will even lie outright" (Professor Hereward Price, *Julius Caesar*, Introduction, p. ix).

He is unscrupulous but not dissolute. Cassius is unscrupulous in whetting Brutus against Caesar; Antony is whetting the Roman people against Cassius and Brutus. Antony no doubt plays with words but at times he is as straightforward in his speech or honourable in his tactics than the men to whom he truthfully says :

> "You show'd your teeth like apes, and fawn'd like apes, hounds,
> And bow'd like bondmen, kissing Caesar's feet;
> Whilst damned Casca, like a cur, behind
> Struck Caesar on the neck." (V. i. 41-4)

Equally, there is no sign of his desires to seek honour and power for himself in pursuing his aim, amongst other things, he ignores Cassius's offer to let his share the honour and power that the conspirators anticipates for themselves. Nor does he keep his emotions less securely under lock and key than Cassius in the second and third scenes of the play, or, for that matter, than Brutus when he is quarrelling with Cassius.

His reckless and unprincipled nature is revealed in his avowal to Octavius of his design to use Lepidus as a scapegoat and a shield to cover the faults of his administration and not to share rewards with him. A meaner treatment of a colleague cannot be imagined and open admission of this design makes it more hateful. Except this one flaw, the character shines in the best possible light. The only occasions on which he is shown in any sense at a loss are those on which he matches his will against that of Octavius (V. i. 14-20), certainly not in his encounters with the conspirators. As a general, Antony shows military genius, tact and shrewdness; the victory at Philippi is in a large measure due to his skill. The tribute that he paid to the noble qualities of Brutus, after the philosopher's death, shows him off to the best advantage. It shows that he is not slow to recognize merit where it is; it is a manifestation of the same enthusiasm for great personalities that made him such an admiring follower of Caesar.

The following lines of S. Brooke amply demonstrate the different traits of Antony : "Antony is nobly managed .... In him and in Brutus, craft and simplicity stand face to face with each other, and both the men are true to the character Shakespeare has made for them. As a politician Antony is wise and Brutus is a fool. As a man Brutus is noble and Antony ignoble — and yet not quite ignoble."

Critics on Antony : "The bewilderment of the conspirators in the presence of this unlooked-for force is seen in Cassius's unavailing attempt to bring Antony to the point, as to what compact he will make with them. Antony, on the contrary, reads his men with such nicety that he can indulge himself in sailing close to the wind, and grasps fervently the hands of the assassins while he pours out a flood of bitter grief over the corpse. It is not hypocrisy, nor a trick to gain time, this conciliation of his enemies. Steeped in the political spirit of the age, Antony knows, as no other man, the mob which governs Rome, and is conscious of the mighty engine he possesses in his oratory to sway the mob..." — R.G. Moulton in *Shakespeare as a Dramatic Artist,* 1885.

"Antony is an intriguer, a Machiavellian. He knows Brutus and fully utilizes the opportunity that has been offered to him by the folly of Brutus. He is cunning as well as cruel. He puts to death about a hundred senators whereas Brutus decided to kill no one except Caesar. He is cynical in his attitude to Lepidus. He retains some of his cynicism even in the other play. He becomes a hero in defeat only.'' – R.B. Sharma in *Essays on Shakespearean Tragedy*.

4. **Caius Cassius**

Shakespeare puts into the mouth of Caesar a masterly character-sketch of Cassius which brings out one side of him clearly, and which, for what else it tells us of him, is worth-noting :

> ''. . . . He reads much,
> He is a great observer, and he looks
> Quite through the deads of men. He loves no plays,
> As thou dost, Antony; he hears no music.
> . . . .
> Such men as he be never at heart's ease
> Whiles they behold a greater than themselves,
> And therefore are they very dangerous.'' (I. 11. 198-20).

Here Shakespeare is concerned to show Cassius as the type of the ''scheming malcontent, a man whom we could easily visualize as plotting the murder of a great national leader; and in Caesar's description of Cassius he has hit such a man to the life. Cadaverous and hungry-looking, much given to brooding ('he thinks too much'), he is a bitter and unhappy man.'' When he allows himself to smile at all the way in which he smiles betrays his frustrated nature, and Caesar has the insight to see that he is very dangerous. Thus, Shakespeare puts Cassius, the man of passion, in strong contrast to Brutus, the philosopher.

Barker says, ''Egoist he is, yet not intellectually arrogant'' (Harley Granville-Barker, *Prefaces to Shakespeare)*. As an egoist, he is unfitted for the role of tempter but as an intellectual he persuades Brutus to join the conspiracy. He exploits the vacillating nature of Brutus by calculated weighing of his name with Caesar's :

> ''Brutus and Caesar. What should be in that 'Caesar'?
> Why should that name be sounded more than yours?

He sees in Brutus the nobler nature and a finer mind, and yields to his judgment even when he strongly feels that it is leading them astray. It is to be noted that whenever critical decisions are to be taken, Cassius proves himself more clear-sighted than Brutus; and though he allows himself each time to be over-borne by Brutus with a good enough grace, we are aware that, had his counsels prevailed, especially in regard to Antony, the republican cause would have had a much greater chance of success. He advised Brutus not to proceed to Philippi. But his advice meets the usual fate.

Cassius is a perfect artist in conspiracy. Caesar is afraid of Cassius, afraid of his insight, his depth of soul: afraid, primarily, of something he cannot understand. In point of profundity and earnestness Cassius is similar to the Duke in *Measure for Measure.* The Duke had 'ancient skill' in reading other's characters (IV. ii. 164). He contended 'to know himself' (III. ii. 253). The Duke was also critical of music and as for pleasures, he was to see others rejoice. Like the Duke, he hates shows and ceremonies. Cassius despises Caesar as a 'person'. Nor can he see him, as Brutus does, a national hero. The adulation of Rome is absurd. He does not even blame Caesar at all. The fault is his countrymen's :

"He were no lion, were not Romans hinds" (I. iii.103). Cassius has nothing but contempt for Caesar, his glory is merely a madness in his admirers. He does not, like Brutus, see two Caesars : he sees only one — a frail, weak, contemptible man; and, next, the hero-worship of Rome. He, like Antony, knows his mind. Throughout the first act we hear mainly Cassius's opinion, expressed at length to Brutus and Casca. Cassius's motive is clearly a sort of envy but it is a fully conscious envy, which stands the test of his reasoning. To him the end justifies any means. The conspiracy is necessary. He wants Brutus. Why? Because Caesar loves Brutus and not him. If Caesar loves him, no amount of reasoning will persuade him to the conspiracy. He himself would never betray love. "Cassius always follows personal emotions."

Politics is a dirty game, and a successful politician must be less studious of moral perfection, must be unscrupulous, cruel, reckless, bold, cautious and wise. For a politician to be troubled with the qualms of conscience, is tantamount to putting a knife to the throat of his plot. Hence Cassius, untroubled by any pricks of conscience, had suggested that if the murder of the tyrant had to be accomplished it must be done in all its fullness. No follower or confederate of the tyrant was to be spared. Then in the battle-field he did not hesitate to levy forced contributions from the area under military control, though it was not strictly moral. He knew that the battle-field was no place for sermons and that morality has little place in politics. Hence he raised money, the sinews of war, to carry on the war to a successful issue. Thus we find that as a politician Cassius is immensely superior to Brutus, though humanly he is much inferior. As a soldier and general, too, Cassius shows the same wisdom and resourcefulness. He gave better advice that they should wait for the enemy's attack and not leave a position where they could entrench themselves strongly, and stake everything on a single battle in an unknown country. But the moralist Brutus sets aside this suggestion too and marches to Philippi, with a result which we all know.

Of Cassius Wilson Knight says, "A certain golden star burns in his heart : a great longing for love." Throughout the play Cassius's love of Brutus is emphasized. In the famous quarrel-scene, Cassius is passionate in anger, grief, or love. "Brutus is cold, aureoled in self-righteousness, unreachable, remote: but beneath emotion surges, too, in him." Brutus loves him not : a 'friendly eye' would not see such faults. Brutus's ethical scorn still lacerates him unmercifully. Cassius is wrung with sorrow at Portia's death, and shows more grief than Brutus. His love for Brutus, in spite of the flaw in military expeditions, saves the conspiracy from the final disgrace of 'division', enables it to meet its end intact.

Plutarch's Cassius is not so noble as Shakespeare has painted him. We are told that "Brutus could evil away with the tyranny and that Cassius hated the tyrant." Skottowe says, "Shakespeare has made Cassius's hatred for Caesar sufficiently apparent; but so repeatedly is his love for liberty enforced that the patriot rather than the malignant avenger of his own wrongs appears to strike against the tyrant."

Critics on Cassius : "Brutus is a political Girodin when he is placed in contrast with his brother-in-law Cassius, the political Jacobin" —Dowden.

"The leading distinctions between the two remarkable men, as drawn by Shakespeare, appear to us to be these : Brutus acts only upon principle; Cassius partly upon impulse. Brutus acts only when he has reconciled the contemplation of action with his speculative opinions. Brutus is a philosopher, Cassius is a partisan. Brutus therefore deliberates and spares; Cassius precipitates and denounces. Brutus is the noble instructor, Cassius the better politician" — Knight.

5. **Casca**

Like Cassius, Casca is a malcontent, jealous of Caeser's supremacy. "He was quick mettle when he went to school" (I. ii. 293); but he has grown resentful of those who have outstripped him in the race for power, and bitter with himself that he has let himself be thus out-stripped. Cassius assures Brutus that, despite his "tardy form", he is still quick mettle "in execution of any bold or noble enterprise but Shakespeare gives him no nobility. The clear-sighted Antony sees Casca for what he is. He reserves for him most bitterly ironical courtesy when he takes the conspirators' hands: "my valiant Casca", he calls him; and in his Forum speech he refers to him as "the envious Casca". While Brutus and Cassius are given eulogistic epitaphs, the last we hear of Casca is when Antony recalls how.

> "... damned Casca, like a cur, behind
> Struck Caesar on the neck." (V. i. 43-4)

In the Elizabethan drama, whenever there is an alternation of mood, it is, as Eliot somewhere suggests, generally in the direction of humour, as in the scene in *Julius Caesar* where Casca recounts to Brutus and Cassius the refusal of Caesar to accept the crown thrice by Antony :

> "I can as well be hang'd as tell the manner of it: it was mere foolery; I did not mark it. I saw Mark Antony offer him a crown; yet't was not a crown neither, 't was one of these coronets; and, as I told you, he put it by once; but for all that, to my thinking, he would fain have had it..." (I. ii. 231).

"With Casca the tone is that of the informal, half-mocking conversation of old friends, rhythmic nonetheless for its prose, because the tension is dormant." T.S. Dorsch gives a different interpretation, "He hides his feelings of frustration beneath the affectation of a sour fashion of speech, and of a bluntness that passes for a cross-grained good-humour."

Again, the same speech brings out vividly his aristocratic pride and contempt for the rank-scented multitude. He is superstitious, and the unnatural portents have stirred him to the depth of his being. His description of the storm reveals his power of imagination. In the meeting of the conspirators he shows the want of constancy in his character, by first supporting the proposal of Cassius to include Cicero in the faction, and immediately after going round to the opinion of Brutus.

He prides himself on his bluntness, but is a child in the hands of a clever manipulator. His bluntness is characteristic. It pervades his narration of Caesar rejecting the crown and his acceptance of dinner at Cassius'. Brutus does not like it :

> "What a blunt fellow is this grown to be!" (I. ii. 292)

Cassius is all praise for him and defends him :

> "This rudeness is a sauce to his good wit,
> Which gives men stomach to digest his words
> With bitter appetite." (I. ii. 297-299)

6. Cicero

We get a very imperfect glimpse of Cicero in the play, *Julius Caesar.* He appears only once, and reference to him are not many; yet by a few skilful touches the important characteristics of the orator have been brought out.

He is pre-eminently a man of intellect.

He is a much-respected man in Rome :

> O, let us have him, for his silver hairs
> Will purchase us a good opinion,
> And buy men's voices to commend our deeds." (II. i. 144-47)

But, ironically, Brutus overrules the suggestion on the ground :

> "For he will never follow anything
> That other men begin." (II. i. 151-52)

Brutus refers to his ferret and fiery eyes, when he meets with any opposition in the Senate. This is not a mark of petulance in him but of righteous indignation.

Casca reports that when Caesar recovered from his swoon and hastened to reassure himself of the favour of the commons, Cicero said something in Greek that made those who understood him smile at each other and shake their heads; we may presume that it was a sarcastic comment at the expense of Caesar.

Superstition has no place in his mind, and he is not moved by the unnatural portents. He is sceptical in these matters and does not believe like Casca that "they are portentous things unto the climate that they point upon." We no more hear of Cicero except that he perished by "the order of proscription" of the Triumvirs (IV. iii. 176-79); but we get a memorable picture of him from the few episodes with which he is associated.

7. Portia

William Shakespeare's Portia is a serious, noble and dignified wife of Brutus. She has the stoic strength of her father, Cato and her husband, Brutus. She is a true and honourable wife to Brutus, sharing all his inmost thoughts, pleasures and gifts :

> "... by and by thy bosom shall partake
> The secrets of my heart:
> All my engagements I will construe to thee,
> All the charactery of my sad brows," (II. i. 305-8)

'All', notice — he will conceal from her nothing that is in his heart.

But this is not all that Portia wants. "If this were true, "she says, "then should I know this secret": as the woman that Brutus choose for his wife, and Cato's daughter, she declares, she is worthy to share her husband's secrets and to support him in his anxieties. She has proved her fortitude in bearing physical pain by wounding herself in the thigh, and she has the moral courage to participate in the grief that oppresses Brutus. Brutus can no longer withstand her appeal. "O ye gods, "he cries, "render me worthy of this noble wife!" and he promises to disclose to her all the secrets of his heart. By her love and constancy and dignity, Portia does indeed show herself a wife of whom any man would wish to prove himself worthy.

Barker observes, "She is not seen as a clever woman, nor is she witty, and she speaks without coquetry of her 'once-commended beauty'. She is home-keeping and content, she is yielding, but from good sense, which she does not fear will seem weakness. She has dignity and perfect courage." She is all of a piece. Her gentleness, her reasonableness is her strength. Even her pride has its modesty :

> "I grant I am a woman, but, withal,
> A woman that Lord Brutus took to wife;
> I grant I am a woman, but, withal,
> A woman well-reputed, Cato's daughter", (II. i. 292-295)

"The repeated phrase and the stressed consonants give the verse a sudden vigour." Mrs. Jameson rightly says of her : "She is but a softened reflection of her husband Brutus; in him we see an excess of natural sensibility, an almost womanish tenderness of heart, repressed by the tenets of his austere philosophy; a Stoic by profession, and in reality the reverse-acting deeds, against his nature by the strong force of principle and will. In Portia, there is the same profound and passionate feeling and all her sex's softness and timidity held in check by that self-discipline, that stately dignity, which, she thought, became a woman 'so father'd and so husband'd."

But the Stoic in her does not repress her essential womanliness. She is a woman before a philosopher. Her love and anxiety for Brutus could not be kept in bounds by her philosophy. When the time for action comes, all the woman in her appears and overpowers her will and resolution, and she is about to disclose the conspiracy through a terrible agitation of her mind. Her impatience to learn the issue of the conspiracy is quite womanly and she now discovered for herself "how weak a thing the heart of woman is"

By this scene Shakespeare, in the words of Dorsch, "establishes Portia as a fully rounded character, endowed with a woman's heart as well as the constancy of Cato's daughter" (T.S. Dorsch, *Julius Caesar,* The Arden Edition).

The manner of her death shows how her attempt to struggle against nature ended in failure. Suspense and overwrought feelings have unnerved her, and in a fit of madness she commits suicide. Thus, Portia comes up to the noble conception of womanhood that Wordsworth has depicted in "She was a phantom of delight".

8. **Calpurnia**

Calpurnia is shown as the superstitious, negative and nervous wife of Caesar. In Act II, Scene ii, she appears in mortal terror, frightened like a child in the dark:

> "O Caesar, these things are beyond all use,
> And I do fear them." (II. ii. 25-6)

Or else, she scolds him like a shrew from the excess of her fear :

> "You shall not stir out of your house to-day." (II. ii. 9)

Finally, like Portia, she falls on her knees before him :

> "Let me, upon my knee, prevail in this." (II. ii. 54)

Unlike Brutus, Caesar neither treats her as an equal, nor does he comfort her as her fearful nature requires; instead he speaks in his Olympian mode :

> "What can be avoided
> Whose end is purposed by the mighty gods?
> Yet Caesar shall go forth!" (II. ii. 26-8)

Caesar treats her like a child.

Calpurnia's silence when Decius and the rest come to fetch Caesar to the Senate House is pathetic in its helplessness. She stands isolated and tremulous, watching him go in to taste wine with these good friends.

According to Macmillan, Calpurnia answers Pope's description of a woman having no character at all. She is no doubt a loving and tender wife, who manifests a proper spirit of wifely solitude for her husband's safety. She lives in Caesar's life alone, and by day and night it is her joy. She has no share in the secrets and ambitions of her lord.

The Roman Citizens

Shakespeare's picture of the Roman citizens in *Julius Caesar* is minute as well as vivid. They are represented here in their physical as well as mental characteristics. They are ugly in appearance, with sweaty caps, grimy hands and stinking breath from their mouths. In Casca's description of the refusal of the crown by Caesar at the festival of the Lupercal, we come across the following passage:

> "He put it the third time by; and still as he refus'd it, the rabblement hooted, and clapp'd their chopt hands, and threw up their sweaty might-caps, and uttered such a deal of stinking breath because Caesar refus'd the crown, that it had, almost, choked Caesar; for he swounded, and fell down at it. And for mine own part, I durst not laugh, for fear of opening my lips and receiving the bad air."
>
> (I. ii. 239-247)

Though not an aristocrat himself, Shakespeare had lived under the patronage of English nobles, and had loved the refinement which he found there. His other Roman play, *Coriolanus,* is a study in fickleness of the crowd and in a number of his plays we find the principal characters display their shrinking from the mob on account of physical reasons. In *Antony and Cleopatra,* the physical repulsion of the crowd frightens Cleopatra :

> "...mechanic slaves
> With greasy aprons, rules, and hammers shall
> Uplift us to the view. In their thick breaths,
> Rank of gross diet, shall we be enclouded,
> And forced to drink their vapour," (V. ii. 209-213)

It is not unlikely that Shakespeare formed this opinion in the course of his connection with the theatre when he had to depend for the acting of his plays on the applause of the crowd which assembled in the pit, and formed a great contrast with the refined and well-dressed nobility near the stage. Ben Jonson also refers contemptuously to these unrefined and foul-smelling 'groundlings' as 'the understanding gentlemen of the ground' who decided the fortune of a play.

Mentally they are fickle, capricious, excitable, emotional, unthinking and violent. They do not exercise reason; emotion is their only guide. This has caused them to be easy pawns in the hands of the intriguing politicians. In the first scene, they come out in the streets to honour Caesar; but being rebuked by the tribunes for their ungratefulness to Pompey for whom they had made a god shortly before, they go away as enemies of Caesar. With them the hero of today becomes the villain of tomorrow. They are slavish to a degree. They don't care for abstract ideas like republicanism, patriotism etc. With them personalities count for much. Hence when they found that Caesar provided them with food and show, they wanted to make him king, and placed their confidence in him. Appeal to their intellect or reason were worse than useless. Brutus sought to appeal to them through their reason by dwelling on such abstractions as the duty of patriotism, a share in the commonwealth, etc. They seemed to be convinced of the necessity of the murder of Caesar. But how great must have been the disappointment of the philosopher when they greeted him by saying — "Let him be Caesar." This is the best commentary on the fact that they care more for personalities than principles. The people who a moment back hailed Brutus by saying —"Let him be Caesar"— are turned in the next moment into his bitterest enemies by the wild rhetoric of Antony, who makes him dance to the tune and ultimately sets the mischief afoot. This shows their unstable, unthinking nature, which makes them change their views with every breath of wind. They are violent in their thought and action when they are roused. Witness how they tear the unfortunate poet Cinna to pieces, because he bore the same name as a conspirator! Such is the unenviable light in which Shakespeare has represented the populace of Rome.

Jusserand airly sums up his attitude in this respect :

"In the play (*Julius Caesar*), as in *Coriolanus* one of the most minutely described personages, if it can be so called is the People. Shakespeare who belongs to his time, not to ours, has no tenderness for the people; he depicts with great consistency their exigencies, their credulity, their ignorance, their fits of irresistible but transient ferocity, their contradictions, their violent exaggerations, everything, in fact that history has ever reproached them with...; the people who follow Jack Cade in *Henry VI* are the same as those who now applaud Brutus and Antony, exile Coriolanus, and proclaim Laertes king to console him for the death of his father slain by Hamlet."

Yet, it would be unjust to leave the description of the mob on such disparaging note. They might not show heroic virtues, but "Shakespeare recognises that the heart of the people is sound; their feelings are generally right, but their view of facts is perverted, by interests, by passions and stupidity" (Dowden). Their judgment proceeding from their feelings turned out true in the long run and they had "a Caesar"

*

D. DISCUSSION OF IMPORTANT CRITICAL OPINIONS

1. Edward Dowden

Commenting upon the date of composition of *Julius Caesar,* Dowden suggests 1601 as the most probable year. The play was written during a period when "the profoundest concerns of the individual soul were now pressing upon the imagination of the poet." That is why, even though Shakespeare borrowed themes from history, he laid greater emphasis upon the moral and emotional nature of the characters. He was engaged in writing drama all right. But during this period "subjects taken from history became not chronicles but tragedies. The moral interest is supreme."

Dowden also compares Shakespeare's treatment of Roman themes with Ben Jonson's. *Sejanus* and *Catiline's Conspiracy* are examples of Ben Jonson's method. He crowds the plays with minute and obscure references and the characters of these two plays are made to speak the very words spoken by them in the original Latin, that is in the works of Tacitus and Suetonius. But Shakespeare, who "knew little Latin and less Greek" is not interested in showing off his scholarship, to which — thank God — had hardly any pretensions. Shakespeare, points out Dowden, does not "buttress art with erudition".

The assassination of *Julius Caesar* had a great importance in the domain of history. It heralded the beginning of the end of Republicanism in Rome. Within thirteen years of Julius Caesar's assassination all the "great" Romans were dead — Brutus, Cassius, Casca, Pompey's sons, Mark Antony. In 31 B.C. Julius Caesar's grandnephew, Octavius Caesar became the first Emperor of Rome. But Dowden points out that, Shakespeare was not "interested so much in corporate life". The stress in the play is not on matters political, dynastic, national (*i.e.* Roman) or ecclesiastical. Shakespeare's supreme concern in *Julius Caesar* was with "the life and destiny of the individual man".

The main source for Shakespeare's *Julius Caesar* was North's translation of Plutarch's *Lives.* The material was no doubt treated "with reverent care" by Shakespeare. He did not aim at "a happy falsifying of the facts of history." Shakespeare has not consciously distorted Roman history in *Julius Caesar.* He has attempted rather, "an imaginative rendering" of Roman history, after confining himself to the very facts of that history.

Dowden comments : "While Shakespeare is profoundly faithful to Roman life and character, it is an ideal truth, truth spiritual rather than truth material, which he seeks to discover."

Dowden also *finds* that in Julius Caesar — "an ideal of duty is dominant".

Dowden is of opinion — and rightly so – that the character Shakespeare sees as the central one in *Julius Caesar,* is Brutus. Dowden points out that in Brutus Shakespeare is making "a complete imaginative study of the case of a man predestined to failure." Nevertheless, Brutus retains to the end "the moral integrity which he prized as his highest possession." It is true no doubt that Brutus too commits mistakes in the play. To err, we must remember, is human. But every fresh error that Brutus commits earns greater admiration and love of the audience.

Analysing the character of Brutus in detail, Dowden calls him "the stoic constant, loyal to his ideas, studious of moral perfection, bent upon gaining self-mastery, unsullied and untarnished to the end..."

Brutus, as pointed out by Dowden "is an idealist". He is a lover of books; he draws mental nourishment from philosophies; he keeps himself secluded and aloof from the harsh realities and treacherous intentions of the conspirators; he is more at home in the world of moral ideas and principles; he is jealous of the purity of his own character and does not want even misconception or misrepresentation to stain, or even touch his character. He is, therefore, always engaged in explaining his own conduct and examining all things in terms of his own uncompromising moral principles.

Shakespeare makes of Brutus an idealist. But the flaw of this idealist is his sternness, and since Brutus is shown yielding to the tendencies of idealism, the result is that Brutus loves the "success in the visible, material world".

According to Dowden, Octavius is the typical successful man. In

Julius Caesar he "deals skilfully with life . . . is misled by no enthusiasms." His "cool heart does not disturb his efficient hands"; he "sees the fact with clear-cut edges and achieves the necessary deed with logical precision, which is pitiless but not cruel."

Cassius is a contrast to Brutus. He is not a practiser of moral perfection, as Brutus is. "He is frankly envious, and hates Caesar. Yet, he is not ignoble. Brutus loves him and this fact in itself is a guarantee of his nobility."

"Cassius has a swift and clear perception of facts. He is not, like Brutus, a theorist, but a great observer, who looks quite through the deeds of men. Brutus lives in the abstraction, in the idea, Cassius lives in the concrete, in the fact."

Julius Caesar appears in only three scenes of the play and Shakespeare, in all these scenes, seems anxious to emphasise upon the weakness rather than the strength of Julius Caesar. He swoons when the crown is offered to him. When he recovers, he plays the role of a theatrical hero. Caesar suffers from the falling sickness, as revealed by Cassius. Caesar is also deaf. He is growing old and he does not maintain his youthful vigour. Caesar is also shown as a person who believes hopefully in superstitions. He asks Mark Antony to touch his childless wife Calpurnia during the course of the holy race. He also believes in the evil aspects of omens and doesn't want to go to the Capitol because of the unfavourable signs. But he accepts flattery as his right, and though he claims to be constant and fixed like the North star, he listens to flattery. "He vacillates, while professing unalterable constancy; he has lost in part his gift of perceiving facts, and of dealing efficiently with men and with events."

Why is it that Shakespeare dwells more upon the infirmities of Caesar in the first part of the play? This question is discussed by Dowden at some length. Another question related to the above is whether the title of the play, *Julius Caesar* is justified or not? Dowden examines critically the view held by Gervinus and Hudson on the subject and finds their opinions inadequate. Dowden maintains : "Julius Caesar is indeed protagonist of the tragedy; but it is not the Caesar whose bodily presence is weak, whose mind is declining in strength and sure-footed energy, the Caesar who stands exposed to all the accidents of fortune. This bodily presence of Caesar is but of secondary importance....*It is the spirit of Caesar which is the dominant power of the tragedy.*"

Brutus *fought* against this spirit of Julius Caesar. But Brutus is fallible and commits errors in practical politics. Brutus succeeds only in destroying Caesar's body. Caesar, while alive was physically weak and subject to many human infirmities. But after his death Caesar "rises as pure spirit, strong and terrible and avenges himself upon the conspirators. ...." Brutus's error was an error of judgment. He could not perceive where lay the true power of Caesar "and acted with short-sighted eagerness and violence".

Dowden points out that Shakespeare emphasised upon Caesar's physical infirmities in the early parts of the play, and brought out by way of contrast the mighty, over-awing power of Caesar's spiritual presence in the latter half of the play for a definite purpose. Shakespeare wanted to show dramatically "the vast posthumous power of the dictator... with strict propriety, therefore, the play bears the name of *Julius Caesar.*"

Dowden calls Antony "a man of genius without moral fibre; a nature of a rich, sensitive, pleasure-loving kind, the prey of good impulses and of bad; looking on life as a game, in which he has a distinguished part to play, and playing that part with magnificent grace and skill."

Antony is deeply devoted to Julius Caesar, but hardly shows any devotion to the principles of either Republicanism or Monarchy. He is a gifted subordinate and that is why he succeeds as a confidant and trusted lieutenant of Caesar, and later on, as a dutiful lover to the imperious Cleopatra. As a complement to his attitude towards his superiors, is Antony's behaviour towards his subordinates. He nurtures great contempt for inefficient people and he has the Machiavellian trait of making others scapegoats for his own evil deeds. His cynical attitude towards Lepidus (Act IV, Scene 1) and the devilish plan hatched to liquidate all those in Rome who are opposed to him, illustrate his character.

Brutus is pre-eminently ethical and all the weaknesses of Brutus spring from this nobility of his nature. He cannot credit or conceive the base facts of life. He doesn't possess the capacity to understand the littleness of little minds like Casca and other conspirators.

But it is ironical that the Stoic Brutus, who criticised Cato for having committed suicide should himself embrace a self-inflicted death. Brutus's famous soliloquy in the Orchard scene is an excellent example of the peculiar brooding style which has been used by Shakespeare in the great soliloquies of the great tragedies.

Coleridge cannot understand "the rationale" of this soliloquy. But

Dowden comments that here Shakespeare "wishes to show upon what grounds the political idealist acts."

The spectacle of a moral idealist (Brutus) whose abstract principles spur him to stab his best friend (Caesar) is truly ironical, in the tragic sense. Dowden comments: "Idealists like Brutus perform deeds which are at once beautiful and hideous".

Brutus has a deep-rooted conviction in moral ideals and wants to see them in operation in the real world inhabited by envious conspirators. That is why he refuses to accept the proposal for needless blood-shedding. He spares Mark Antony. Subsequent events show that this was a blunder. Another thing that Brutus lacked was the capacity to understand the cruel message of practical politics. As pointed out by Bernard Shaw in his play *Caesar and Cleopatra* (ironically enough spoken by Caesar himself), murder breeds murder and prophetically enough Caesar's assassination unleashed the hounds of civil war, leading to more bloodshed.

According to Dowden, Portia is "the ideal of moral loveliness, heroic and feminine". She is painted as more than a mere woman and wife to Brutus. She is "an ideal of august and adorable heroism". "We read of no embrace, no touch of hands or lips between Brutus and Portia, but we know that they are inseparably one."

"No relation of man and woman in the plays of Shakespeare is altogether so noble as that of Portia and Brutus" (E. Dowden).

Portia is Cato's daughter and a Stoic like her husband Brutus. In the fourth scene of the Second Act, Brutus has gone forth to bring Caesar to the Capitol, and Portia is alone at home. She is on the tenterhooks of suspense and anxiety. She is restless and hardly able to control herself. . . . Her death took place under the pressure of her anxious solicitude for the welfare of her husband, Brutus, and aptly illustrates the poet Landor's line, —"It is the strongest hearts that are the soonest broke."

Like the true Stoic, Brutus bears the tragedy of Portia's death with calm heroism. When he is accused by Cassius of not using his philosophy for curing his own griefs Brutus quietly announces, —"Portia is dead."

This was the fittest tribute that could be given to Portia. Herself a Stoic, she would have disapproved of a tumultuous grief, or its theatrical display.

Uncompromisingly harsh with moral lapses, Brutus is considerate and gentle towards everyone. There is hardly any scene more tender in the plays of Shakespeare than the one in which Lucius, Brutus's boy servant, goes to sleep while playing on the lyre. The tenderness of a man who is stern is the only tenderness which is wholly delicate and refined" (E. Dowden).

"The life of Brutus, as the lives of such men must be, was good life, in spite of its disastrous fortunes. The idealist was predestined to failure in the materialist world. But for Brutus true failure would have been disloyalty to his ideals. Of such failure he suffered none. Octavius and Mark Antony became victors at Philippi. Yet the purest wreath of victory rests on the forehead of the defeated conspirator."

Dramatic suspense is built up by Shakespeare up to the moment of Caesar's death by constant references to the passage of time. It is the Ides of March. In Act II, Scene I, at Brutus's house, Cinna speaks of "yon grey lines/That fret the clouds are messengers of the day." Soon afterwards, when the clock strikes three, Brutus draws the attention of the conspirators to the time. In scene II, Caesar asks the conspirators "what is't o'clock?" and Brutus informs him "Caesar, 'tis strucken eight." In scene IV Portia asks the Soothsayer on the streets, "What is't o'clock," and the reply is, — "About the ninth hour, lady." Again in Scene I of Act III, Caesar mockingly tells the Soothsayer, "The Ides of March are come."

The emphasis on time, *i.e.* night, dawn, 3-o'clock, eight-o'clock, nine-o'clock, builds up and hightens the suspense and our interest is kept upon the strain.

2. **A.C. Bradley**

Bradley is of opinion that *Antony and Cleopatra, Richard II* and *Julius Caesar* are "tragic histories," or "historical tragedies." Inasmuch as the material of these plays is drawn from history, Shakespeare had "to practise a certain obligation to follow his authority," that is to say, the sources from which he borrowed the story. But Bradley is of opinion that what he got from history was "an undramatic material".

Bradley's opinion regarding the relative importance of Caesar and Brutus is interesting, "Caesar, whose murder comes in Act III is in a sense the dominating figure in the story, but Brutus is the hero". Where Dowden declares categorically that the play properly bears the name of Julius Caesar, Bradley states that Caesar is only "the dominating figure in the story" and that the hero is Brutus.

Discussing "the fatal flaw" of the tragic hero, Bradley maintains that the tragic error involves no conscious breach of right. "Brutus helps in getting Caesar assassinated and participates in the actual act of killing impelled" by a full conviction of right.

Brutus thus offers a contrast to both Macbeth and Richard III. Both of these tragic protagonists launched upon a career of murderous ambition deliberately and with full conscious knowledge that what they were doing was 'wrong'. Brutus alone of the all the tragic heroes of Shakespeare acts from a conviction of being 'right'.

Bradley also points out that in his mature plays Shakespeare is not content with showing his tragic hero in a mere external combat with antagonists. "There is an outward conflict of persons and groups; there is also a conflict of forces in the hero's soul." This is equally applicable to the play *Julius Caesar* in which Brutus is in political conflict with Mark Antony, Octavius and others. But this conflict does not exceed the conflict going inside the soul of Brutus. As a matter of fact, there seems to be several struggles going on in Brutus's bosom. At first, it was a conflict between his loyalty towards his friend Caesar and his staunch belief in the ideology of Republicanism. Subsequently his idealist morality struggled to adjust itself with the base nature of the conspirators. What must have tormented Brutus's mind towards the end of his life is the irony of fate which caused his "right" act to yield "wrong" fruits. The ultimate refuge for all such idealists, whose acts in the practical world lead to disaster, is a Stoic acceptance of welcome death.

Bradley also discusses the concept of "fatality" in the tragedies of Shakespeare. The following words of Hamlet are applicable to all tragic heroes and their acts :

"Our thoughts are ours, their ends none of our own." The thoughts of Brutus are idealistic, noble inasmuch as they champion the sanctity of the individual resisting the tyranny of a would-be dictator. But when he pursues his ideals and acts in the practical world of corrupt conspirators, the result is tragedy. The tragic heroes "fight blindly in the dark. They act freely and yet their action binds them hand and foot. And it makes no difference whether they meant well or ill. No one could mean better than Brutus, but he contrives misery for his country and death for himself."

It is generally believed that "the catastrophe" of tragedy is an example of justice. But Bradley points out that it is not always so. It may be 'poetic justice' but it is hardly 'just'. Why should Richard III and

Brutus share the same fate? In many Greek tragedies we are forced to think that "justice" and "retribution" are different things. This is also true with regard to Brutus.

Another point which sets *Julius Caesar* apart from all the other tragic plays of Shakespeare is the nature of the tragic flaw in the protagonist. In all the other plays, evil is pitted against goodness. *Julius Caesar* is the only play of Shakespeare in which the question posed before it is a much more fundamental and moral one : "Is the hero doing right or wrong?" In his other plays Shakespeare takes a categorical stand — Macbeth, Richard III, Othello, Hamlet — all have committed a palpably wrong act. But we are not so sure in *Julius Caesar*. Bradley concludes that "this is one of the reasons why that play (*Julius Caesar*) has something of a classic air."

Usually in Shakespearean tragedy "the main source of the convulsion which produces suffering and death is never good...it is in almost every case evil in the fullest sense, not mere imperfection but plain moral evil."

Julius Caesar is the only play in which we find an exception to the above rule.

The tragic sequence of events in *Julius Caesar* makes it structurally very simple. The fortunes of the conspiracy move in rising action which leads to Act III culminating in the crisis of Caesar's assassination. Thereafter came the vicissitudes of falling action leading gradually to the final catastrophe, where Brutus and Cassius perish.

Shakespeare pays special attention to his opening scenes particularly in the great tragedies. "His usual plan in tragedy is to begin with a short scene or part of a scene, either full of life and stir, or in some other way arresting." In *Julius Caesar* too Shakespeare presents an arresting spectacle, — "a crowd in commotion".

This crowd is symbolically and literally an "antagonist" which is pitted against the "great men" of Rome. We receive at the very outset a strong impression of the force which is to prove fatal to the hero's happiness. In *Macbeth,* the three Weird Sisters, who are brought in the opening scene, weave the sinister web of temptation reinforced with treacherous prophecies in which Macbeth is so inexonerably caught. In *Julius Caesar* the crowd plays the role of a sinister shadow of fate. With its fickleness the crowd is so impersonal, so gullible, so much susceptible to the exhortations of a theatrical speaker, that any thing can be expected from it.

Marullus rightly castigates the crowd for its fickleness. Subsequent events show that the crowd owes loyalty to no one. It welcomed both Pompey and Caesar with equal enthusiasm. It applauded Brutus and very soon afterwards was transformed into "the rabble" roused by the clever speech of Mark Antony and forced Brutus and company to fly from Rome. The crowd lives from moment to moment and can be manipulated by clever people in any way they want. It is "these qualities of the crowd" that render hopeless the enterprise of Brutus and wreck the ambition of Coriolanus in Shakespeare's play of that name.

The movement of the tragic conflict is given great clearness and force in *Julius Caesar* by the dramatic movement of the opposing forces at work in the play. The forces represented by Cassius and the other conspirators advance to a decisive success. They are thereafter driven downward towards defeat by the reaction provoked by the crisis.

Immediately after the crisis, however, Shakespeare's usual practice in his great tragedies is to introduce a momentary pause followed by a slowing, mounting counter-movement. This momentary pause represents a lull and some critics have brought the charge that some of Shakespeare's great tragedies fall off in Act IV.

It is said about *Julius Caesar* too that the movement of the play has tendency "to drag" in Act IV.

But an analysis of the play's movement will bring out an interesting pattern. In *Julius Caesar* the ascending force reaches its zenith in the Third Act with the assassination of Julius Caesar. But Shakespeare does not allow any let-up in the dramatic tension in this play as he does elsewhere. In *Macbeth,* for example, Duncan's assassination is followed by the Porter's scene, offering some kind of tragic relief. But in *Julius Caesar* the assassination of Caesar is followed quickly by Antony's speech in the forum which rouses the fickle crowd to a storm of sympathy for Caesar and of fury against the conspirators.

Shakespeare is here following up the tension of Caesar's murder with the counter-tension of a furious mob crying for revenge against Brutus and his 'friends' and actually killing Cinna.

During the scene of Mark Antony's speech we are shown that very crowd of unstable Romans which was so easily led this way or that, in the opening scene. The crowd shows that the enterprise of Brutus is hopeless and that the days of the Republic are numbered. This repetition of a first effect produces a fateful feeling.

The fourth Act is used in *Julius Caesar* also for indicating the inward changes in the tragic hero. The quarrel-scene between Brutus and Cassius serves this purpose. It has another function too. "In this section of a tragedy Shakespeare often appeals to an emotion different from any of those excited in the first half of the play, and so provides novelty and generally also relief. As a rule, this new emotion is pathetic, and the pathos is not terrible or lacerating." The reconciliation of Brutus and Cassius, the arrival of the news of Portia's death and the tenderness of Brutus towards Lucius, the boy-servant — all evoke tender feelings — feelings completely opposed to those roused in the blood-thirsty III Act.

Although "a battle is not the most favourable place for the exhibition of tragic character", it thrills the imagination of the readers. It is worth remembering that Brutus and Cassius do not die fighting, but commit suicide after defeat."

There are certain obvious similarities between Brutus and Hamlet. Both are highly intellectual by nature and reflective by habit. Both may even be called, in a popular sense, philosophic. But Brutus is so in a stricter sense. Both are good men and both evince a sensitive and almost painful anxiety to do right. Both Hamlet and Brutus fail in the practical affairs of the world because their reflective natures make them unpractical and incapable of understanding correctly the nature of evil in the world.

This is why Prof. Dowden call *Julius Caesar* "a tragedy of thought", distinguishing it from the later tragedies of Shakespeare which may be called "tragedies of passion", because they deal with wilder and stormier aspects of the human heart.

Bradley is of opinion that "in *Julius Caesar* everybody means well." In *Hamlet* the hero is trying to do his duty. He means well but there are other characters in *Hamlet* who are decidedly evil. In the later tragedies the forces of evil come more blatantly to the surface. Human nature now inspires "not mere sadness or repulsion, but horror and dismay."

But in *Julius Caesar* there is an absence of "abnormal or appalling forms of evil". This indicates that at this stage of his career Shakespeare was not so much scrutinising moral evil as he was in the later tragedies.

Julius Caesar is distinguished, according to A.C. Bradley, "by a deliberate endeavour after a dignified and unadorned simplicity — a Roman simplicity perhaps". *Julius Caesar* belongs to the end of the second period of Shakespeare when he reaches "a limited perfection". "We receive an impression of easy mastery and complete harmony, but not so strong an impression of inner power bursting into outer life." "In his great anxiety to do right Hamlet most resembles Brutus."

"It (the supernatural) gives a confirmation and a distinct form to inward movements already present and exerting an influence; to the sense of failure in Brutus."

3. David Daiches

According to Daiches it is "the ambiguity of innocence" that brings about the tragedy in Shakespeare's tragic plays. There is a simple innocence in the sensitive idealism of Hamlet, the credulousness of Othello and the stern virtuousness of Brutus. It was this innocence that brought disaster upon them.

This innocence is a positive quality in the personal life of Brutus. But what makes Brutus great in his private life was a distinct handicap to him as a political figure and public man. David Daiches is, therefore, of the view that "the relation between private and public virtue... is in some degree the theme of *Julius Caesar*". The fault of Brutus was that he lacked sophistication. He was not worldly enough. He was, to borrow a slang term — a sucker. His innocence makes him a ready and pathetic victim of the unscrupulous conspirators. "The case of Brutus is that of the liberal intellectual in a world of Realpolitik."

"Cassius is the co-hero of the play." He is a skilled politician and has no scruples. He doesn't hesitate to play upon the finer feelings of Brutus (his wife's brother) in order to make Brutus a co-conspirator. But Brutus is undoubtedly the greater of the two, and in all matters gains ascendancy over Cassius. David Daiches makes the following comment on this association between Brutus and Cassius. "When the coarse nature of Cassius is dominated by the finer one of Brutus, both are destroyed." Brutus's plan to give a fight to the forces of Octavius and Mark Antony at Philippi was ill-advised. But since Brutus was the dominating figure, Cassius agreed. Brutus was, therefore, solely responsible for the disaster that followed. At the end of the play the Epicurean Cassius is almost converted into a Stoic. He commits suicide out of shame for having lived on even after his best friend Brutus had been taken prisoner (as Cassius wrongly believed).

Cassius is more shrewd and more practical than Brutus. But Daiches says that "he (Cassius) is basically an idealist too".

This, in my opinion, is not correct, David Daiches draws his opinion from Caesar's comment on Cassius —"he thinks too much". But Cassius's 'thinking' is hardly of the intellctual type. Cassius suffers from a deep-rooted feeling of inferiority complex and it is the poison of his envy that makes him kill Caesar. This is evident in the following speech :

> "The fault, dear Brutus, is not in our stars, But in ourselves, that we are underlings" (Act I. ii. 140-1).

What rankles in Cassius's mind is not the awareness that persons like him are "petty men" (I. ii. 136) and must find "dishonourable graves" (I. ii. 138) under the shadow of Caesar who bestrides the narrow world like a Colossus (I. ii. 135-36). A man with such bitter feelings of envy can never be an idealist. The thinking which Caesar discovered in Cassius is obviously what is known as brooding.

David Daiches' comments on Mark Antony are equally superficial. D. Daiches comments that Antony is the man without innocence, and in *Julius Caesar,* Antony's is the success story; he knows how to come to terms with life. There is no villainy, no evil in him. He is, on the contrary, generous, noble and kind-hearted. But he has the ability to manipulate people.

"Antony is the great puppeteer of the play, and his famous oration is the work of a supreme puppet-master. He manipulates other people's innocence. "Antony is too good to be a tragic villain, too bad to be a tragic hero. He is rather the tarnished, sensual man standing midway between innocence and evil." "Octavius Caesar is Shakespeare's ideal, practical man, shrewd cool-headed, altogether a cold fish."

4. Irving Ribner

Ribner breaks new grounds in the criticism of Shakespearean tragedy. He defines tragedy as "an exploration of man's relation to the forces of evil in the world." The tragic hero comes to grief because he makes "the wrong moral choice", which goes counter to "a purposive, ordered universe".

Ribner also says that Shakespeare attempts "through *Julius Caesar* to embody political as well as ethical ideas in dramatic form." History is supposed to be a mere chronicle of events and Tragedy tries to answer ethical questions about man's involvement with evil. But it will be wrong to say that if a writer uses historical material, he won't be able to wrestle with questions about man's predicament in the universe, which is the province of Tragedy. The hero of a tragedy has usually a symbolic function. But in historical tragedies like *Julius Caesar* characters have a historic dimension too. "The fate of Brutus, or Caesar is secondary to that of Rome and as tragic heroes they also reflect in specific human terms principles of general political conduct."

The historical tragedies "use the past in order to teach political wisdom to the present." Coming to *Julius Caesar,* Ribner calls it a "tragedy of moral choice, drawing upon the tradition of the English morality play." In other words, in such a tragedy the hero (Brutus) is confronted with a choice between good and evil. Brutus is not a practical, worldly man. He is too much of an idealist and his imperfections lead him to make a wrong choice. Of course, Brutus comes to realise that his choice was erroneous when suffering visits him as a result of his error. The final act of the tragic hero is to renounce his error and life too.

Certain critics see *Julius Caesar* as the story of a great hero (Caesar) trying to establish monarchy in a corrupt society. But the critics continue, Caesar is frustrated and killed by rebels who also plunge the country into a civil war. Plutarch and some other writers saw Caesar as a great hero no doubt. But they have also showed how Caesar became puffed up with pride and ambition and how it was Caesar himself who was chiefly responsible for the end of Republican Rome.

Brutus's motive for assassinating Caesar is pure and seems to be ethically all right. He agrees to destroy Caesar not because Caesar has been a tyrant, but because Caesar aspires to unlawful power, that is, to become a king, although Caesar did not belong to any dynasty of kings.

Brutus's famous soliloquy in the orchard scene has been called by many critics bad logic. But Ribner defends the argument used by Brutus in lines 10-28, Act II, Scene i. The logic is that of Renaissance England specially with reference to the political background of the Tudor dynasty. The king is God's deputy upon earth and only God can sanction kingship to a person. This is the divine theory of kingship in which the contemporaries of Shakespeare (and obviously Shakespeare too) firmly believed. Without God's sanction Caesar won't have the check of responsibility to God. An ordinary man, no matter how great, could not aspire to kingship. If he does, as Caesar was doing, he could aspire only to tyranny, and this is what Brutus fears and resolves to prevent.

But Brutus commits a sin when he helps to assassinate Caesar, because "to attain a public good he commits a private crime." The tragedy of Brutus illustrates the dictum that public morality can be built only upon private virtue.

Ribner is of opinion that "there are two tragic heroes in the play *Julius Caesar.* Each brings about his own destruction, and together they bring chaos to Rome".

Both Caesar and Brutus are among the greatest men the world has ever known. But both Caesar and Brutus make wrong moral choices. Let us quote Montaigne's opinion on Caesar : "All his noble inclinations were stifled and corrupted by that furious passion of ambition by which he was so forcibly carried away."

"This inordinate desire for kingship is the height of Caesar's tragic folly, the 'hubris' (tragic flaw) which will destroy him" (I. Ribner).

Caesar's inordinate pride is amply illustrated in his pompous, boastful speeches (Act II. ii. 44-47) and throughout the first three Acts. Shakespeare portrays Caesar as a strutting, vainglorious fellow who spurns his normal relationship to ordinary men and claims the qualities and stature of a god. There is a pathetic irony in Caesar's boast of being "constant as the Northern star," because soon afterwards he is stabbed to death. His pretensions, one feels, are after all, ludicrous posturings, and Caesar's assassination shows that he is as much bound by the mortal limitations of flesh and blood as any other Roman.

"Caesar's wrong moral choice is his decision to go to the Senate to accept a crown to which he has no moral claim."

Antony triumphs, but he is more evil than good, as will be seen in his immorality, his cunning manipulation of the mob for personal revenge, and his ruthless, cold-blooded selection of Romans whom he wants to eliminate (IV. i. 1-6). In order to make his own position secure, Antony indulges in those very evils that Brutus had tried to eradicate by killing Caesar.

Caesar never becomes aware of his sin which led to his downfall. Brutus, however, late in the play, realises his sin of wrong moral choice. He is an idealist philosopher, lacking in those public virtues that make for a successful political leader. His rejection of the conspiratorial oath, his refusal to assassinate Mark Antony, his permitting Antony to speak at the funeral of Caesar, — all these were tactical errors and show the refusal of Brutus to recognise the fact that the assassination of Caesar was a sinful act.

"In order to attain a goal of public good, Brutus commits a private crime : he murders his friend. This is his wrong moral choice and the source of his tragedy. The crime of Brutus, the virtuous murderer, is a violation of the closest bonds which tie man to man, bonds which the audience instinctively identifies. We have a sharp dramatic antithesis between an abstract political ideal and the ordinary human goodness which it violates."

In *Julius Caesar* Shakespeare shows the Aristotelian principle that the final test of government is virtue and that public morality must be grounded firmly upon private morality.

Brutus attempts to raise the bloody murder of his friend Caesar to the status of a ritual, sacramental act. But the irony and pathos of Brutus's position is that he forgets to recognise that an evil act (the assassination of Caesar) can never produce good. Another irony implicit in the situation is that though Brutus wants to kill the spirit of Caesar, he succeeds in killing only Caesar's body and that the spirit returns to haunt him at Philippi.

Shakespeare does not condemn Brutus wholly. Brutus's decision that Caesar is a threat to Rome is not a sin. Rather, Brutus's decision to join Cassius in conspiracy and murder was the fateful error.

5. Tucker Brooke

"*Julius Caesar* can be called a Senecan tragedy, complete with ghost and revenge-motif; but it is given a bias-movement by the character of Brutus."

"Brutus is not a thoroughly harmonised portrait. He is a preliminary drawing for Shakespeare's Hamlet, who has many of the same difficulties to face and is of similar mental fibre."

6. G. Wilson Knight

Wilson Knight's criticism of Shakespeare's tragedies examines the imagery used in them, and from this draws conclusions about the theme and pattern of the great tragedies.

According to Wilson Knight "the *Julius Caesar* world is fiery-bright with a brilliant erotic vision which sees a flaming spirit in history, in action, in man."

"All here is fiery, spiritual ardour, in love, honour, insurrection, revenge, high intent of whatever kind. So the lights of heaven burn down, sun and stars, dawn, 'exhalations', comets; all take part in an action whose fiery spirit is worthy of their company. Darkness shot with light characterises this play."

Wilson Knight lists the important groups of images in *Julius Caesar*. Images denoting beasts, flash of metals, personal appearances and body nourishment, the life-forces of eating, drinking, sleeping, frequent suggestions of the opposite — disease, infirmity, weakness, and the fiery spirit world are found everywhere.

'Blood' is an important image. Calpurnia's dream and the conspirators' ritual dipping of their hands in Caesar's blood are the key-images. Blood is, Wilson Knight says, "lovingly, almost erotically described". "There is an almost brutal enjoyment evident in the imagery of slaughter, wounds and blood; yet it is so flamed with imagination's joy that there is no sense of disgust."

Caesar is portrayed as a weak, ailing, small man; yet his life-blood drenches the play. Shakespeare is pointing towards a body-spirit contrast. "In the spirit of men there is no blood" (II. i. 168) — but in the blood of men there is spirit : hence the power of Caesar's blood throughout the play. 'Blood' also means vitality in *Julius Caesar*. 'Blood' is very close to 'spirit'. So in *Julius Caesar* blood imagery does not horrify. It rather excites — it is a brilliant stream of rich life, sacrificially, poured out in a drama of vivid, erotic perception, dynamic and spiritualised humanity.

The central theme is : Caesar's personal weakness in body, even in mind; and his colossal spirit : the spirit of empire and order. "Spirit" and "fire" are words that recur again and again in the play.

In *Julius Caesar* there are two sides, and each side sees the other as the cause of disorder : thus, absolutely, the disorder is one of inharmonious relation only.

That the chaos and disorder are political and presage the liquidation of the Republic, is a point which Wilson Knight conveniently forgets. He is of opinion that Caesar represents "order", "harmony", and that the conspirators destroy it.

But actually the matter is not so simple. The historical events presented in *Julius Caesar* form only the middle part of the Roman Civil War. Caesar had himself fought and vanquished Pompey. Caesar was assassinated by Brutus, Cassius and company who in their turn, were defeated by Antony and Octavius. But even Antony did not last long, and finally it was Octavius who established a monarchy in Rome.

But Wilson Knight opines, — "Caesar is the fiery symbol of Rome's spirit. He blazes in a fine majesty, supreme . . . . Caesar compares himself to a star, his starry greatness a thing of steady light unquenchable, unshaken (III, i, 56-60). Caesar is thus infinite as eternity itself. . . ."

Wilson Knight further comments : ". . . Love is here the regal, the conquering reality : the murder of Caesar is a gash in the body of Rome, and this gash is healed by love, so that the play's action emphasises first the disjointing of spirit from matter, and then the remating of these two elements into the close fusion which is love, order, peace."

"Caesar is a sublime figure-head, but.... We (also) see him as a man, weak, egotistical, petulant." He often vacillates. Indeed there seem to be two Caesars, the ailing and petulant old man, and the giant spirit standing colossal over all others. As his death approaches, he is shown as two incompatibles, shifting, rocking like a ship about to sink. His speech is alternately resonant of imperial glory and drenched with absurdities. When Metellus Cimber approaches him, he is intent, not on justice, but on preserving his own constancy. He wants to show off. His egotism then knows no bounds. But it is ludicrous too, in spite of the rhetorical hyperboles of egocentricity.

But in Wilson Knight's opinion, "Whatever we may think of Caesar as a man, we must see him also as a symbol of something of vast import, resplendent majesty, and starry purpose."

"The central act in the play is Caesar's assassination, shown as a rough breaking of spirit from body whether of Caesar or Rome. Antony's love alone heals the dualism."

According to Wilson Knight, Brutus sacrifices love to his "honour". Honour first, love second. This is so even with Portia. That is why she invokes the strength of love in Act II, scene i, lines 267-76. The love-honour dualism in Brutus's experience results in disorder, failure. He trusts to his abstractions pitifully. That is why he expects the citizens to be convinced by his prose-speech and appeals to cold reason . . . . Cassius is more in touch with realities of love, conspiracy and war : Brutus is more at home with his ethical abstractions.

The famous quarrel scene between Cassius and Brutus marks the failure of their joint venture. It also suggests the failure of ideals unrelated to practical expediency. We see Brutus's ship of honour foundering on the hard rocks of finance. Brutus is always so enwrapped in a sense of his own honour that others can made no headway against his will (IV. iii. 63-66). In fact, Brutus is a continual hindrance because of his exaggerated sense of honour. Yet we admire the consistency and the steadiness of purpose in Brutus. In the speech just before his death (V. v. 34-36), Brutus expresses the simple and only joy that his followers have been true to him. There is a resignation here, a knowledge of failure and a stoic acceptance of life's tragedy.

Brutus is the only "ethical" force in the play, *Julius Caesar* : the rest act by emotion. Brutus's tragedy is that he pursues an ethical ideal in and for itself, unrelated to the time and people around. Wilson Knight comments : "It is a selfishness. His ethic is no ethic, rather a projection of himself. A phantasma of his own mind." Because Brutus is a sensitive idealist, he alone of all the conspirators nurtures anguished sense of guilt. That is why, only his conscience projects an evil spirit the Ghost of Caesar. And yet, Brutus is glorious till the very end. He suffers because he is far greater than all the conspirators.

Looked at from a different angle, Brutus' uncompromising love for 'honour' makes him 'impossible'. He remains ice-cold, appalingly impregnable in the 'honour' in the famous quarrel-scene. He is impossibly noble.

Cassius is strongly contrasted with Brutus. A man with a lean, hungry look. Cassius provokes fear in Caesar who calls him "dangerous". His seriousness makes him sombre, gloomy, ashamed of all trivialities. He has no disorder in his soul. So he takes deliberate pleasure in barring his "bosom to the thunder storm". He has little sense of abstract honour. To him the end justifies any means. He dupes Brutus through the bogus letters so that Brutus may join the conspiracy. The key to the personality of Cassius is his own speech in Act I, scene ii (lines 312-19) which is suffused with a sense of cynicism. In a Machiavellian mood he realises that Brutus's "honourable" loyalty can be easily converted into "honourable" conspiracy. He is dark with thwarted ambition and envy.

But Wilson Knight thinks that "a certain golden star burns in his (Cassius) heart : a great longing for love."

Throughout the play Cassius's love for Brutus is emphasised. Envy, ardour of love, a certain spiritual loneliness, propensity to gloom and foreboding, are some of the characteristics of Cassius's personality, according to Wilson Knight. Cassius does not understand Brutus's ethical finesse. Yet, respect for his friend causes him to give way to Brutus time after time, thereby ruining the conspiracy.

Cassius's motive is clearly a sort of envy. Throughout the quarrel-scene Cassius is passionate in anger, grief, or love. "Brutus is cold, aureoled in self-righteousness, unreachable, remote :" but emotion surges in him too.

Caesar is seen from various angles. At the start we often see him as Cassius sees him. In the middle section we see him with Brutus's indecisive vision. After the murder, we tend to see Caesar through the eyes of Mark Antony.

7. Brents Stirling

The main thesis of Stirling, the American critic, is that the element of ceremony, ritual and incantation is an important one in *Julius Caesar*. Plutarch also mentions the feast of Lupercalia and the touching of barren women by the holy runners. This element is further strengthened by the introduction of the Soothsayer. Even while Cassius and Brutus are talking, in the distance can be heard the shouts and flourishes of a symbolic spectacle. This is a touch given by Shakespeare who has most dramatically reinforced the element of ritual by making it into a major theme of *Julius Caesar*. But Shakespeare, while bringing the serious ritual into prominence, also takes pains to subject it to satirical treatment....

The view of the Elizabethans was that Brutus's virtues were complicated by self-deception and doubtful principle. This Elizabethan view of Brutus as tragically misguided is consistent with Antony's pronouncement that Brutus was the only disinterested member of the conspiracy. But Brutus is not to be summed up in an epitaph. "As the impersonal member of a conspiracy motivated largely by personal ends, he sought in a complex way to resolve his contradiction by depersonalising, ritualising the means."

Modern readers find the tragedy of Brutus in his rigid devotion to justice and fair play. But in spite of his disinterested honour and liberality, modern readers do perceive a conflict between questionable goals and honourable action, a contradiction lying in his attempt to redeem morally confused ends by morally clarified means. The Elizabethan tragedy of Brutus, like that of Othello, is marked by an integrity of conduct which leads the protagonist into evil and reassures him in his error. But Brutus attempts to purify assassination through ceremony. This act, not to be found in Plutarch, symbolises the "Elizabethan" Brutus who is compelled by honour to join with conspirators but persuaded by his conscience to reject conspiracy.

Shakespeare's Brutus plans the killing of Cacsar as a ritual, while Plutarch presents it as the very opposite of this. Plutarch's description of the assassination runs thus : "Caesar turned him nowhere but he was stricken at by some...and was hacked and mangled among them, as a wild beast taken of hunters."

Shakespeare gives Plutarch's words to Antony, and by making Brutus lay emphasis on the ritual element, Shakespeare creates a truly significant dramatic tension.

In the well known speech in Act II, i, lines 166-80, Brutus expands the theme which ends his hesitation and frees his moral imagination. This is his conversion of bloodshed to ritual. Brutus's soliloquy in Act II, scene i, 63-69, uses the conventional symbol of political convulsion by inward "insurrection"

Antony's soliloquy which renders his prophecy of "domestic fury and fierce civil strife" should be taken as a choric interpretation of Caesar's death, and compared to Carlisle's prophecy on the deposition of Richard II.

8. Martin S. Day

By all logic of play construction *Julius Caesar* should be a failure. The title role is ended in Act III, scene i. Brutus does not emerge as a hero till the play is half over. But the play owes its great success to a superb presentation of dramatic conflict on the stage and to its incomparable rhetoric.

Brutus rebels against constituted authority, brings sedition and chaos into the political fabric. Although his intentions are splendid, his achievement is a catastrophe. Shakespeare shows no sympathy for the Republicanism of Brutus. Rather, Brutus is portrayed as the most dangerous of subversives, the misguided intellectual and idealist. Caesar, as he briefly appears, is blinded by his own divinity; but he is a majestic figure and remains throughout the play, even after his death, the martyred symbol of order.

Neither Antony nor Octavius gains stature as the avenger from a Revenge Tragedy, though Shakespeare shows Senecan leanings in the appearance of Caesar's ghost before the battle at Philippi and in the

Stoicism of Brutus. The play's worth may be summed up as "sublime spectacle in masterful language".

9. J.C. Maxwell

Maxwell finds *Julius Caesar* a "transitional" play serving as a link between the English histories and the great tragedies that follow.

On account of its psychological probing (brought in for the first time) *Julius Caesar* is Shakespeare's" first major tragedy".

The Elizabethan "crisis in humanism" finds its highest expression in Shakespeare's great tragedies and even in *Julius Caesar,* the prelude to the great tragedies, we can see "Shakespeare's many sided perception of conflict within humanism" in the form of "cleavage between society and individual greatness."

Julius Caesar is also a worthy prelude to the great tragedies for two other reasons. For the first time Shakespeare handles rhetoric as an art which can distort, intensify, or amplify the emotion of the speaker in *Julius Caesar,* and we are all admiration for the sharp realism of this new theatrical technique. Secondly, it is in *Julius Caesar* that Shakespeare handles properly the Senecan philosophy of Stoicism in Brutus, which brings out the inner tension of the Renaissance.

A peculiarity of *Julius Caesar* is that its construction takes its unity notably from single event — the death of Caesar, the central secular event in world history. Critics have tried to explain it by introducing the abstraction of 'Caesarism' which invokes the spirit of Caesar even when his body has fallen.

Brutus resembles Hamlet only as illustrating the Shakespearean theme of "disparity between the man and what he does". Hamlet is a mystery, Brutus is a puzzle. In him Shakespeare is presenting a doctrinaire intellectual with whose doctrine (classical Republicanism) Shakespeare has no spontaneous imaginative sympathy. This is why in Brutus' soliloquy in Act II, scene i, Shakespeare seems to be whittling down the whole meaning of theoretical Republicanism. Brutus, in this soliloquy, is and is not a Republican, as reflected in the obscurities of this speech. He seems to have been suddenly overshadowed by a terrible doubt. Maxwell is partly correct when he comments that in his famous soliloquy on the crowning of Caesar (II. i. 10-34), Brutus "is and is not a Republican". The soliloquy is not only the expression of Roman Republicanism but paradoxically enough — Renaissance monarchism too — the latter only as a submerged motif. Ribner's analysis of the soliloquy is more convincing. Brutus has here become the mouthpiece of Shakespeare's views on the Divine theory of kingship. The king is divinely annointed as such, and this divinity is the only check, or brake which will effectively restrain a King from becoming a tyrant. Caesar, being an ordinary man, can never have that restraint. He is, therefore, sure to become a tyrant. So, he must be assassinated.

The greatest quality of *Julius Caesar* according to Maxwell is its "moral and political realism". The interpretations of the fall of Caesar generally follow two opposite traditions, partisan to the monarchical or republican side. But Shakespeare shows his preference for a more humanised treatment. He has toned down the bombastic elements in Caesar and yet he has made Caesar stand out. But his fluster and assertion of his rigid and absolute power are mere psychological covers for the first falterings of approaching senility.

Pope was shocked by Brutus's speech (III. i. 107-14) exhorting the conspirators to "bathe our hands in Caesar's blood". But Maxwell is of opinion that "there is nothing which better displays clarity and sanity of moral vision than Act III of *Julius Caesar,* with Brutus's high-minded, sacrificial attitude towards murder displayed without comment."

*

TEXT OF JULIUS CAESAR

DRAMATIS PERSONAE

JULIUS CAESAR

OCTAVIUS CAESAR, MARCUS ANTONIUS, M. AEMILIUS LEPIDUS — triumvirs after death of Julius Caesar

CICERO, PUBLIUS, POPILIUS LENA — senators

MARCUS BRUTUS, CASSIUS, CASCA, TREBONIUS, LIGARIUS, DECIUS BRUTUS, METELLUS CIMBER, CINNA — conspirators against Julius Caesar

FLAVIUS and MARULUS, tribunes.

ARTEMIDORUS of Cnidos, a teacher of rhetoric.

A Soothsayer.

CINNA, a poet. Another Poet.

LUCILIUS, TITINIUS, MESSALA, YOUNG CATO, VOLUMNIUS — friends to Brutus and Cassius

VARRO, CLITUS, CLAUDIUS, STRATO, LLUCIUS, DARDANIUS — servants to Brutus

PINDARUS, servant to Cassius

CALPURNIA, wife to Caesar.

PORTIA, wife to Brutus

SCENE : *Rome : the neighborhood of Sardis : the neighborhood of Philippi.*

ACT I.

Scene I. *Rome. A street.*

Enter Flavius, Marullus, *and certain* Commoners.

Flav. Hence! home, you idle creatures get you home:
Is this a holiday? what! know you not,
Being mechanical, you ought not walk
Upon a laboring day without the sign
Of your profession? Speak, what trade art thou?

First Com. Why, sir, a carpenter.

Mar. Where is thy leather apron and thy rule?
What dost thou with thy best apparel on?
You, sir, what trade are you?

Sec. Com. Truly, sir, in respect of a fine workman, I am but, as you would say, a cobbler.

Mar. But what trade art thou? answer me directly.

Sec. Com. A trade, sir, that, I hope, I may use with a safe conscience; which is, indeed, sir, a mender of bad soles.

Mar. What trade, thou knave? thou naughty knave, what trade?

Sec. Com. Nay, I beseech you, sir, be not out with me: yet, if you be out, sir, I can mend you.

Mar. What meanest thou by that? mend me, thou saucy fellow!

Sec. Com. Why, sir, cobble you.

Flav. Thou art a cobbler, art thou?

Sec. Com. Truly, sir, all that I live by is with the awl: I meddle with no tradesman's matters, nor women's matters, but with awl. I am, indeed, sir, a surgeon to old shoes; when they are in great danger, I recover them. As proper men as ever trod upon neat's leather have gone upon my handiwork.

Flav. But wherefore art not in thy shop today?
Why dost thou lead these men about the streets?

Sec. Com. Truly, sir, to wear out their shoes, to get myself into more work. But, indeed, sir, we make holiday, to see Cæsar and to rejoice in his triumph.

Mar. Wherefore rejoice? What conquest brings he home?
What tributaries follow him to Rome,
To grace in captive bonds his chariot-wheels?
You blocks, you stones, you worse than senseless things!
O you hard hearts, you cruel men of Rome,
Knew you not Pompey? Many a time and oft
Have you climb'd up to walls and battlements,
To towers and windows, yea, to chimney-tops,
Your infants in your arms, and there have sat
The live-long day, with patient expectation,
To see great Pompey pass the streets of Rome:
And when you saw his chariot but appear,
Have you not made an universal shout,
That Tiber trembled underneath her banks,
To hear the replication of your sounds
Made in her concave shores?
And do you now put on your best attire?
And do you now cull out a holiday?
And do you now strew flowers in his way
That comes in triumph over Pompey's blood?
Be gone!
Run to your houses, fall upon your knees,
Pray to the gods to intermit the plague
That needs must light on this ingratitude.

Flav. Go, go, good countrymen, and, for this fault,
Assemble all the poor men of your sort;
Draw them to Tiber banks, and weep your tears
Into the channel, till the lowest stream
Do kiss the most exalted shores of all.
[*Exeunt all the Commoners.*
See whether their basest metal be not moved;
They vanish tongue-tied in their guiltiness.
Go you down that way towards the Capitol;
This way will I: disrobe the images,
If you do find them deck'd with ceremonies.

Mar. May we do so?
You know it is the feast of Lupercal.

Flav. It is no matter; let no images
Be hung with Cæsar's trophies. I'll about,
And drive away the vulgar from the streets:
So do you too, where you perceive them thick.
These growing feathers pluck'd from Cæsar's wing
Will make him fly an ordinary pitch,
Who else would soar above the view of men
And keep us all in servile fearfulness.
[*Exeunt.*

Scene II. *A public place.*

Flourish. Enter Cæsar; Antony, *for the course;* Calpurnia, Portia, Decius, Cicero, Brutus, Cassius, *and* Casca; *a great crowd following, among them a* Soothsayer.

Cæs. Calpurnia!

Casca. Peace, ho! Cæsar speaks.

Cæs. Calpurnia!

Cal. Here, my lord.

Cæs. Stand you directly in Antonius' way,
When he doth run his course. Antonius!

Ant. Cæsar, my lord?

Cæs. Forget not, in your speed, Antonius,
To touch Calpurnia; for our elders say,
The barren, touched in this holy chase,
Shake off their sterile curse.

Ant. I shall remember:
When Cæsar says 'do this,' it is perform'd.

Cæs. Set on; and leave no ceremony out.
[*Flourish.*

Sooth. Cæsar!

Cæs. Ha! who calls?

Casca. Bid every noise be still: peace yet again!

Cæs. Who is it in the press that calls on me?
I hear a tongue, shriller than all the music,
Cry 'Cæsar!' Speak; Cæsar is turn'd to hear.

Sooth. Beware the ides of March.

Cæs. What man is that?

Bru. A soothsayer bids you beware the ides of March.

Cæs. Set him before me; let me see his face.

Cas. Fellow, come from the throng; look upon Cæsar.

Cæs. What say'st thou to me now? speak once again.

Sooth. Beware the ides of March.

Cæs. He is a dreamer; let us leave him: pass. [*Sennet. Exeunt all except Brutus and Cassius.*

Cas. Will you go see the order of the course?

Bru. Not I.

Cas. I pray you, do.

Bru. I am not gamesome: I do lack some part
Of that quick spirit that is in Antony.
Let me not hinder, Cassius, your desires;
I'll leave you.

Cas. Brutus, I do observe you now of late:
I have not from your eyes that gentleness
And show of love as I was wont to have:
You bear too stubborn and too strange a hand
Over your friend that loves you.

Bru. Cassius,
Be not deceived: if I have veil'd my look,
I turn the trouble of my countenance
Merely upon myself. Vexed I am
Of late with passions of some difference,
Conceptions only proper to myself,
Which give some soil perhaps to my behaviors;
But let not therefore my good friends be grieved—
Among which number, Cassius, be you one—
Nor construe any further my neglect,
Than that poor Brutus, with himself at war,
Forgets the shows of love to other men.

Cas. Then, Brutus, I have much mistook your passion;
By means whereof this breast of mine hath buried
Thoughts of great value, worthy cogitations.
Tell me, good Brutus, can you see your face?

Bru. No, Cassius; for the eye sees not itself,
But by reflection, by some other things.

Cas. 'Tis just:
And it is very much lamented, Brutus,
That you have no such mirrors as will turn
Your hidden worthiness into your eye,
That you might see your shadow. I have heard,
Where many of the best respect in Rome,
Except immortal Cæsar, speaking of Brutus
And groaning underneath this age's yoke,
Have wish'd that noble Brutus had his eyes.

Bru. Into what dangers would you lead me, Cassius,
That you would have me seek into myself
For that which is not in me?

Cas. Therefore, good Brutus, be prepared to hear:
And since you know you cannot see yourself
So well as by reflection, I, your glass,
Will modestly discover to yourself
That of yourself which you yet know not of.
And be not jealous on me, gentle Brutus:
Were I a common laugher, or did use
To stale with ordinary oaths my love
To every new protester; if you know
That I do fawn on men and hug them hard
And after scandal them, or if you know
That I profess myself in banqueting
To all the rout, then hold me dangerous. [*Flourish, and shout.*

Bru. What means this shouting? I do fear, the people
Choose Cæsar for their king.

Cas. Ay, do you fear it?
Then must I think you would not have it so.

Bru. I would not, Cassius; yet I love him well.
But wherefore do you hold me here so long?
What is it that you would impart to me?
If it be aught toward the general good,
Set honor in one eye and death i' the other,
And I will look on both indifferently,
For let the gods so speed me as I love
The name of honor more than I fear death.

Cas. I know that virtue to be in you, Brutus,
As well as I do know your outward favor.
Well, honor is the subject of my story.
I cannot tell what you and other men
Think of this life; but, for my single self,
I had as lief not be as live to be
In awe of such a thing as I myself.
I was born free as Cæsar; so were you:
We both have fed as well, and we can both
Endure the winter's cold as well as he:
For once, upon a raw and gusty day,
The troubled Tiber chafing with her shores,
Cæsar said to me 'Darest thou, Cassius, now
Leap in with me into this angry flood,
And swim to yonder point?' Upon the word,
Accoutred as I was, I plunged in
And bade him follow; so indeed he did.
The torrent roar'd, and we did buffet it
With lusty sinews, throwing it aside
And stemming it with hearts of controversy;
But ere we could arrive the point proposed,
Cæsar cried 'Help me, Cassius, or I sink!'
I, as Æneas, our great ancestor,
Did from the flames of Troy upon his shoulder
The old Anchises bear, so from the waves of Tiber
Did I the tired Cæsar. And this man
Is now become a god, and Cassius is
A wretched creature and must bend his body,
If Cæsar carelessly but nod on him.
He had a fever when he was in Spain,
And when the fit was on him, I did mark
How he did shake: 'tis true, this god did shake;
His coward lips did from their color fly,
And that same eye whose bend doth awe the world
Did lose his lustre: I did hear him groan:
Ay, and that tongue of his that bade the Romans
Mark him and write his speeches in their books,
Alas, it cried 'Give me some drink, Titinius,'
As a sick girl. Ye gods, it doth amaze me
A man of such a feeble temper should
So get the start of the majestic world
And bear the palm alone. [*Shout. Flourish.*

Bru. Another general shout!
I do believe that these applauses are
For some new honors that are heap'd on Cæsar.

Cas. Why, man, he doth bestride the narrow world
Like a Colossus, and we petty men
Walk under his huge legs and peep about
To find ourselves dishonorable graves.
Men at some time are masters of their fates:
The fault, dear Brutus, is not in our stars,
But in ourselves, that we are underlings.
Brutus and Cæsar: what should be in that 'Cæsar'?
Why should that name be sounded more than yours?

Write them together, yours is as fair a name;
Sound them, it doth become the mouth as well;
Weigh them, it is as heavy; conjure with 'em,
Brutus will start a spirit as soon as Cæsar.
Now, in the names of all the gods at once,
Upon what meat doth this our Cæsar feed,
That he is grown so great? Age, thou art shamed!
Rome, thou hast lost the breed of noble bloods!
When went there by an age, since the great flood,
But it was famed with more than with one man?
When could they say till now, that talk'd of Rome,
That her wide walls encompass'd but one man?
Now is it Rome indeed and room enough,
When there is in it but one only man.
O, you and I have heard our fathers say,
There was a Brutus once that would have brook'd
The eternal devil to keep his state in Rome
As easily as a king.

Bru. That you do love me, I am nothing jealous;
What you would work me to, I have some aim:
How I have thought of this and of these times,
I shall recount hereafter; for this present,
I would not, so with love I might entreat you,
Be any further moved. What you have said
I will consider; what you have to say
I will with patience hear, and find a time
Both meet to hear and answer such high things.
Till then, my noble friend, chew upon this:
Brutus had rather be a villager
Than to repute himself a son of Rome
Under these hard conditions as this time
Is like to lay upon us.

Cas. I am glad that my weak words
Have struck but thus much show of fire from Brutus.

Bru. The games are done and Cæsar is returning.

Cas. As they pass by, pluck Casca by the sleeve;
And he will, after his sour fashion, tell you
What hath proceeded worthy note to-day.

Re-enter CÆSAR *and his Train.*

Bru. I will do so. But, look you, Cassius,
The angry spot doth glow on Cæsar's brow,
And all the rest look like a chidden train:
Calpurnia's cheek is pale; and Cicero
Looks with such ferret and such fiery eyes
As we have seen him in the Capitol,
Being cross'd in conference by some senators.

Cas. Casca will tell us what the matter is.

Cæs. Antonius!

Ant. Cæsar?

Cæs. Let me have men about me that are fat;
Sleek-headed men and such as sleep o' nights:
Yond Cassius has a lean and hungry look;
He thinks too much: such men are dangerous.

Ant. Fear him not, Cæsar; he's not dangerous;
He is a noble Roman and well given.

Cæs. Would he were fatter! But I fear him not:
Yet if my name were liable to fear,
I do not know the man I should avoid
So soon as that spare Cassius. He reads much;
He is a great observer and he looks
Quite through the deeds of men: he loves no plays,
As thou dost, Antony; he hears no music;
Seldom he smiles, and smiles in such a sort
As if he mock'd himself and scorn'd his spirit
That could be moved to smile at any thing
Such men as he be never at heart's ease
Whiles they behold a greater than themselves,
And therefore are they very dangerous.
I rather tell thee what is to be fear'd
Than what I fear; for always I am Cæsar.
Come on my right hand, for this ear is deaf,
And tell me truly what thou think'st of him.

[*Sennet. Exeunt Cæsar and all his Train, but Casca.*

Casca. You pull'd me by the cloak; would you speak with me?

Bru. Ay, Casca; tell us what hath chanced to-day,
That Cæsar looks so sad.

Casca. Why, you were with him, were you not?

Bru. I should not then ask Casca what had chanced.

Casca. Why, there was a crown offered him: and being offered him, he put it by with the back of his hand, thus; and then the people fell a-shouting.

Bru. What was the second noise for?

Casca. Why, for that too.

Cas. They shouted thrice: what was the last cry for?

Casca. Why, for that too.

Bru. Was the crown offered him thrice?

Casca. Ay, marry, was't, and he put it by thrice, every time gentler than other, and at every putting-by mine honest neighbors shouted.

Cas. Who offered him the crown?

Casca. Why, Antony.

Bru. Tell us the manner of it, gentle Casca.

Casca. I can as well be hanged as tell the manner of it: it was mere foolery; I did not mark it. I saw Mark Antony offer him a crown;—yet 'twas not a crown neither, 'twas one of these coronets;—and, as I told you, he put it by once: but, for all that, to my thinking, he would fain have had it. Then he offered it to him again; then he put it by again: but, to my thinking, he was very loath to lay his fingers off it. And then he offered it the third time; he put it the third time by: and still as he refused it, the rabblement hooted and clapped their chapped hands and threw up their sweaty night-caps and uttered such a deal of stinking breath because Cæsar refused the crown that it had almost choked Cæsar; for he swounded and fell down at it: and for mine own part, I durst not laugh, for fear of opening my lips and receiving the bad air.

Cas. But, soft, I pray you: what, did Cæsar swound?

Casca. He fell down in the market-place, and foamed at mouth, and was speechless.

Bru. 'Tis very like: he hath the falling sickness.

Cas. No, Cæsar hath it not; but you and I,
And honest Casca, we have the falling sickness.

Casca. I know not what you mean by that; but, I am sure, Cæsar fell down. If the tag-rag people did not clap him and hiss him, according as he pleased and displeased them, as they use to do the players in the theatre, I am no true man.

Bru. What said he when he came unto himself?

Casca. Marry, before he fell down, when he perceived the common herd was glad he refused the crown, he plucked me ope his doublet and offered them his throat to cut. An I had been a man of any occupation, if I would not have taken him at a word, I would I might go to hell among the rogues. And so he fell. When he came to himself again, he said, If he had done or said any thing amiss, he desired their worships to think it was his infirmity. Three or four wenches, where I stood, cried 'Alas, good soul!' and forgave him with all their hearts: but there's no heed to be taken of them; if Cæsar had stabbed their mothers, they would have done no less.

Bru. And after that, he came, thus sad, away?

Casca. Ay.

Cas. Did Cicero say any thing?

Casca. Ay, he spoke Greek.

Cas. To what effect?

Casca. Nay, an I tell you that, I'll ne'er look you i' the face again: but those that understood him smiled at one another and shook their heads; but, for mine own part, it was Greek to me. I could tell you more news too: Marullus and Flavius, for pulling scarfs off Cæsar's images, are put to silence. Fare you well. There was more foolery yet, if I could remember it.

Cas. Will you sup with me to-night, Casca?

Casca. No, I am promised forth.

Cas. Will you dine with me to-morrow?

Casca. Ay, if I be alive and your mind hold and your dinner worth the eating.

Cas. Good: I will expect you.

Casca. Do so. Farewell, both. [*Exit.*

Bru. What a blunt fellow is this grown to be!
He was quick mettle when he went to school.

Cas. So is he now in execution
Of any bold or noble enterprise,
However he puts on this tardy form.
This rudeness is a sauce to his good wit,
Which gives men stomach to digest his words
With better appetite.

Bru. And so it is. For this time I will leave you:
To-morrow, if you please to speak with me,
I will come home to you; or, if you will,
Come home to me, and I will wait for you.

Cas. I will do so: till then, think of the world. [*Exit Brutus.*
Well, Brutus, thou art noble; yet, I see,
Thy honorable metal may be wrought
From that it is disposed: therefore it is meet
That noble minds keep ever with their likes;
For who so firm that cannot be seduced?
Cæsar doth bear me hard; but he loves Brutus:
If I were Brutus now and he were Cassius,
He should not humor me. I will this night,
In several hands, in at his windows throw,
As if they came from several citizens,
Writings all tending to the great opinion
That Rome holds of his name; wherein obscurely
Cæsar's ambition shall be glanced at:
And after this let Cæsar seat him sure;
For we will shake him, or worse days endure. [*Exit.*

SCENE III. *The same. A street.*

Thunder and lightning. Enter from opposite sides, CASCA, *with his sword drawn, and* CICERO.

Cic. Good even, Casca: brought you Cæsar home?
Why are you breathless? and why stare you so?

Casca. Are not you moved, when all the sway of earth
Shakes like a thing unfirm? O Cicero,
I have seen tempests, when the scolding winds
Have rived the knotty oaks, and I have seen
The ambitious ocean swell and rage and foam,
To be exalted with the threatening clouds:
But never till to-night, never till now,
Did I go through a tempest dropping fire.
Either there is a civil strife in heaven,
Or else the world, too saucy with the gods,
Incenses them to send destruction.

Cic. Why, saw you any thing more wonderful?

Casca. A common slave—you know him well by sight—
Held up his left hand, which did flame and burn
Like twenty torches join'd, and yet his hand,
Not sensible of fire, remain'd unscorch'd.
Besides—I ha' not since put up my sword—
Against the Capitol I met a lion,
Who glared upon me, and went surly by,
Without annoying me: and there were drawn
Upon a heap a hundred ghastly women,
Transformed with their fear; who swore they saw
Men all in fire walk up and down the streets.
And yesterday the bird of night did sit
Even at noon-day upon the market-place,
Hooting and shrieking. When these prodigies
Do so conjointly meet, let not men say
'These are their reasons; they are natural;'
For, I believe, they are portentous things
Unto the climate that they point upon.

Cic. Indeed, it is a strange-disposed time:
But men may construe things after their fashion,
Clean from the purpose of the things themselves.
Come Cæsar to the Capitol to-morrow?

Casca. He doth; for he did bid Antonius
Send word to you he would be there to-morrow.

Cic. Good night then, Casca: this disturbed sky
Is not to walk in.

Casca. Farewell, Cicero. [*Exit Cicero.*

Enter CASSIUS.

Cas. Who's there?
Casca. A Roman.
Cas. Casca, by your voice.
Casca. Your ear is good. Cassius, what night is this!
Cas. A very pleasing night to honest men.
Casca. Who ever knew the heavens menace so?
Cas. Those that have known the earth so full of faults.
For my part, I have walk'd about the streets,
Submitting me unto the perilous night,
And, thus unbraced, Casca, as you see,
Have bared my bosom to the thunder-stone;
And when the cross blue lightning seem'd to open
The breast of heaven, I did present myself
Even in the aim and very flash of it.
Casca. But wherefore did you so much tempt the heavens?
It is the part of men to fear and tremble,
When the most mighty gods by tokens send
Such dreadful heralds to astonish us.
Cas. You are dull, Casca, and those sparks of life
That should be in a Roman you do want,
Or else you use not. You look pale and gaze
And put on fear and cast yourself in wonder,
To see the strange impatience of the heavens:
But if you would consider the true cause
Why all these fires, why all these gliding ghosts,
Why birds and beasts from quality and kind,
Why old men fool and children calculate,
Why all these things change from their ordinance
Their natures and preformed faculties
To monstrous quality,—why, you shall find
That heaven hath infused them with these spirits,
To make them instruments of fear and warning
Unto some monstrous state.
Now could I, Casca, name to thee a man
Most like this dreadful night,
That thunders, lightens, opens graves, and roars
As doth the lion in the Capitol,
A man no mightier than thyself or me
In personal action, yet prodigious grown
And fearful, as these strange eruptions are.
Casca. 'Tis Cæsar that you mean; is it not, Cassius?
Cas. Let it be who it is: for Romans now
Have thews and limbs like to their ancestors;
But, woe the while! our fathers' minds are dead,
And we are govern'd with our mothers' spirits;
Our yoke and sufferance show us womanish.
Casca. Indeed, they say the senators to-morrow
Mean to establish Cæsar as a king;
And he shall wear his crown by sea and land,
In every place, save here in Italy.
Cas. I know where I will wear this dagger then;
Cassius from bondage will deliver Cassius:
Therein, ye gods, you make the weak most strong;
Therein, ye gods, you tyrants do defeat:
Nor stony tower, nor walls of beaten brass,
Nor airless dungeon, nor strong links of iron,
Can be retentive to the strength of spirit;
But life, being weary of these worldly bars,
Never lacks power to dismiss itself.
If I know this, know all the world besides,
That part of tyranny that I do bear
I can shake off at pleasure. [*Thunder still.*
Casca. So can I:
So every bondman in his own hand bears
The power to cancel his captivity.
Cas. And why should Cæsar be a tyrant then?
Poor man! I know he would not be a wolf,
But that he sees the Romans are but sheep:
He were no lion, were not Romans hinds.
Those that with haste will make a mighty fire
Begin it with weak straws: what trash is Rome,
What rubbish and what offal, when it serves
For the base matter to illuminate
So vile a thing as Cæsar! But, O grief,
Where hast thou led me? I perhaps speak this
Before a willing bondman; then I know
My answer must be made. But I am arm'd,
And dangers are to me indifferent.
Casca. You speak to Casca, and to such a man
That is no fleering tell-tale. Hold, my hand:
Be factious for redress of all these griefs,
And I will set this foot of mine as far
As who goes farthest.
Cas. There's a bargain made.
Now know you, Casca, I have moved already
Some certain of the noblest-minded Romans
To undergo with me an enterprise
Of honorable-dangerous consequence;
And I do know, by this, they stay for me
In Pompey's porch: for now, this fearful night,
There is no stir or walking in the streets;
And the complexion of the element
In favor's like the work we have in hand,
Most bloody, fiery, and most terrible.
Casca. Stand close awhile, for here comes one in haste.
Cas. 'Tis Cinna; I do know him by his gait;
He is a friend.

Enter CINNA.

Cinna, where haste you so?
Cin. To find out you. Who's that? Metellus Cimber?
Cas. No, it is Casca; one incorporate
To our attempts. Am I not stay'd for, Cinna?
Cin. I am glad on 't. What a fearful night is this!
There's two or three of us have seen strange sights.
Cas. Am I not stay'd for? tell me.
Cin. Yes, you are.
O Cassius, if you could
But win the noble Brutus to our party—
Cas. Be you content: good Cinna, take this paper,
And look you lay it in the prætor's chair,
Where Brutus may but find it; and throw this
In at his window; set this up with wax
Upon old Brutus' statue: all this done,

Repair to Pompey's porch, where you shall find us.
Is Decius Brutus and Trebonius there?

Cin. All but Metellus Cimber; and he's gone
To seek you at your house. Well, I will hie,
And so bestow these papers as you bade me.

Cas. That done, repair to Pompey's theatre. [*Exit Cinna.*
Come, Casca, you and I will yet ere day
See Brutus at his house: three parts of him
Is ours already, and the man entire
Upon the next encounter yields him ours.

Casca. O, he sits high in all the people's hearts:
And that which would appear offence in us,
His countenance, like richest alchemy,
Will change to virtue and to worthiness.

Cas. Him and his worth and our great need of him
You have right well conceited. Let us go,
For it is after midnight; and ere day
We will awake him and be sure of him. [*Exeunt.*

ACT II.

SCENE I. *Rome. Brutus's orchard.*

Enter BRUTUS.

Bru. What, Lucius, ho!
I cannot, by the progress of the stars,
Give guess how near to day. Lucius, I say!
I would it were my fault to sleep so soundly.
When, Lucius, when? awake, I say! what, Lucius!

Enter LUCIUS.

Luc. Call'd you, my lord?

Bru. Get me a taper in my study, Lucius:
When it is lighted, come and call me here.

Luc. I will, my lord. [*Exit.*

Bru. It must be by his death: and for my part,
I know no personal cause to spurn at him,
But for the general. He would be crown'd:
How that might change his nature, there's the question.
It is the bright day that brings forth the adder;
And that craves wary walking. Crown him?—that;—
And then, I grant, we put a sting in him,
That at his will he may do danger with.
The abuse of greatness is, when it disjoins
Remorse from power: and, to speak truth of Cæsar,
I have not known when his affections sway'd
More than his reason. But 'tis a common proof,
That lowliness is young ambition's ladder,
Whereto the climber-upward turns his face;
But when he once attains the upmost round,
He then unto the ladder turns his back,
Looks in the clouds, scorning the base degrees
By which he did ascend. So Cæsar may.
Then, lest he may, prevent. And, since the quarrel
Will bear no color for the thing he is,
Fashion it thus; that what he is, augmented,
Would run to these and these extremities:
And therefore think him as a serpent's egg
Which, hatch'd, would, as his kind, grow mischievous,
And kill him in the shell.

Re-enter LUCIUS.

Luc. The taper burneth in your closet, sir.
Searching the window for a flint, I found
This paper, thus seal'd up; and, I am sure,
It did not lie there when I went to bed. [*Gives him the letter.*

Bru. Get you to bed again; it is not day.
Is not to-morrow, boy, the ides of March?

Luc. I know not, sir.

Bru. Look in the calendar, and bring me word.

Luc. I will, sir. [*Exit.*

Bru. The exhalations whizzing in the air
Give so much light that I may read by them. [*Opens the letter and reads.*
'Brutus, thou sleep'st: awake, and see thyself.
Shall Rome, &c. Speak, strike, redress!
Brutus, thou sleep'st: awake!'
Such instigations have been often dropp'd
Where I have took them up.
'Shall Rome, &c.' Thus must I piece it out:
Shall Rome stand under one man's awe? What, Rome?
My ancestors did from the streets of Rome
The Tarquin drive, when he was call'd a king.
'Speak, strike, redress!' Am I entreated
To speak and strike? O Rome, I make thee promise:
If the redress will follow, thou receivest
Thy full petition at the hand of Brutus!

Re-enter LUCIUS.

Luc. Sir, March is wasted fourteen days. [*Knocking within.*

Bru. 'Tis good. Go to the gate; somebody knocks. [*Exit Lucius.*
Since Cassius first did whet me against Cæsar,
I have not slept.
Between the acting of a dreadful thing
And the first motion, all the interim is
Like a phantasma, or a hideous dream:
The Genius and the mortal instruments
Are then in council; and the state of man,
Like to a little kingdom, suffers then
The nature of an insurrection.

Re-enter LUCIUS.

Luc. Sir, 'tis your brother Cassius at the door,
Who doth desire to see you.

Bru. Is he alone?

Luc. No, sir, there are moe with him.

Bru. Do you know them?

Luc. No, sir; their hats are pluck'd about their ears,
And half their faces buried in their cloaks,
That by no means I may discover them
By any mark of favor.

Bru. Let 'em enter. [*Exit Lucius.*
They are the faction. O conspiracy,
Shamest thou to show thy dangerous brow by night,
When evils are most free? O, then by day
Where wilt thou find a cavern dark enough
To mask thy monstrous visage? Seek none, conspiracy;
Hide it in smiles and affability:
For if thou path, thy native semblance on,

Not Erebus itself were dim enough
To hide thee from prevention.

Enter the conspirators, Cassius, Casca, Decius, Cinna, Metellus Cimber, *and* Trebonius.

Cas. I think we are too bold upon your rest:
Good morrow, Brutus; do we trouble you?
Bru. I have been up this hour, awake all night.
Know I these men that come along with you?
Cas. Yes, every man of them, and no man here
But honors you; and every one doth wish
You had but that opinion of yourself
Which every noble Roman bears of you.
This is Trebonius.
Bru. He is welcome hither.
Cas. This, Decius Brutus.
Bru. He is welcome too.
Cas. This, Casca; this, Cinna; and this, Metellus Cimber.
Bru. They are all welcome.
What watchful cares do interpose themselves
Betwixt your eyes and night?
Cas. Shall I entreat a word?
[*Brutus and Cassius whisper.*
Dec. Here lies the east: doth not the day break here?
Casca. No.
Cin. O, pardon, sir, it doth; and yon gray lines
That fret the clouds are messengers of day.
Casca. You shall confess that you are both deceived.
Here, as I point my sword, the sun arises,
Which is a great way growing on the south,
Weighing the youthful season of the year.
Some two months hence up higher toward the north
He first presents his fire; and the high east
Stands, as the Capitol, directly here.
Bru. Give me your hands all over, one by one.
Cas. And let us swear our resolution.
Bru. No, not an oath: if not the face of men,
The sufferance of our souls, the time's abuse,—
If these be motives weak, break off betimes,
And every man hence to his idle bed;
So let high-sighted tyranny range on,
Till each man drop by lottery. But if these,
As I am sure they do, bear fire enough
To kindle cowards and to steel with valor
The melting spirits of women, then, countrymen,
What need we any spur but our own cause,
To prick us to redress? what other bond
Than secret Romans, that have spoke the word,
And will not palter? and what other oath
Than honesty to honesty engaged,
That this shall be, or we will fall for it?
Swear priests and cowards and men cautelous,
Old feeble carrions and such suffering souls
That welcome wrongs; unto bad causes swear
Such creatures as men doubt; but do not stain
The even virtue of our enterprise,
Nor the insuppressive mettle of our spirits,
To think that or our cause or our performance
Did need an oath; when every drop of blood
That every Roman bears, and nobly bears,
Is guilty of a several bastardy,
If he do break the smallest particle
Of any promise that hath pass'd from him.
Cas. But what of Cicero? shall we sound him?
I think he will stand very strong with us.
Casca. Let us not leave him out.
Cin. No, by no means.
Met. O, let us have him, for his silver hairs
Will purchase us a good opinion
And buy men's voices to commend our deeds:
It shall be said, his judgment ruled our hands;
Our youths and wildness shall no whit appear,
But all be buried in his gravity.
Bru. O, name him not: let us not break with him;
For he will never follow any thing
That other men begin.
Cas. Then leave him out.
Casca. Indeed he is not fit.
Dec. Shall no man else be touch'd but only Cæsar?
Cas. Decius, well urged: I think it is not meet,
Mark Antony, so well beloved of Cæsar,
Should outlive Cæsar: we shall find of him
A shrewd contriver; and, you know, his means,
If he improve them, may well stretch so far
As to annoy us all: which to prevent,
Let Antony and Cæsar fall together.
Bru. Our course will seem too bloody, Caius Cassius,
To cut the head off and then hack the limbs,
Like wrath in death and envy afterwards;
For Antony is but a limb of Cæsar:
Let us be sacrificers, but not butchers, Caius.
We all stand up against the spirit of Cæsar;
And in the spirit of men there is no blood:
O, that we then could come by Cæsar's spirit,
And not dismember Cæsar! But, alas,
Cæsar must bleed for it! And, gentle friends,
Let's kill him boldly, but not wrathfully;
Let's carve him as a dish fit for the gods,
Not hew him as a carcass fit for hounds:
And let our hearts, as subtle masters do,
Stir up their servants to an act of rage,
And after seem to chide 'em. This shall make
Our purpose necessary and not envious:
Which so appearing to the common eyes,
We shall be call'd purgers, not murderers.
And for Mark Antony, think not of him;
For he can do no more than Cæsar's arm
When Cæsar's head is off.
Cas. Yet I fear him;
For in the ingrafted love he bears to Cæsar—
Bru. Alas, good Cassius, do not think of him:
If he love Cæsar, all that he can do
Is to himself, take thought and die for Cæsar:
And that were much he should; for he is given
To sports, to wildness and much company.
Treb. There is no fear in him; let him not die;
For he will live, and laugh at this hereafter.
[*Clock strikes.*
Bru. Peace! count the clock.
Cas. The clock hath stricken three.
Treb. 'Tis time to part.

Cas. But it is doubtful yet,
Whether Cæsar will come forth to-day, or no;
For he is superstitious grown of late,
Quite from the main opinion he held once
Of fantasy, of dreams and ceremonies:
It may be, these apparent prodigies,
The unaccustom'd terror of this night,
And the persuasion of his augurers,
May hold him from the Capitol to-day.

Dec. Never fear that: if he be so resolved,
I can o'ersway him; for he loves to hear
That unicorns may be betray'd with trees,
And bears with glasses, elephants with holes,
Lions with toils and men with flatterers;
But when I tell him he hates flatterers,
He says he does, being then most flattered.
Let me work;
For I can give his humor the true bent,
And I will bring him to the Capitol.

Cas. Nay, we will all of us be there to fetch him.

Bru. By the eighth hour: is that the uttermost?

Cin. Be that the uttermost, and fail not then.

Met. Caius Ligarius doth bear Cæsar hard,
Who rated him for speaking well of Pompey:
I wonder none of you have thought of him.

Bru. Now, good Metellus, go along by him:
He loves me well, and I have given him reasons;
Send him but hither, and I'll fashion him.

Cas. The morning comes upon 's: we'll leave you, Brutus.
And, friends, disperse yourselves; but all remember
What you have said, and show yourselves true Romans.

Bru. Good gentlemen, look fresh and merrily;
Let not our looks put on our purposes,
But bear it as our Roman actors do,
With untired spirits and formal constancy:
And so good morrow to you every one.

[*Exeunt all but Brutus.*

Boy! Lucius! Fast asleep? It is no matter;
Enjoy the honey-heavy dew of slumber:
Thou hast no figures nor no fantasies,
Which busy care draws in the brains of men;
Therefore thou sleep'st so sound.

Enter PORTIA.

Por. Brutus, my lord!

Bru. Portia, what mean you? wherefore rise you now?
It is not for your health thus to commit
Your weak condition to the raw cold morning.

Por. Nor for yours neither. You've ungently, Brutus,
Stole from my bed: and yesternight, at supper,
You suddenly arose, and walk'd about,
Musing and sighing, with your arms across,
And when I ask'd you what the matter was,
You stared upon me with ungentle looks;
I urged you further; then you scratch'd your head,
And too impatiently stamp'd with your foot;
Yet I insisted, yet you answer'd not,
But, with an angry wafture of your hand,
Gave sign for me to leave you: so I did;
Fearing to strengthen that impatience
Which seem'd too much enkindled, and withal
Hoping it was but an effect of humor,
Which sometime hath his hour with every man.
It will not let you eat, nor talk, nor sleep,
And could it work so much upon your shape
As it hath much prevail'd on your condition
I should not know you, Brutus. Dear my lord
Make me acquainted with your cause of grief

Bru. I am not well in health, and that is all.

Por. Brutus is wise, and, were he not in health,
He would embrace the means to come by it

Bru. Why, so I do. Good Portia, go to bed.

Por. Is Brutus sick? and is it physical
To walk unbraced and suck up the humors
Of the dank morning? What, is Brutus sick
And will he steal out of his wholesome bed,
To dare the vile contagion of the night
And tempt the rheumy and unpurged air
To add unto his sickness? No, my Brutus;
You have some sick offence within your mind
Which, by the right and virtue of my place,
I ought to know of: and, upon my knees,
I charm you, by my once-commended beauty
By all your vows of love and that great vow
Which did incorporate and make us one,
That you unfold to me, yourself, your half,
Why you are heavy, and what men to-night
Have had resort to you: for here have been
Some six or seven, who did hide their faces
Even from darkness.

Bru. Kneel not, gentle Portia

Por. I should not need, if you were gentle Brutus.
Within the bond of marriage, tell me, Brutus
Is it excepted I should know no secrets
That appertain to you? Am I yourself
But, as it were, in sort or limitation,
To keep with you at meals, comfort your bed
And talk to you sometimes? Dwell I but in the suburbs
Of your good pleasure? If it be no more,
Portia is Brutus' harlot, not his wife.

Bru. You are my true and honorable wife
As dear to me as are the ruddy drops
That visit my sad heart.

Por. If this were true, then should I know this secret.
I grant I am a woman; but withal
A woman that Lord Brutus took to wife:
I grant I am a woman; but withal
A woman well-reputed, Cato's daughter.
Think you I am no stronger than my sex,
Being so father'd and so husbanded?
Tell me your counsels, I will not disclose 'em
I have made strong proof of my constancy,
Giving myself a voluntary wound
Here, in the thigh: can I bear that with patience,
And not my husband's secrets?

Bru. O ye gods,
Render me worthy of this noble wife!

[*Knocking within*

Hark, hark! one knocks: Portia, go in awhile;
And by and by thy bosom shall partake
The secrets of my heart.
All my engagements I will construe to thee,

All the charactery of my sad brows:
Leave me with haste. [*Exit Portia.*] Lucius, who's that knocks?

Re-enter LUCIUS *with* LIGARIUS.

Luc. He is a sick man that would speak with you.
Bru. Caius Ligarius, that Metellus spake of.
Boy, stand aside. Caius Ligarius! how?
Lig. Vouchsafe good morrow from a feeble tongue.
Bru. O, what a time have you chose out, brave Caius,
To wear a kerchief! Would you were not sick!
Lig. I am not sick, if Brutus have in hand
Any exploit worthy the name of honor.
Bru. Such an exploit have I in hand, Ligarius,
Had you a healthful ear to hear of it.
Lig. By all the gods that Romans bow before,
I here discard my sickness! Soul of Rome!
Brave son, derived from honorable loins!
Thou, like an exorcist, hast conjured up
My mortified spirit. Now bid me run,
And I will strive with things impossible;
Yea, get the better of them. What's to do?
Bru. A piece of work that will make sick men whole.
Lig. But are not some whole that we must make sick?
Bru. That must we also. What it is, my Caius,
I shall unfold to thee, as we are going
To whom it must be done.
Lig. Set on your foot,
And with a heart new-fired I follow you,
To do I know not what: but it sufficeth
That Brutus leads me on.
Bru. Follow me, then. [*Exeunt.*

SCENE II. *Cæsar's house.*

Thunder and lightning. Enter CÆSAR, *in his night-gown.*

Cæs. Nor heaven nor earth have been at peace to-night:
Thrice hath Calpurnia in her sleep cried out,
'Help, ho! they murder Cæsar!' Who's within?

Enter a Servant.

Serv. My lord?
Cæs. Go bid the priests do present sacrifice
And bring me their opinions of success.
Serv. I will, my lord. [*Exit.*

Enter CALPURNIA.

Cal. What mean you, Cæsar? think you to walk forth?
You shall not stir out of your house to-day.
Cæs. Cæsar shall forth: the things that threaten'd me
Ne'er look'd but on my back; when they shall see
The face of Cæsar, they are vanished.
Cal. Cæsar, I never stood on ceremonies,
Yet now they fright me. There is one within,
Besides the things that we have heard and seen,
Recounts most horrid sights seen by the watch.
A lioness hath whelped in the streets;
And graves have yawn'd, and yielded up their dead;
Fierce fiery warriors fought upon the clouds,
In ranks and squadrons and right form of war,
Which drizzled blood upon the Capitol;
The noise of battle hurtled in the air,
Horses did neigh, and dying men did groan,
And ghosts did shriek and squeal about the streets.
O Cæsar! these things are beyond all use,
And I do fear them.
Cæs. What can be avoided
Whose end is purposed by the mighty gods?
Yet Cæsar shall go forth; for these predictions
Are to the world in general as to Cæsar.
Cal. When beggars die, there are no comets seen;
The heavens themselves blaze forth the death of princes.
Cæs. Cowards die many times before their deaths;
The valiant never taste of death but once.
Of all the wonders that I yet have heard,
It seems to me most strange that men should fear;
Seeing that death, a necessary end,
Will come when it will come.

Re-enter Servant.

What say the augurers?
Serv. They would not have you to stir forth to-day.
Plucking the entrails of an offering forth,
They could not find a heart within the beast.
Cæs. The gods do this in shame of cowardice:
Cæsar should be a beast without a heart,
If he should stay at home to-day for fear.
No, Cæsar shall not: danger knows full well
That Cæsar is more dangerous than he:
We are two lions litter'd in one day,
And I the elder and more terrible:
And Cæsar shall go forth.
Cal. Alas, my lord,
Your wisdom is consumed in confidence.
Do not go forth to-day: call it my fear
That keeps you in the house, and not your own.
We'll send Mark Antony to the senate-house:
And he shall say you are not well to-day:
Let me, upon my knee, prevail in this.
Cæs. Mark Antony shall say I am not well,
And, for thy humor, I will stay at home.

Enter DECIUS.

Here's Decius Brutus, he shall tell them so.
Dec. Cæsar, all hail! good morrow, worthy Cæsar:
I come to fetch you to the senate-house.
Cæs. And you are come in very happy time,
To bear my greeting to the senators
And tell them that I will not come to-day:
Cannot, is false, and that I dare not, falser:
I will not come to-day: tell them so, Decius.
Cal. Say he is sick.
Cæs. Shall Cæsar send a lie?
Have I in conquest stretch'd mine arm so far,
To be afraid to tell graybeards the truth?

Decius, go tell them Cæsar will not come.
Dec. Most mighty Cæsar, let me know some cause,
Lest I be laugh'd at when I tell them so.
Cæs. The cause is in my will : I will not come ;
That is enough to satisfy the senate.
But for your private satisfaction,
Because I love you, I will let you know :
Calpurnia here, my wife, stays me at home :
She dreamt to-night she saw my statua,
Which, like a fountain with an hundred spouts,
Did run pure blood : and many lusty Romans
Came smiling, and did bathe their hands in it :
And these does she apply for warnings, and portents,
And evils imminent ; and on her knee
Hath begg'd that I will stay at home to-day.
Dec. This dream is all amiss interpreted ;
It was a vision fair and fortunate :
Your statue spouting blood in many pipes,
In which so many smiling Romans bathed,
Signifies that from you great Rome shall suck
Reviving blood, and that great men shall press
For tinctures, stains, relics and cognizance.
This by Calpurnia's dream is signified.
Cæs. And this way have you well expounded it.
Dec. I have, when you have heard what I can say :
And know it now : the senate have concluded
To give this day a crown to mighty Cæsar.
If you shall send them word you will not come,
Their minds may change. Besides, it were a mock
Apt to be render'd, for some one to say
'Break up the senate till another time,
When Cæsar's wife shall meet with better dreams.'
If Cæsar hide himself, shall they not whisper
'Lo, Cæsar is afraid'?
Pardon me, Cæsar ; for my dear dear love
To your proceeding bids me tell you this ;
And reason to my love is liable.
Cæs. How foolish do your fears seem now, Calpurnia !
I am ashamed I did yield to them.
Give me my robe, for I will go.

Enter PUBLIUS, BRUTUS, LIGARIUS, METELLUS, CASCA, TREBONIUS, *and* CINNA.

And look where Publius is come to fetch me.
Pub. Good morrow, Cæsar.
Cæs. Welcome, Publius.
What, Brutus, are you stirr'd so early too ?
Good morrow, Casca. Caius Ligarius,
Cæsar was ne'er so much your enemy
As that same ague which hath made you lean.
What is 't o'clock ?
Bru. Cæsar, 'tis strucken eight.
Cæs. I thank you for your pains and courtesy.

Enter ANTONY.

See ! Antony, that revels long o' nights,
Is notwithstanding up. Good morrow, Antony.
Ant. So to most noble Cæsar.
Cæs. Bid them prepare within :
I am to blame to be thus waited for.
Now, Cinna : now, Metellus : what, Trebonius !
I have an hour's talk in store for you ;
Remember that you call on me to-day :
Be near me, that I may remember you.
Treb. Cæsar, I will : [*Aside*] and so ne will I be,
That your best friends shall wish I had bee further.
Cæs. Good friends, go in, and taste som wine with me ;
And we, like friends, will straightway go t gether.
Bru. [*Aside*] That every like is not th same, O Cæsar,
The heart of Brutus yearns to think upon !
[*Exeun*

SCENE III. *A street near the Capitol.*

Enter ARTEMIDORUS, *reading a paper.*

Art. 'Cæsar, beware of Brutus ; take hee of Cassius ; come not near Casca ; have an ey to Cinna, trust not Trebonius : mark we Metellus Cimber : Decius Brutus loves the not : thou hast wronged Caius Ligarius. The is but one mind in all these men, and it is ben against Cæsar. If thou beest not immorta look about you : security gives way to con spiracy. The mighty gods defend thee ! Th lover,

'ARTEMIDORUS

Here will I stand till Cæsar pass along,
And as a suitor will I give him this.
My heart laments that virtue cannot live
Out of the teeth of emulation.
If thou read this, O Cæsar, thou mayst live ;
If not, the Fates with traitors do contrive.
[*Exi*

SCENE IV. *Another part of the same stree before the house of Brutus.*

Enter PORTIA *and* LUCIUS.

Por. I prithee, boy, run to the senat house ;
Stay not to answer me, but get thee gone :
Why dost thou stay ?
Luc. To know my errand, madam
Por. I would have had thee there, and her again,
Ere I can tell thee what thou shouldst do there
O constancy, be strong upon my side,
Set a huge mountain 'tween my heart an tongue !
I have a man's mind, but a woman's might.
How hard it is for women to keep counsel !
Art thou here yet ?
Luc. Madam, what should I do ?
Run to the Capitol, and nothing else ?
And so return to you, and nothing else ?
Por. Yes, bring me word, boy, if thy lor look well,
For he went sickly forth : and take good note
What Cæsar doth, what suitors press to him.
Hark, boy ! what noise is that ?
Luc. I hear none, madam.
Por. Prithee, listen well
I heard a bustling rumor, like a fray,
And the wind brings it from the Capitol.
Luc. Sooth, madam, I hear nothing.

Enter the Soothsayer.

Por. Come hither, fellow : which way has thou been ?
Sooth. At mine own house, good lady.
Por. What is't o'clock ?

Sooth. About the ninth hour, lady.
Por. Is Cæsar yet gone to the Capitol?
Sooth. Madam, not yet: I go to take my stand,
To see him pass on to the Capitol.
Por. Thou hast some suit to Cæsar, hast thou not?
Sooth. That I have, lady: if it will please Cæsar
To be so good to Cæsar as to hear me,
I shall beseech him to befriend himself.
Por. Why, know'st thou any harm's intended towards him?
Sooth. None that I know will be, much that I fear may chance.
Good morrow to you. Here the street is narrow:
The throng that follows Cæsar at the heels,
Of senators, of prætors, common suitors,
Will crowd a feeble man almost to death:
I'll get me to a place more void, and there
Speak to great Cæsar as he comes along. [*Exit.*
Por. I must go in. Ay me, how weak a thing
The heart of woman is! O Brutus,
The heavens speed thee in thine enterprise!
Sure, the boy heard me: Brutus hath a suit
That Cæsar will not grant. O, I grow faint.
Run, Lucius, and commend me to my lord;
Say I am merry: come to me again,
And bring me word what he doth say to thee. [*Exeunt severally.*

ACT III.

SCENE I. *Rome. Before the Capitol; the Senate sitting above.*

A crowd of people; among them ARTEMIDORUS *and the* Soothsayer. *Flourish. Enter* CÆSAR, BRUTUS, CASSIUS, CASCA, DECIUS, METULLUS, TREBONIUS, CINNA, ANTONY, LEPIDUS, POPILIUS, PUBLIUS, *and others.*

Cæs. [*To the Soothsayer*] The ides of March are come.
Sooth. Ay, Cæsar; but not gone.
Art. Hail, Cæsar! read this schedule.
Dec. Trebonius doth desire you to o'er-read,
At your best leisure, this his humble suit.
Art. O Cæsar, read mine first; for mine's a suit
That touches Cæsar nearer: read it, great Cæsar.
Cæs. What touches us ourself shall be last served.
Art. Delay not, Cæsar; read it instantly.
Cæs. What, is the fellow mad?
Pub. Sirrah, give place.
Cas. What, urge you your petitions in the street?
Come to the Capitol.

CÆSAR *goes up to the Senate-House, the rest following.*

Pop. I wish your enterprise to-day may thrive.
Cas. What enterprise, Popilius?
Pop. Fare you well. [*Advances to Cæsar.*
Bru. What said Popilius Lena?
Cas. He wish'd to-day our enterprise might thrive.
I fear our purpose is discovered.
Bru. Look, how he makes to Cæsar; mark him.
Cas. Casca, be sudden, for we fear prevention.
Brutus, what shall be done? If this be known,
Cassius or Cæsar never shall turn back,
For I will slay myself.
Bru. Cassius, be constant:
Popilius Lena speaks not of our purposes;
For, look, he smiles, and Cæsar doth not change.
Cas. Trebonius knows his time; for, look you, Brutus.
He draws Mark Antony out of the way. [*Exeunt Antony and Trebonius.*
Dec. Where is Metellus Cimber? Let him go,
And presently prefer his suit to Cæsar.
Bru. He is address'd: press near and second him.
Cin. Casca, you are the first that rears your hand.
Cæs. Are we all ready? What is now amiss
That Cæsar and his senate must redress?
Met. Most high, most mighty, and most puissant Cæsar,
Metellus Cimber throws before thy seat
An humble heart,— [*Kneeling.*
Cæs. I must prevent thee, Cimber.
These couchings and these lowly courtesies
Might fire the blood of ordinary men,
And turn pre-ordinance and first decree
Into the law of children. Be not fond,
To think that Cæsar bears such rebel blood
That will be thaw'd from the true quality
With that which melteth fools; I mean, sweet words,
Low-crooked court'sies and base spaniel-fawning.
Thy brother by decree is banished:
If thou dost bend and pray and fawn for him,
I spurn thee like a cur out of my way.
Know, Cæsar doth not wrong, nor without cause
Will he be satisfied.
Met. Is there no voice more worthy than my own
To sound more sweetly in great Cæsar's ear
For the repealing of my banish'd brother?
Bru. I kiss thy hand, but not in flattery, Cæsar;
Desiring thee that Publius Cimber may
Have an immediate freedom of repeal.
Cæs. What, Brutus!
Cas. Pardon, Cæsar; Cæsar, pardon:
As low as to thy foot doth Cassius fall,
To beg enfranchisement for Publius Cimber.
Cæs. I could be well moved, if I were as you:
If I could pray to move, prayers would move me:
But I am constant as the northern star,
Of whose true-fix'd and resting quality
There is no fellow in the firmament.
The skies are painted with unnumber'd sparks,
They are all fire and every one doth shine,
But there's but one in all doth hold his place:
So in the world; 'tis furnish'd well with men,

And men are flesh and blood, and apprehensive ;
Yet in the number I do know but one
That unassailable holds on his rank,
Unshaked of motion : and that I am he,
Let me a little show it, even in this ;
That I was constant Cimber should be banish'd,
And constant do remain to keep him so.
Cin. O Cæsar,—
Cæs. Hence ! wilt thou lift up Olympus ?
Dec. Great Cæsar,—
Cæs. Doth not Brutus bootless kneel ?
Casca. Speak, hands, for me !
[*Casca first, then the other Conspirators and Marcus Brutus stab Cæsar.*
Cæs. Et tu, Brute ! Then fall, Cæsar. [*Dies.*
Cin. Liberty ! Freedom ! Tyranny is dead !
Run hence, proclaim, cry it about the streets.
Cas. Some to the common pulpits, and cry out
'Liberty, freedom, and enfranchisement !'
Bru. People and senators, be not affrighted ;
Fly not ; stand still : ambition's debt is paid.
Casca. Go to the pulpit, Brutus.
Dec. And Cassius too.
Bru. Where's Publius ?
Cin. Here, quite confounded with this mutiny.
Met. Stand fast together, lest some friend of Cæsar's
Should chance—
Bru. Talk not of standing. Publius, good cheer ;
There is no harm intended to your person,
Nor to no Roman else : so tell them, Publius.
Cas. And leave us, Publius ; lest that the people,
Rushing on us, should do your age some mischief.
Bru. Do so : and let no man abide this deed,
But we the doers.

Re-enter TREBONIUS.

Cas. Where is Antony ?
Treb. Fled to his house amazed :
Men, wives and children stare, cry out and run
As it were doomsday.
Bru. Fates, we will know your pleasures :
That we shall die, we know ; 'tis but the time
And drawing days out, that men stand upon.
Cas. Why, he that cuts off twenty years of life
Cuts off so many years of fearing death.
Bru. Grant that, and then is death a benefit :
So are we Cæsar's friends, that have abridged
His time of fearing death. Stoop, Romans, stoop,
And let us bathe our hands in Cæsar's blood
Up to the elbows, and besmear our swords :
Then walk we forth, even to the market-place,
And, waving our red weapons o'er our heads,
Let's all cry 'Peace, freedom and liberty !'
Cas. Stoop, then, and wash. How many ages hence
Shall this our lofty scene be acted over
In states unborn and accents yet unknown !
Bru. How many times shall Cæsar bleed in sport,
That now on Pompey's basis lies along
No worthier than the dust !
Cas. So oft as that shall be
So often shall the knot of us be call'd
The men that gave their country liberty.
Dec. What, shall we forth ?
Cas. Ay, every man away
Brutus shall lead ; and we will grace his heels
With the most boldest and best hearts o
Rome.

Enter a Servant.

Bru. Soft ! who comes here ? A friend o Antony's.
Serv. Thus, Brutus, did my master bid m kneel :
Thus did Mark Antony bid me fall down ;
And, being prostrate, thus he bade me say :
Brutus is noble, wise, valiant, and honest ;
Cæsar was mighty, bold, royal, and loving :
Say I love Brutus, and I honor him ;
Say I fear'd Cæsar, honor'd him and love him.
If Brutus will vouchsafe that Antony
May safely come to him, and be resolved
How Cæsar hath deserved to lie in death,
Mark Antony shall not love Cæsar dead
So well as Brutus living ; but will follow
The fortunes and affairs of noble Brutus
Thorough the hazards of this untrod state
With all true faith. So says my master Antony
Bru. Thy master is a wise and valiant Roman ;
I never thought him worse.
Tell him, so please him come unto this place,
He shall be satisfied ; and, by my honor,
Depart untouch'd.
Serv. I'll fetch him presently. [*Exi*
Bru. I know that we shall have him well t friend.
Cas. I wish we may : but yet have I a min
That fears him much ; and my misgiving sti
Falls shrewdly to the purpose.
Bru. But here comes Antony.

Re-enter ANTONY.

Welcome, Mark Antony
Ant. O mighty Cæsar ! dost thou lie s low ?
Are all thy conquests, glories, triumphs, spoils
Shrunk to this little measure ? Fare thee wel
I know not, gentlemen, what you intend,
Who else must be let blood, who else is rank
If I myself, there is no hour so fit
As Cæsar's death hour, nor no instrument
Of half that worth as those your swords, mad rich
With the most noble blood of all this world.
I do beseech ye, if you bear me hard,
Now, whilst your purpled hands do reek an smoke,
Fulfil your pleasure. Live a thousand years,
I shall not find myself so apt to die :
No place will please me so, no mean of deat
As here by Cæsar, and by you cut off,
The choice and master spirits of this age.
Bru. O Antony, beg not your death of u
Though now we must appear bloody and crue
As, by our hands and this our present act,
You see we do, yet see you but our hands
And this the bleeding business they have done
Our hearts you see not ; they are pitiful ;
And pity to the general wrong of Rome—

As fire drives out fire, so pity pity—
Hath done this deed on Cæsar. For your part,
To you our swords have leaden points, Mark Antony :
Our arms, in strength of malice, and our hearts
Of brothers' temper, do receive you in
With all kind love, good thoughts, and reverence.

Cas. Your voice shall be as strong as any man's
In the disposing of new dignities.

Bru. Only be patient till we have appeased
The multitude, beside themselves with fear,
And then we will deliver you the cause,
Why I, that did love Cæsar when I struck him,
Have thus proceeded.

Ant. I doubt not of your wisdom.
Let each man render me his bloody hand :
First, Marcus Brutus, will I shake with you ;
Next, Caius Cassius, do I take your hand ;
Now, Decius Brutus, yours : now yours, Metellus ;
Yours, Cinna ; and, my valiant Casca, yours ;
Though last, not least in love, yours, good Trebonius.
Gentlemen all,—alas, what shall I say ?
My credit now stands on such slippery ground,
That one of two bad ways you must conceit me,
Either a coward or a flatterer.
That I did love thee, Cæsar, O, 'tis true :
If then thy spirit look upon us now,
Shall it not grieve thee dearer than thy death,
To see thy Antony making his peace,
Shaking the bloody fingers of thy foes,
Most noble ! in the presence of thy corse ?
Had I as many eyes as thou hast wounds,
Weeping as fast as they stream forth thy blood,
It would become me better than to close
In terms of friendship with thine enemies.
Pardon me, Julius ! Here wast thou bay'd, brave hart ;
Here didst thou fall ; and here thy hunters stand,
Sign'd in thy spoil, and crimson'd in thy lethe.
O world, thou wast the forest to this hart ;
And this, indeed, O world, the heart of thee.
How like a deer, strucken by many princes,
Dost thou here lie !

Cas. Mark Antony,—

Ant. Pardon me, Caius Cassius :
The enemies of Cæsar shall say this ;
Then, in a friend, it is cold modesty.

Cas. I blame you not for praising Cæsar so ;
But what compact mean you to have with us ?
Will you be prick'd in number of our friends ;
Or shall we on, and not depend on you ?

Ant. Therefore I took your hands, but was, indeed,
Sway'd from the point, by looking down on Cæsar.
Friends am I with you all and love you all,
Upon this hope, that you shall give me reasons
Why and wherein Cæsar was dangerous.

Bru. Or else were this a savage spectacle :
Our reasons are so full of good regard
That were you, Antony, the son of Cæsar,
You should be satisfied.

Ant. That's all I seek :
And am moreover suitor that I may
Produce his body to the market-place ;
And in the pulpit, as becomes a friend,
Speak in the order of his funeral.

Bru. You shall, Mark Antony.

Cas. Brutus, a word with you.
[*Aside to Bru.*] You know not what you do : do not consent
That Antony speak in his funeral :
Know you how much the people may be moved
By that which he will utter ?

Bru. By your pardon ;
I will myself into the pulpit first,
And show the reason of our Cæsar's death :
What Antony shall speak, I will protest
He speaks by leave and by permission,
And that we are contented Cæsar shall
Have all true rites and lawful ceremonies.
It shall advantage more than do us wrong.

Cas. I know not what may fall ; I like it not.

Bru. Mark Antony, here, take you Cæsar's body.
You shall not in your funeral speech blame us,
But speak all good you can devise of Cæsar,
And say you do't by our permission ;
Else shall you not have any hand at all
About his funeral : and you shall speak
In the same pulpit whereto I am going,
After my speech is ended.

Ant. Be it so ;
I do desire no more.

Bru. Prepare the body then, and follow us.
[*Exeunt all but Antony.*

Ant. O, pardon me, thou bleeding piece of earth,
That I am meek and gentle with these butchers !
Thou art the ruins of the noblest man
That ever lived in the tide of times.
Woe to the hand that shed this costly blood !
Over thy wounds now do I prophesy,—
Which, like dumb mouths, do ope their ruby lips,
To beg the voice and utterance of my tongue—
A curse shall light upon the limbs of men ;
Domestic fury and fierce civil strife
Shall cumber all the parts of Italy ;
Blood and destruction shall be so in use
And dreadful objects so familiar
That mothers shall but smile when they behold
Their infants quarter'd with the hands of war ;
All pity choked with custom of fell deeds :
And Cæsar's spirit, ranging for revenge,
With Ate by his side come hot from hell,
Shall in these confines with a monarch's voice
Cry 'Havoc,' and let slip the dogs of war ;
That this foul deed shall smell above the earth
With carrion men, groaning for burial.

Enter a Servant.

You serve Octavius Cæsar, do you not ?

Serv. I do, Mark Antony.

Ant. Cæsar did write for him to come to Rome.

Serv. He did receive his letters, and is coming ;
And bid me say to you by word of mouth—
O Cæsar !— [*Seeing the body.*

Ant. Thy heart is big, get thee apart and weep.
Passion, I see, is catching ; for mine eyes,
Seeing those beads of sorrow stand in thine,
Began to water. Is thy master coming ?

Serv. He lies to-night within seven leagues of Rome.
Ant. Post back with speed, and tell him what hath chanced:
Here is a mourning Rome, a dangerous Rome,
No Rome of safety for Octavius yet;
Hie hence, and tell him so. Yet, stay awhile;
Thou shalt not back till I have borne this corse
Into the market-place: there shall I try
In my oration, how the people take
The cruel issue of these bloody men;
According to the which, thou shalt discourse
To young Octavius of the state of things.
Lend me your hand.
[*Exeunt with Cæsar's body.*

SCENE II. *The Forum.*

Enter BRUTUS *and* CASSIUS, *and a throng of* Citizens.

Citizens. We will be satisfied; let us be satisfied.
Bru. Then follow me, and give me audience, friends.
Cassius, go you into the other street,
And part the numbers.
Those that will hear me speak, let 'em stay here;
Those that will follow Cassius, go with him;
And public reasons shall be rendered
Of Cæsar's death.
First Cit. I will hear Brutus speak.
Sec. Cit. I will hear Cassius; and compare their reasons,
When severally we hear them rendered.
[*Exit Cassius, with some of the Citizens. Brutus goes into the pulpit.*
Third Cit. The noble Brutus is ascended: silence!
Bru. Be patient till the last.

Romans, countrymen, and lovers! hear me for my cause, and be silent, that you may hear: believe me for mine honor, and have respect to mine honor, that you may believe: censure me in your wisdom, and awake your senses, that you may the better judge. If there be any in this assembly, any dear friend of Cæsar's, to him I say, that Brutus' love to Cæsar was no less than his. If then that friend demand why Brutus rose against Cæsar, this is my answer:—Not that I loved Cæsar less, but that I loved Rome more. Had you rather Cæsar were living and die all slaves, than that Cæsar were dead, to live all free men? As Cæsar loved me, I weep for him; as he was fortunate, I rejoice at it; as he was valiant, I honor him: but, as he was ambitious, I slew him. There is tears for his love; joy for his fortune; honor for his valor; and death for his ambition. Who is here so base that would be a bondman? If any, speak; for him have I offended. Who is here so rude that would not be a Roman? If any, speak; for him have I offended. Who is here so vile that will not love his country? If any, speak; for him have I offended. I pause for a reply.

All. None, Brutus, none.

Bru. Then none have I offended. I have done no more to Cæsar than you shall do to Brutus. The question of his death is enrolled in the Capitol; his glory not extenuated, wherein he was worthy, nor his offences enforced, for which he suffered death.

Enter ANTONY *and others, with* CÆSAR'S *body.*

Here comes his body, mourned by Mark Antony: who, though he had no hand in his death, shall receive the benefit of his dying, a place in the commonwealth; as which of you shall not? With this I depart,—that, as I slew my best lover for the good of Rome, I have the same dagger for myself, when it shall please my country to need my death.

All. Live, Brutus! live, live!
First Cit. Bring him with triumph home unto his house.
Sec. Cit. Give him a statue with his ancestors.
Third Cit. Let him be Cæsar.
Fourth Cit. Cæsar's better parts
Shall be crown'd in Brutus.
First Cit. We'll bring him to his house
With shouts and clamors.
Bru. My countrymen,—
Sec. Cit. Peace, silence! Brutus speaks.
First Cit. Peace, ho!
Bru. Good countrymen, let me depart alone,
And, for my sake, stay here with Antony:
Do grace to Cæsar's corpse, and grace his speech
Tending to Cæsar's glories; which Mark Antony,
By our permission, is allow'd to make.
I do entreat you, not a man depart,
Save I alone, till Antony have spoke. [*Exit.*
First Cit. Stay, ho! and let us hear Mark Antony.
Third Cit. Let him go up into the public chair;
We'll hear him. Noble Antony, go up.
Ant. For Brutus' sake, I am beholding to you. [*Goes into the pulpit.*
Fourth Cit. What does he say of Brutus?
Third Cit. He says, for Brutus' sake,
He finds himself beholding to us all.
Fourth Cit. 'Twere best he speak no harm of Brutus here.
First Cit. This Cæsar was a tyrant.
Third Cit. Nay, that's certain:
We are blest that Rome is rid of him.
Sec. Cit. Peace! let us hear what Antony can say.
Ant. You gentle Romans,—
Citizens. Peace, ho! let us hear him.
Ant. Friends, Romans, countrymen, lend me your ears;
I come to bury Cæsar, not to praise him.
The evil that men do lives after them;
The good is oft interred with their bones;
So let it be with Cæsar. The noble Brutus
Hath told you Cæsar was ambitious:
If it were so, it was a grievous fault,
And grievously hath Cæsar answer'd it.
Here, under leave of Brutus and the rest—
For Brutus is an honorable man;
So are they all, all honorable men—
Come I to speak in Cæsar's funeral.
He was my friend, faithful and just to me:
But Brutus says he was ambitious;
And Brutus is an honorable man.
He hath brought many captives home to Rome
Whose ransoms did the general coffers fill:
Did this in Cæsar seem ambitious?
When that the poor have cried, Cæsar hath wept:

Ambition should be made of sterner stuff:
Yet Brutus says he was ambitious;
And Brutus is an honorable man.
You all did see that on the Lupercal
I thrice presented him a kingly crown,
Which he did thrice refuse: was this ambition?
Yet Brutus says he was ambitious;
And, sure, he is an honorable man.
I speak not to disprove what Brutus spoke,
But here I am to speak what I do know.
You all did love him once, not without cause:
What cause withholds you then, to mourn for him?
O judgment! thou art fled to brutish beasts,
And men have lost their reason. Bear with me;
My heart is in the coffin there with Cæsar,
And I must pause till it come back to me.

First Cit. Methinks there is much reason in his sayings.

Sec. Cit. If thou consider rightly of the matter,
Cæsar has had great wrong.

Third Cit. Has he, masters?
I fear there will a worse come in his place.

Fourth Cit. Mark'd ye his words? He would not take the crown;
Therefore 'tis certain he was not ambitious.

First Cit. If it be found so, some will dear abide it.

Sec. Cit. Poor soul! his eyes are red as fire with weeping.

Third Cit. There's not a nobler man in Rome than Antony.

Fourth Cit. Now mark him, he begins again to speak.

Ant. But yesterday the word of Cæsar might
Have stood against the world; now lies he there.
And none so poor to do him reverence.
O masters, if I were disposed to stir
Your hearts and minds to mutiny and rage,
I should do Brutus wrong, and Cassius wrong,
Who, you all know, are honorable men:
I will not do them wrong; I rather choose
To wrong the dead, to wrong myself and you,
Than I will wrong such honorable men.
But here's a parchment with the seal of Cæsar;
I found it in his closet, 'tis his will:
Let but the commons hear this testament—
Which, pardon me, I do not mean to read—
And they would go and kiss dead Cæsar's wounds
And dip their napkins in his sacred blood,
Yea, beg a hair of him for memory,
And, dying, mention it within their wills,
Bequeathing it as a rich legacy
Unto their issue.

Fourth Cit. We'll hear the will: read it, Mark Antony.

All. The will, the will! we will hear Cæsar's will.

Ant. Have patience, gentle friends, I must not read it;
It is not meet you know how Cæsar loved you.
You are not wood, you are not stones, but men;
And, being men, hearing the will of Cæsar,
It will inflame you, it will make you mad:
'Tis good you know not that you are his heirs;
For, if you should, O, what would come of it!

Fourth Cit. Read the will; we'll hear it, Antony;
You shall read us the will, Cæsar's will.

Ant. Will you be patient? will you stay awhile?
I have o'ershot myself to tell you of it:
I fear I wrong the honorable men
Whose daggers have stabb'd Cæsar; I do fear it.

Fourth Cit. They were traitors: honorable men!

All. The will! the testament!

Sec. Cit. They were villains, murderers: the will! read the will.

Ant. You will compel me, then, to read the will?
Then make a ring about the corpse of Cæsar,
And let me show you him that made the will.
Shall I descend? and will you give me leave?

Several Cit. Come down.

Sec. Cit. Descend.

Third Cit. You shall have leave.

[*Antony comes down.*

Fourth Cit. A ring; stand round.

First Cit. Stand from the hearse, stand from the body.

Sec. Cit. Room for Antony, most noble Antony.

Ant. Nay, press not so upon me; stand far off.

Several Cit. Stand back; room; bear back.

Ant. If you have tears, prepare to shed them now.
You all do know this mantle: I remember
The first time ever Cæsar put it on;
'Twas on a summer's evening, in his tent,
That day he overcame the Nervii:
Look, in this place ran Cassius' dagger through:
See what a rent the envious Casca made:
Through this the well-beloved Brutus stabb'd;
And as he pluck'd his cursed steel away,
Mark how the blood of Cæsar follow'd it,
As rushing out of doors, to be resolved
If Brutus so unkindly knock'd, or no;
For Brutus, as you know, was Cæsar's angel:
Judge, O you gods, how dearly Cæsar loved him!
This was the most unkindest cut of all;
For when the noble Cæsar saw him stab,
Ingratitude, more strong than traitors' arms,
Quite vanquish'd him: then burst his mighty heart;
And, in his mantle muffling up his face,
Even at the base of Pompey's statua,
Which all the while ran blood, great Cæsar fell.
O, what a fall was there, my countrymen!
Then I, and you, and all of us fell down,
Whilst bloody treason flourish'd over us.
O, now you weep; and, I perceive, you feel
The dint of pity: these are gracious drops.
Kind souls, what, weep you when you but behold
Our Cæsar's vesture wounded? Look you here,
Here is himself, marr'd, as you see, with traitors.

First Cit. O piteous spectacle!

Sec. Cit. O noble Cæsar!

Third Cit. O woful day!
Fourth Cit. O traitors, villains!
First Cit. O most bloody sight!
Sec. Cit. We will be revenged.
All. Revenge! About! Seek! Burn! Fire! Kill! Slay! Let not a traitor live!
Ant. Stay, countrymen.
First Cit. Peace there! hear the noble Antony.
Sec. Cit. We'll hear him, we'll follow him, we'll die with him.
Ant. Good friends, sweet friends, let me not stir you up
To such a sudden flood of mutiny.
They that have done this deed are honorable:
What private griefs they have, alas, I know not,
That made them do it: they are wise and honorable,
And will, no doubt, with reasons answer you.
I come not, friends, to steal away your hearts:
I am no orator, as Brutus is;
But, as you know me all, a plain blunt man,
That love my friend; and that they know full well
That gave me public leave to speak of him:
For I have neither wit, nor words, nor worth,
Action, nor utterance, nor the power of speech,
To stir men's blood: I only speak right on;
I tell you that which you yourselves do know;
Show you sweet Cæsar's wounds, poor poor dumb mouths,
And bid them speak for me: but were I Brutus,
And Brutus Antony, there were an Antony
Would ruffle up your spirits and put a tongue
In every wound of Cæsar that should move
The stones of Rome to rise and mutiny.
All. We'll mutiny.
First Cit. We'll burn the house of Brutus.
Third Cit. Away, then! come, seek the conspirators.
Ant. Yet hear me, countrymen; yet hear me speak.
All. Peace, ho! Hear Antony. Most noble Antony!
Ant. Why, friends, you go to do you know not what:
Wherein hath Cæsar thus deserved your loves?
Alas, you know not: I must tell you, then:
You have forgot the will I told you of.
All. Most true. The will! Let's stay and hear the will.
Ant. Here is the will, and under Cæsar's seal.
To every Roman citizen he gives,
To every several man, seventy-five drachmas.
Sec. Cit. Most noble Cæsar! We'll revenge his death.
Third Cit. O royal Cæsar!
Ant. Hear me with patience.
All. Peace, ho!
Ant. Moreover, he hath left you all his walks,
His private arbors and new-planted orchards,
On this side Tiber; he hath left them you,
And to your heirs for ever, common pleasures,
To walk abroad, and recreate yourselves.
Here was a Cæsar! when comes such another?
First Cit. Never, never. Come, awa away!
We'll burn his body in the holy place,
And with the brands fire the traitors' hous
Take up the body.
Sec. Cit. Go fetch fire.
Third Cit. Pluck down benches.
Fourth Cit. Pluck down forms, window any thing.
[*Exeunt Citizens with the bod*
Ant. Now let it work. Mischief, thou a afoot,
Take thou what course thou wilt!

Enter a Servant.

How now, fellov
Serv. Sir, Octavius is already come Rome.
Ant. Where is he?
Serv. He and Lepidus are at Cæsa house.
Ant. And thither will I straight to vi him:
He comes upon a wish. Fortune is merry,
And in this mood will give us any thing.
Serv. I heard him say, Brutus and Cassi
Are rid like madmen through the gates Rome.
Ant. Belike they had some notice of t people,
How I had moved them. Bring me to Oct vius. [*Exeu*

Scene III. *A street.*

Enter Cinna *the poet.*

Cin. I dreamt to-night that I did feast wi Cæsar,
And things unlucky charge my fantasy:
I have no will to wander forth of doors,
Yet something leads me forth.

Enter Citizens.

First Cit. What is your name?
Sec. Cit. Whither are you going?
Third Cit. Where do you dwell?
Fourth Cit. Are you a married man or bachelor?
Sec. Cit. Answer every man directly.
First Cit. Ay, and briefly.
Fourth Cit. Ay, and wisely.
Third Cit. Ay, and truly, you were best
Cin. What is my name? Whither am I g ing? Where do I dwell? Am I a married ma or a bachelor? Then, to answer every man d rectly and briefly, wisely and truly: wisely say, I am a bachelor.
Sec. Cit. That's as much as to say, they a fools that marry: you'll bear me a bang f that, I fear. Proceed; directly.
Cin. Directly, I am going to Cæsar's f neral.
First Cit. As a friend or an enemy?
Cin. As a friend.
Sec. Cit. That matter is answered directl
Fourth Cit. For your dwelling,—briefly.
Cin. Briefly, I dwell by the Capitol.
Third Cit. Your name, sir, truly.
Cin. Truly, my name is Cinna.
First Cit. Tear him to pieces; he's a co spirator.
Cin. I am Cinna the poet, I am Cinna t poet.

Fourth Cit. Tear him for his bad verses, ear him for his bad verses.

Cin. I am not Cinna the conspirator.

Fourth Cit. It is no matter, his name's inna; pluck but his name out of his heart, nd turn him going.

Third Cit. Tear him, tear him! Come, rands, ho! fire-brands: to Brutus', to Cas-ius'; burn all: some to Decius' house, and ome to Casca's; some to Ligarius': away, o! [*Exeunt.*

ACT IV.

SCENE I. *A house in Rome.*

NTONY, OCTAVIUS, *and* LEPIDUS, *seated at a table.*

Ant. These many, then, shall die; their names are prick'd.
Oct. Your brother too must die; consent you, Lepidus?
Lep. I do consent—
Oct. Prick him down, Antony.
Lep. Upon condition Publius shall not live,
Vho is your sister's son, Mark Antony.
Ant. He shall not live; look, with a spot I damn him.
But, Lepidus, go you to Cæsar's house;
etch the will hither, and we shall determine
How to cut off some charge in legacies.
Lep. What, shall I find you here?
Oct. Or here, or at the Capitol. [*Exit Lepidus.*
Ant. This is a slight unmeritable man,
Meet to be sent on errands: is it fit,
The three-fold world divided, he should stand
One of the three to share it?
Oct. So you thought him;
And took his voice who should be prick'd to die,
In our black sentence and proscription.
Ant. Octavius, I have seen more days than you:
And though we lay these honors on this man,
To ease ourselves of divers slanderous loads,
He shall but bear them as the ass bears gold,
To groan and sweat under the business,
Either led or driven, as we point the way;
And having brought our treasure where we will,
Then take we down his load, and turn him off,
Like to the empty ass, to shake his ears,
And graze in commons.
Oct. You may do your will;
But he's a tried and valiant soldier.
Ant. So is my horse, Octavius; and for that
I do appoint him store of provender:
It is a creature that I teach to fight,
To wind, to stop, to run directly on,
His corporal motion govern'd by my spirit.
And, in some taste, is Lepidus but so;
He must be taught and train'd and bid go forth;
A barren-spirited fellow; one that feeds
On abjects, orts and imitations,
Which, out of use and staled by other men,
Begin his fashion: do not talk of him,
But as a property. And now, Octavius,
Listen great things:—Brutus and Cassius
Are levying powers: we must straight make head:
Therefore let our alliance be combined,
Our best friends made, our means stretch'd;
And let us presently go sit in council,
How covert matters may be best disclosed,
And open perils surest answered.
Oct. Let us do so: for we are at the stake,
And bay'd about with many enemies;
And some that smile have in their hearts, I fear,
Millions of mischiefs. [*Exeunt.*

SCENE II. *Camp near Sardis. Before Brutus's tent.*

Drum. Enter BRUTUS, LUCILIUS, LUCIUS, *and* Soldiers; TITINIUS *and* PINDARUS *meeting them.*

Bru. Stand, ho!
Lucil. Give the word, ho! and stand.
Bru. What now, Lucilius! is Cassius near?
Lucil. He is at hand; and Pindarus is come
To do you salutation from his master.
Bru. He greets me well. Your master, Pindarus,
In his own change, or by ill officers,
Hath given me some worthy cause to wish
Things done, undone: but, if he be at hand,
I shall be satisfied.
Pin. I do not doubt
But that my noble master will appear
Such as he is, full of regard and honor.
Bru. He is not doubted. A word, Lucilius;
How he received you, let me be resolved.
Lucil. With courtesy and with respect enough;
But not with such familiar instances,
Nor with such free and friendly conference,
As he hath used of old.
Bru. Thou hast described
A hot friend cooling: ever note, Lucilius,
When love begins to sicken and decay,
It useth an enforced ceremony.
There are no tricks in plain and simple faith;
But hollow men, like horses hot at hand,
Make gallant show and promise of their mettle;
But when they should endure the bloody spur,
They fall their crests, and, like deceitful jades,
Sink in the trial. Comes his army on?
Lucil. They mean this night in Sardis to be quarter'd;
The greater part, the horse in general,
Are come with Cassius.
Bru. Hark! he is arrived. [*Low march within.*
March gently on to meet him.

Enter CASSIUS *and his powers.*

Cas. Stand, ho!
Bru. Stand, ho! Speak the word along.
First Sol. Stand!
Sec. Sol. Stand!
Third Sol. Stand!
Cas. Most noble brother, you have done me wrong.
Bru. Judge me, you gods! wrong I mine enemies?
And, if not so, how should I wrong a brother?
Cas. Brutus, this sober form of yours hides wrongs;

And when you do them—
Bru. Cassius, be content;
Speak your griefs softly: I do know you well.
Before the eyes of both our armies here,
Which should perceive nothing but love from us,
Let us not wrangle: bid them move away;
Then in my tent, Cassius, enlarge your griefs,
And I will give you audience.
Cas. Pindarus,
Bid our commanders lead their charges off
A little from this ground.
Bru. Lucilius, do you the like; and let no man
Come to our tent till we have done our conference.
Let Lucius and Titinius guard our door.
[*Exeunt.*

SCENE III. *Brutus's tent.*

Enter BRUTUS *and* CASSIUS.

Cas. That you have wrong'd me doth appear in this:
You have condemn'd and noted Lucius Pella
For taking bribes here of the Sardians;
Wherein my letters, praying on his side,
Because I knew the man, were slighted off.
Bru. You wronged yourself to write in such a case.
Cas. In such a time as this it is not meet
That every nice offence should bear his comment.
Bru. Let me tell you, Cassius, you yourself
Are much condemn'd to have an itching palm;
To sell and mart your offices for gold
To undeservers.
Cas. I an itching palm!
You know that you are Brutus that speak this,
Or, by the gods, this speech were else your last.
Bru. The name of Cassius honors this corruption,
And chastisement doth therefore hide his head.
Cas. Chastisement!
Bru. Remember March, the ides of March remember:
Did not great Julius bleed for justice' sake?
What villain touch'd his body, that did stab,
And not for justice? What, shall one of us,
That struck the foremost man of all this world
But for supporting robbers, shall we now
Contaminate our fingers with base bribes,
And sell the mighty space of our large honors
For so much trash as may be grasped thus?
I had rather be a dog, and bay the moon,
Than such a Roman.
Cas. Brutus, bay not me;
I'll not endure it: you forget yourself,
To hedge me in; I am a soldier, I,
Older in practice, abler than yourself
To make conditions.
Bru. Go to; you are not, Cassius.
Cas. I am.
Bru. I say you are not.
Cas. Urge me no more, I shall forget myself;
Have mind upon your health, tempt me no further.
Bru. Away, slight man!
Cas. Is't possible?
Bru. Hear me, for I will speak.
Must I give way and room to your rash choler?
Shall I be frighted when a madman stares?
Cas. O ye gods, ye gods! must I endure all this?
Bru. All this! ay, more: fret till your proud heart break;
Go show your slaves how choleric you are,
And make your bondmen tremble. Must I budge?
Must I observe you? must I stand and crouch
Under your testy humor? By the gods
You shall digest the venom of your spleen,
Though it do split you; for, from this day forth,
I'll use you for my mirth, yea, for my laughter,
When you are waspish.
Cas. Is it come to this?
Bru. You say you are a better soldier:
Let it appear so; make your vaunting true,
And it shall please me well: for mine own part,
I shall be glad to learn of noble men.
Cas. You wrong me every way; you wrong me, Brutus;
I said, an elder soldier, not a better:
Did I say 'better'?
Bru. If you did, I care not.
Cas. When Cæsar lived, he durst not thus have moved me.
Bru. Peace, peace! you durst not so have tempted him.
Cas. I durst not!
Bru. No.
Cas. What, durst not tempt him!
Bru. For your life you durst not.
Cas. Do not presume too much upon my love;
I may do that I shall be sorry for.
Bru. You have done that you should be sorry for.
There is no terror, Cassius, in your threats,
For I am arm'd so strong in honesty
That they pass by me as the idle wind,
Which I respect not. I did send to you
For certain sums of gold, which you denied me:
For I can raise no money by vile means:
By heaven, I had rather coin my heart,
And drop my blood for drachmas, than to wring
From the hard hands of peasants their vile trash
By any indirection: I did send
To you for gold to pay my legions,
Which you denied me: was that done like Cassius?
Should I have answer'd Caius Cassius so?
When Marcus Brutus grows so covetous,
To lock such rascal counters from his friends,
Be ready, gods, with all your thunderbolts;
Dash him to pieces!
Cas. I denied you not.
Bru. You did.
Cas. I did not: he was but a fool that brought
My answer back. Brutus hath rived my heart:
A friend should bear his friend's infirmities,
But Brutus makes mine greater than they are.
Bru. I do not, till you practice them on me.

Cas. You love me not.

Bru. I do not like your faults.

Cas. A friendly eye could never see such faults.

Bru. A flatterer's would not, though they do appear
As huge as high Olympus.

Cas. Come, Antony, and young Octavius, come,
Revenge yourselves alone on Cassius,
For Cassius is aweary of the world;
Hated by one he loves; braved by his brother;
Check'd like a bondman; all his faults observed,
Set in a note-book, learn'd, and conn'd by rote,
To cast into my teeth. O, I could weep
My spirit from mine eyes! There is my dagger,
And here my naked breast; within, a heart
Dearer than Plutus' mine, richer than gold:
If that thou be'st a Roman, take it forth;
I, that denied thee gold, will give my heart:
Strike, as thou didst at Cæsar; for, I know,
When thou didst hate him worst, thou lovedst him better
Than ever thou lovedst Cassius.

Bru. Sheathe your dagger:
Be angry when you will, it shall have scope;
Do what you will, dishonor shall be humor.
O Cassius, you are yoked with a lamb
That carries anger as the flint bears fire;
Who, much enforced, shows a hasty spark,
And straight is cold again.

Cas. Hath Cassius lived
To be but mirth and laughter to his Brutus,
When grief, and blood ill-temper'd, vexeth him?

Bru. When I spoke that, I was ill-temper'd too.

Cas. Do you confess so much? Give me your hand.

Bru. And my heart too.

Cas. O Brutus!

Bru. What's the matter?

Cas. Have not you love enough to bear with me,
When that rash humor which my mother gave me
Makes me forgetful?

Bru. Yes, Cassius; and, from henceforth,
When you are over-earnest with your Brutus,
He'll think your mother chides, and leave you so.

Poet. [*Within*] Let me go in to see the generals;
There is some grudge between 'em, 'tis not meet
They be alone.

Lucil. [*Within*] You shall not come to them.

Poet. [*Within*] Nothing but death shall stay me.

Enter Poet, *followed by* LUCILIUS, TITINIUS, *and* LUCIUS.

Cas. How now! what's the matter?

Poet. For shame, you generals! what do you mean?
Love, and be friends, as two such men should be;
For I have seen more years, I'm sure, than ye.

Cas. Ha, ha! how vilely doth this cynic rhyme!

Bru. Get you hence, sirrah; saucy fellow, hence!

Cas. Bear with him, Brutus; 'tis his fashion.

Bru. I'll know his humor, when he knows his time:
What should the wars do with these jigging fools?
Companion, hence!

Cas. Away, away, be gone.
[*Exit Poet.*

Bru. Lucilius and Titinius, bid the commanders
Prepare to lodge their companies to-night.

Cas. And come yourselves, and bring Messala with you
Immediately to us.
[*Exeunt Lucilius and Titinius.*

Bru. Lucius, a bowl of wine! [*Exit Lucius.*

Cas. I did not think you could have been so angry.

Bru. O Cassius, I am sick of many griefs.

Cas. Of your philosophy you make no use,
If you give place to accidental evils.

Bru. No man bears sorrow better. Portia is dead.

Cas. Ha! Portia!

Bru. She is dead.

Cas. How 'scaped I killing when I cross'd you so?
O insupportable and touching loss!
Upon what sickness?

Bru. Impatient of my absence,
And grief that young Octavius with Mark Antony
Have made themselves so strong:—for with her death
That tidings came;—with this she fell distract,
And, her attendants absent, swallow'd fire.

Cas. And died so?

Bru. Even so.

Cas. O ye immortal gods!

Re-enter LUCIUS, *with wine and taper.*

Bru. Speak no more of her. Give me a bowl of wine.
In this I bury all unkindness, Cassius.

Cas. My heart is thirsty for that noble pledge.
Fill, Lucius, till the wine o'erswell the cup;
I cannot drink too much of Brutus' love.

Bru. Come in, Titinius! [*Exit Lucius.*

Re-enter TITINIUS, *with* MESSALA.

Welcome, good Messala.
Now sit we close about this taper here,
And call in question our necessities.

Cas. Portia, art thou gone?

Bru. No more, I pray you.
Messala, I have here received letters,
That young Octavius and Mark Antony
Come down upon us with a mighty power,
Bending their expedition toward Philippi.

Mes. Myself have letters of the selfsame tenor.

Bru. With what addition?

Mes. That by proscription and bills of outlawry,
Octavius, Antony, and Lepidus,
Have put to death an hundred senators.

Bru. Therein our letters do not well agree;
Mine speak of seventy senators that died
By their proscriptions, Cicero being one.
Cas. Cicero one!
Mes. Cicero is dead,
And by that order of proscription.
Had you your letters from your wife, my lord?
Bru. No, Messala.
Mes. Nor nothing in your letters writ of her?
Bru. Nothing, Messala.
Mes. That, methinks, is strange.
Bru. Why ask you? hear you aught of her in yours?
Mes. No, my lord.
Bru. Now, as you are a Roman, tell me true.
Mes. Then like a Roman bear the truth I tell:
For certain she is dead, and by strange manner.
Bru. Why, farewell, Portia. We must die, Messala:
With meditating that she must die once,
I have the patience to endure it now.
Mes. Even so great men great losses should endure.
Cas. I have as much of this in art as you,
But yet my nature could not bear it so.
Bru. Well, to our work alive. What do you think
Of marching to Philippi presently?
Cas. I do not think it good.
Bru. Your reason?
Cas. This it is:
'Tis better that the enemy seek us:
So shall he waste his means, weary his soldiers,
Doing himself offence; whilst we, lying still,
Are full of rest, defence, and nimbleness.
Bru. Good reasons must, of force, give place to better.
The people 'twixt Philippi and this ground
Do stand but in a forced affection;
For they have grudged us contribution:
The enemy, marching along by them,
By them shall make a fuller number up,
Come on refresh'd, new-added, and encouraged;
From which advantage shall we cut him off,
If at Philippi we do face him there,
These people at our back.
Cas. Hear me, good brother.
Bru. Under your pardon. You must note beside,
That we have tried the utmost of our friends,
Our legions are brim-full, our cause is ripe:
The enemy increaseth every day;
We, at the height, are ready to decline.
There is a tide in the affairs of men,
Which, taken at the flood, leads on to fortune;
Omitted, all the voyage of their life
Is bound in shallows and in miseries.
On such a full sea are we now afloat;
And we must take the current when it serves,
Or lose our ventures.
Cas. Then, with your will, go on;
We'll along ourselves, and meet them at Philippi.
Bru. The deep of night is crept upon our talk,
And nature must obey necessity;
Which we will niggard with a little rest.
There is no more to say?
Cas. No more. Good night:
Early to-morrow will we rise, and hence.
Bru. Lucius! [*Enter Lucius.*] My gown. [*Exit Lucius.*] Farewell, good Messala:
Good night, Titinius. Noble, noble Cassius,
Good night, and good repose.
Cas. O my dear brother!
This was an ill beginning of the night:
Never come such division 'tween our souls!
Let it not, Brutus.
Bru. Every thing is well.
Cas. Good night, my lord.
Bru. Good night, good brother.
Tit. Mess. Good night, Lord Brutus.
Bru. Farewell, every one.
[*Exeunt all but Brutus.*

Re-enter LUCIUS, *with the gown.*

Give me the gown. Where is thy instrument?
Luc. Here in the tent.
Bru. What, thou speak'st drowsily?
Poor knave, I blame thee not; thou art o'er-watch'd.
Call Claudius and some other of my men:
I'll have them sleep on cushions in my tent.
Luc. Varro and Claudius!

Enter VARRO *and* CLAUDIUS.

Var. Calls my lord?
Bru. I pray you, sirs, lie in my tent and sleep;
It may be I shall raise you by and by
On business to my brother Cassius.
Var. So please you, we will stand and watch your pleasure.
Bru. I will not have it so: lie down, good sirs;
It may be I shall otherwise bethink me.
Look, Lucius, here's the book I sought for so;
I put it in the pocket of my gown.
[*Var. and Clau. lie down.*
Luc. I was sure your lordship did not give it me.
Bru. Bear with me, good boy, I am much forgetful.
Canst thou hold up thy heavy eyes awhile,
And touch thy instrument a strain or two?
Luc. Ay, my lord, an't please you.
Bru. It does, my boy:
I trouble thee too much, but thou art willing.
Luc. It is my duty, sir.
Bru. I should not urge thy duty past thy might;
I know young bloods look for a time of rest.
Luc. I have slept, my lord, already.
Bru. It was well done; and thou shalt sleep again;
I will not hold thee long: if I do live,
I will be good to thee. [*Music, and a song.*
This is a sleepy tune. O murderous slumber,
Lay'st thou thy leaden mace upon my boy,
That plays thee music? Gentle knave, good night;
I will not do thee so much wrong to wake thee:
If thou dost nod, thou break'st thy instrument;
I'll take it from thee; and, good boy, good night.

Let me see, let me see; is not the leaf turn'd down
Where I left reading? Here it is, I think.

Enter the Ghost of CÆSAR.

How ill this taper burns! Ha! who comes here?
I think it is the weakness of mine eyes
That shapes this monstrous apparition.
It comes upon me. Art thou any thing?
Art thou some god, some angel, or some devil,
That makest my blood cold and my hair to stare?
Speak to me what thou art.

Ghost. Thy evil spirit, Brutus.

Bru. Why comest thou?

Ghost. To tell thee thou shalt see me at Philippi.

Bru. Well; then I shall see thee again?

Ghost. Ay, at Philippi.

Bru. Why, I will see thee at Philippi, then. [*Exit Ghost.*
Now I have taken heart thou vanishest:
Ill spirit, I would hold more talk with thee.
Boy, Lucius! Varro! Claudius! Sirs, awake!
Claudius!

Luc. The strings, my lord, are false.

Bru. He thinks he still is at his instrument.
Lucius, awake!

Luc. My lord?

Bru. Didst thou dream, Lucius, that thou so criedst out?

Luc. My lord, I do not know that I did cry.

Bru. Yes, that thou didst: didst thou see any thing?

Luc. Nothing, my lord.

Bru. Sleep again, Lucius. Sirrah Claudius!
[*To Var.*] Fellow thou, awake!

Var. My lord?

Clau. My lord?

Bru. Why did you so cry out, sirs, in your sleep?

Var. Clau. Did we, my lord?

Bru. Ay: saw you any thing?

Var. No, my lord, I saw nothing.

Clau. Nor I, my lord.

Bru. Go and commend me to my brother Cassius;
Bid him set on his powers betimes before,
And we will follow.

Var. Clau. It shall be done, my lord. [*Exeunt.*

ACT V.

SCENE I. *The plains of Philippi.*

Enter OCTAVIUS, ANTONY, *and their* army.

Oct. Now, Antony, our hopes are answered:
You said the enemy would not come down,
But keep the hills and upper regions;
It proves not so: their battles are at hand;
They mean to warn us at Philippi here,
Answering before we do demand of them.

Ant. Tut, I am in their bosoms, and I know
Wherefore they do it: they could be content
To visit other places; and come down
With fearful bravery, thinking by this face
To fasten in our thoughts that they have courage;
But 'tis not so.

Enter a Messenger.

Mess. Prepare you, generals:
The enemy comes on in gallant show;
Their bloody sign of battle is hung out,
And something to be done immediately.

Ant. Octavius, lead your battle softly on,
Upon the left hand of the even field.

Oct. Upon the right hand I; keep thou the left.

Ant. Why do you cross me in this exigent?

Oct. I do not cross you; but I will do so. [*March.*

Drum. Enter BRUTUS, CASSIUS, *and their* Army; LUCILIUS, TITINIUS, MESSALA, *and others.*

Bru. They stand, and would have parley.

Cas. Stand fast, Titinius: we must out and talk.

Oct. Mark Antony, shall we give sign of battle?

Ant. No, Cæsar, we will answer on their charge.
Make forth; the generals would have some words.

Oct. Stir not until the signal.

Bru. Words before blows: is it so, countrymen?

Oct. Not that we love words better, as you do.

Bru. Good words are better than bad strokes, Octavius.

Ant. In your bad strokes, Brutus, you give good words:
Witness the hole you made in Cæsar's heart,
Crying 'Long live! hail, Cæsar!'

Cas. Antony,
The posture of your blows are yet unknown;
But for your words, they rob the Hybla bees,
And leave them honeyless.

Ant. Not stingless too.

Bru. O, yes, and soundless too;
For you have stol'n their buzzing, Antony,
And very wisely threat before you sting.

Ant. Villains, you did not so, when your vile daggers
Hack'd one another in the sides of Cæsar:
You show'd your teeth like apes, and fawn'd like hounds,
And bow'd like bondmen, kissing Cæsar's feet;
Whilst damned Casca, like a cur, behind
Struck Cæsar on the neck. O you flatterers!

Cas. Flatterers! Now, Brutus, thank yourself:
This tongue had not offended so to-day,
If Cassius might have ruled.

Oct. Come, come, the cause: if arguing make us sweat,
The proof of it will turn to redder drops.
Look;
I draw a sword against conspirators;
When think you that the sword goes up again?
Never, till Cæsar's three and thirty wounds
Be well avenged; or till another Cæsar
Have added slaughter to the sword of traitors.

Bru. Cæsar, thou canst not die by traitors' hands,
Unless thou bring'st them with thee.
Oct. So I hope;
I was not born to die on Brutus' sword.
Bru. O, if thou wert the noblest of thy strain,
Young man, thou couldst not die more honorable.
Cas. A peevish schoolboy, worthless of such honor,
Join'd with a masker and a reveller!
Ant. Old Cassius still!
Oct. Come, Antony, away!
Defiance, traitors, hurl we in your teeth:
If you dare fight to-day, come to the field;
If not, when you have stomachs.
[*Exeunt Octavius, Antony, and their army.*
Cas. Why, now, blow wind, swell billow and swim bark!
The storm is up, and all is on the hazard.
Bru. Ho, Lucilius! hark, a word with you.
Lucil. [*Standing forth*] My lord?
[*Brutus and Lucilius converse apart.*
Cas. Messala!
Mes. [*Standing forth*] What says my general?
Cas. Messala,
This is my birth-day; as this very day
Was Cassius born. Give me thy hand, Messala:
Be thou my witness that against my will,
As Pompey was, am I compell'd to set
Upon one battle all our liberties.
You know that I held Epicurus strong
And his opinion: now I change my mind,
And partly credit things that do presage.
Coming from Sardis, on our former ensign
Two mighty eagles fell, and there they perch'd,
Gorging and feeding from our soldiers' hands;
Who to Philippi here consorted us:
This morning are they fled away and gone;
And in their steads do ravens, crows and kites,
Fly o'er our heads and downward look on us,
As we were sickly prey: their shadows seem
A canopy most fatal, under which
Our army lies, ready to give up the ghost.
Mes. Believe not so.
Cas. I but believe it partly;
For I am fresh of spirit and resolved
To meet all perils very constantly.
Bru. Even so, Lucilius.
Cas. Now, most noble Brutus,
The gods to-day stand friendly, that we may,
Lovers in peace, lead on our days to age!
But since the affairs of men rest still incertain,
Let's reason with the worst that may befall.
If we do lose this battle, then is this
The very last time we shall speak together:
What are you then determined to do?
Bru. Even by the rule of that philosophy
By which I did blame Cato for the death
Which he did give himself, I know not how,
But I do find it cowardly and vile,
For fear of what might fall, so to prevent
The time of life: arming myself with patience
To stay the providence of some high powers
That govern us below.
Cas. Then, if we lose this battle,
You are contented to be led in triumph
Thorough the streets of Rome?
Bru. No, Cassius, no: think not, thou noble Roman,
That ever Brutus will go bound to Rome;
He bears too great a mind. But this same day
Must end that work the ides of March begun;
And whether we shall meet again I know not.
Therefore our everlasting farewell take:
For ever, and for ever, farewell, Cassius!
If we do meet again, why, we shall smile;
If not, why then, this parting was well made.
Cas. For ever, and for ever, farewell, Brutus!
If we do meet again, we'll smile indeed;
If not, 'tis true this parting was well made.
Bru. Why, then, lead on. O, that a man might know
The end of this day's business ere it come!
But it sufficeth that the day will end,
And then the end is known. Come, ho! away!
[*Exeunt.*

SCENE II. *The same. The field of battle.*

Alarum. Enter BRUTUS *and* MESSALA.

Bru. Ride, ride, Messala, ride, and give these bills
Unto the legions on the other side.
[*Loud alarum.*
Let them set on at once; for I perceive
But cold demeanor in Octavius' wing,
And sudden push gives them the overthrow.
Ride, ride, Messala: let them all come down.
[*Exeunt.*

SCENE III. *Another part of the field.*

Alarums. Enter CASSIUS *and* TITINIUS.

Cas. O, look, Titinius, look, the villains fly!
Myself have to mine own turn'd enemy:
This ensign here of mine was turning back;
I slew the coward, and did take it from him.
Tit. O Cassius, Brutus gave the word too early;
Who, having some advantage on Octavius,
Took it too eagerly: his soldiers fell to spoil,
Whilst we by Antony are all enclosed.

Enter PINDARUS.

Pin. Fly further off, my lord, fly further off;
Mark Antony is in your tents, my lord:
Fly, therefore, noble Cassius, fly far off.
Cas. This hill is far enough. Look, look, Titinius;
Are those my tents where I perceive the fire?
Tit. They are, my lord.
Cas. Titinius, if thou lovest me,
Mount thou my horse, and hide thy spurs in him,
Till he have brought thee up to yonder troops,
And here again; that I may rest assured
Whether yond troops are friend or enemy.
Tit. I will be here again, even with a thought. [*Exit.*
Cas. Go, Pindarus, get higher on that hill;
My sight was ever thick; regard Titinius,
And tell me what thou notest about the field.
[*Pindarus ascends the hill.*
This day I breathed first: time is come round,
And where I did begin, there shall I end;
My life is run his compass. Sirrah, what news?

Pin. [*Above*] O my lord!
Cas. What news?
Pin. [*Above*] Titinius is enclosed round about
With horsemen, that make to him on the spur;
Yet he spurs on. Now they are almost on him.
Now, Titinius! Now some light. O, he lights too.
He's ta'en. [*Shout.*] And, hark! they shout for joy.
Cas. Come down, behold no more.
O, coward that I am, to live so long,
To see my best friend ta'en before my face!

PINDARUS *descends.*

Come hither, sirrah:
In Parthia did I take thee prisoner;
And then I swore thee, saving of thy life,
That whatsoever I did bid thee do,
Thou shouldst attempt it. Come now, keep thine oath;
Now be a freeman: and with this good sword,
That ran through Cæsar's bowels, search this bosom.
Stand not to answer: here, take thou the hilts;
And, when my face is cover'd, as 'tis now,
Guide thou the sword. [*Pindarus stabs him.*] Cæsar, thou art revenged,
Even with the sword that kill'd thee. [*Dies.*
Pin. So, I am free; yet would not so have been,
Durst I have done my will. O Cassius,
Far from this country Pindarus shall run,
Where never Roman shall take note of him.
[*Exit.*

Re-enter TITINIUS *with* MESSALA.

Mes. It is but change, Titinius; for Octavius
Is overthrown by noble Brutus' power,
As Cassius' legions are by Antony.
Tit. These tidings will well comfort Cassius.
Mes. Where did you leave him?
Tit. All disconsolate,
With Pindarus his bondman, on this hill.
Mes. Is not that he that lies upon the ground?
Tit. He lies not like the living. O my heart!
Mes. Is not that he?
Tit. No, this was he, Messala,
But Cassius is no more. O setting sun,
As in thy red rays thou dost sink to-night,
So in his red blood Cassius' day is set;
The sun of Rome is set! Our day is gone;
Clouds, dews, and dangers come; our deeds are done!
Mistrust of my success hath done this deed.
Mes. Mistrust of good success hath done this deed.
O hateful error, melancholy's child,
Why dost thou show to the apt thoughts of men
The things that are not? O error, soon conceived,
Thou never comest unto a happy birth,
But kill'st the mother that engender'd thee!
Tit. What, Pindarus! where art thou, Pindarus?
Mes. Seek him, Titinius, whilst I go to meet
The noble Brutus, thrusting this report
Into his ears; I may say, thrusting it;
For piercing steel and darts envenomed
Shall be as welcome to the ears of Brutus
As tidings of this sight.
Tit. Hie you, Messala,
And I will seek for Pindarus the while.
[*Exit Messala.*
Why didst thou send me forth, brave Cassius?
Did I not meet thy friends? and did not they
Put on my brows this wreath of victory,
And bid me give it thee? Didst thou not hear their shouts?
Alas, thou hast misconstrued every thing!
But, hold thee, take this garland on thy brow;
Thy Brutus bid me give it thee, and I
Will do his bidding. Brutus, come apace,
And see how I regarded Caius Cassius.
By your leave, gods:—this is a Roman's part:
Come, Cassius' sword, and find Titinius' heart.
[*Kills himself.*

Alarum. Re-enter MESSALA, *with* BRUTUS, *young* CATO, STRATO, VOLUMNIUS, *and* LUCILIUS.

Bru. Where, where, Messala, doth his body lie?
Mes. Lo, yonder, and Titinius mourning it.
Bru. Titinius' face is upward.
Cato. He is slain.
Bru. O Julius Cæsar, thou art mighty yet!
Thy spirit walks abroad, and turns our swords
In our own proper entrails. [*Low alarums.*
Cato. Brave Titinius!
Look, whether he have not crown'd dead Cassius!
Bru. Are yet two Romans living such as these?
The last of all the Romans, fare thee well!
It is impossible that ever Rome
Should breed thy fellow. Friends, I owe more tears
To this dead man than you shall see me pay.
I shall find time, Cassius, I shall find time.
Come, therefore, and to Thasos send his body:
His funerals shall not be in our camp,
Lest it discomfort us. Lucilius, come;
And come, young Cato; let us to the field.
Labeo and Flavius, set our battles on:
'Tis three o'clock; and, Romans, yet ere night
We shall try fortune in a second fight.
[*Exeunt.*

SCENE IV. *Another part of the field.*

Alarum. Enter fighting, Soldiers *of both armies; then* BRUTUS, *young* CATO, LUCILIUS, *and others.*

Bru. Yet, countrymen, O, yet hold up your heads!
Cato. What bastard doth not? Who will go with me?
I will proclaim my name about the field:
I am the son of Marcus Cato, ho!
A foe to tyrants, and my country's friend;
I am the son of Marcus Cato, ho!
Bru. And I am Brutus, Marcus Brutus, I;
Brutus, my country's friend; know me for Brutus!
[*Exit.*

Lucil. O young and noble Cato, art thou down?
Why, now thou diest as bravely as Titinius;
And mayst be honor'd, being Cato's son.

First Sold. Yield, or thou diest.

Lucil. Only I yield to die:
There is so much that thou wilt kill me straight; [*Offering money.*
Kill Brutus, and be honor'd in his death.

First Sold. We must not. A noble prisoner!

Sec. Sold. Room, ho! Tell Antony, Brutus is ta'en.

First Sold. I'll tell the news. Here comes the general.

Enter ANTONY.

Brutus is ta'en, Brutus is ta'en, my lord.

Ant. Where is he?

Lucil. Safe, Antony; Brutus is safe enough:
I dare assure thee that no enemy
Shall ever take alive the noble Brutus:
The gods defend him from so great a shame!
When you do find him, or alive or dead,
He will be found like Brutus, like himself.

Ant. This is not Brutus, friend; but, I assure you,
A prize no less in worth: keep this man safe;
Give him all kindness: I had rather have
Such men my friends than enemies. Go on,
And see whether Brutus be alive or dead;
And bring us word unto Octavius' tent
How every thing is chanced. [*Exeunt.*

SCENE V. *Another part of the field.*

Enter BRUTUS, DARDANIUS, CLITUS, STRATO, *and* VOLUMNIUS.

Bru. Come, poor remains of friends, rest on this rock.

Cli. Statilius show'd the torch-light, but, my lord,
He came not back: he is or ta'en or slain.

Bru. Sit thee down, Clitus: slaying is the word;
It is a deed in fashion. Hark thee, Clitus. [*Whispers.*

Cli. What, I, my lord? No, not for all the world.

Bru. Peace then! no words.

Cli. I'll rather kill myself.

Bru. Hark thee, Dardanius. [*Whispers.*

Dar. Shall I do such a deed?

Cli. O Dardanius!

Dar. O Clitus!

Cli. What ill request did Brutus make to thee?

Dar. To kill him, Clitus. Look, he meditates.

Cli. Now is that noble vessel full of grief,
That it runs over even at his eyes.

Bru. Come hither, good Volumnius; list a word.

Vol. What says my lord?

Bru. Why, this, Volumnius:
The ghost of Cæsar hath appear'd to me
Two several times by night; at Sardis once,
And, this last night, here in Philippi fields:
I know my hour is come.

Vol. Not so, my lord.

Bru. Nay, I am sure it is, Volumnius.
Thou seest the world, Volumnius, how it goes;
Our enemies have beat us to the pit: [*Low alarums.*
It is more worthy to leap in ourselves,
Than tarry till they push us. Good Volumnius,
Thou know'st that we two went to school together:
Even for that our love of old, I prithee,
Hold thou my sword-hilts, whilst I run on it.

Vol. That's not an office for a friend, my lord. [*Alarum still.*

Cli. Fly, fly, my lord; there is no tarrying here.

Bru. Farewell to you; and you; and you, Volumnius.
Strato, thou hast been all this while asleep;
Farewell to thee too, Strato. Countrymen,
My heart doth joy that yet in all my life
I found no man but he was true to me.
I shall have glory by this losing day
More than Octavius and Mark Antony
By this vile conquest shall attain unto.
So fare you well at once; for Brutus' tongue
Hath almost ended his life's history:
Night hangs upon mine eyes; my bones would rest,
That have but labor'd to attain this hour.
[*Alarum. Cry within,* 'Fly, fly, fly!'

Cli. Fly, my lord, fly.

Bru. Hence! I will follow.
[*Exeunt Clitus, Dardanius, and Volumnius.*
I prithee, Strato, stay thou by thy lord:
Thou art a fellow of a good respect;
Thy life hath had some smatch of honor in it:
Hold then my sword, and turn away thy face,
While I do run upon it. Wilt thou, Strato?

Stra. Give me your hand first. Fare you well, my lord.

Bru. Farewell, good Strato. [*Runs on his sword.*] Cæsar, now be still:
I kill'd not thee with half so good a will.
[*Dies.*

Alarum. Retreat. Enter OCTAVIUS, ANTONY, MESSALA, LUCILIUS, *and the army.*

Oct. What man is that?

Mes. My master's man. Strato, where is thy master?

Stra. Free from the bondage you are in, Messala:
The conquerors can but make a fire of him;
For Brutus only overcame himself,
And no man else hath honor by his death.

Lucil. So Brutus should be found. I thank thee, Brutus,
That thou hast proved Lucilius' saying true.

Oct. All that served Brutus, I will entertain them.
Fellow, wilt thou bestow thy time with me?

Stra. Ay, if Messala will prefer me to you.

Oct. Do so, good Messala.

Mes. How died my master, Strato?

Stra. I held the sword, and he did run on it.

Mes. Octavius, then take him to follow thee,
That did the latest service to my master.

Ant. This was the noblest Roman of them all:
All the conspirators save only he
Did that they did in envy of great Cæsar;
He only, in a general honest thought
And common good to all, made one of them.

His life was gentle, and the elements
So mix'd in him that Nature might stand up
And say to all the world 'This was a man!'
Oct. According to his virtue let us use him,
With all respect and rites of burial.
Within my tent his bones to-night shall lie,
Most like a soldier, order'd honorably.
So call the field to rest; and let's away,
To part the glories of this happy day.
[*Exeunt.*

DETAILED SUMMARY OF JULIUS CAESAR

Act I, Scene I: The play opens on a street in Rome. Here, two tribunes, Flavius and Marullus, reprimand the working men who are gathering in the street. The tribunes ask them why, being "mechanical" or working men, they are violating the law by walking about the streets on a working day without their tools or equipment. In answer, a cobbler, the leader of the crowd, at first makes flippant replies. For instance, he makes puns or plays on words that sound alike about his occupation as "a mender of bad soles" who "meddles with awl" (the cobbler's tool); finally he states that he and his companions have taken a holiday "to see Caesar and to rejoice in his triumph".

Act I, Scene 2 : Immediately after the crowd and the tribunes leave, a magnificent procession of patricians or nobles accompanied by musicians begins to wend its way along the street. Caesar, as a hero, is here; so too is Caesar's wife, Calpurnia. Caesar tells his wife, Calpurnia, to be sure to stand directly in Antony's way when the race begins. Then he turns to Antony, telling him to be sure to touch Calpurnia for, according to folk-lore, the touch of a runner in this "holy chase" or race will cure a woman of barrenness. As Antony promises Caesar that he will obey, the procession resumes its march and the musicians play again. Then a voice calling "Caesar" is heard. As the music stops and as the procession halts, the soothsayer comes forward from the rear and tells Caesar : "Beware the Ides of March". Caesar looks at the man, studying him, then dismisses the warning, saying slightingly, "He is a dreamer". The procession recommences but Brutus and Cassius, lagging behind, remain in conversation on the street.

Act I, Scene 3 : Again on the street, some time later, Casca appears, carrying an unsheathed sword. He meets Cicero and tells him of the dreadful unnatural phenomena of the night. Frightened, Casca concluded that either there is battle among the gods or that mankind is undergoing punishment by the gods in this manner. He describes some of the prodigious occurrences and sights : a slave's hand sheathed in fire remained unburned; a lion roamed the street; crowds of women have sworn that they saw men dressed in fire walk about; a night owl shrieked at noon; etc. Cicero, remaining stoically calm, averse only that it is indeed a strange time but adds a remark indicating that he takes little stock in men's interpretation of such events. He finds out from Casca that Caesar will be at the Capitol on the morrow; then Cicero departs.

Act II, Scene I : Before dawn on the Ides of March, Brutus is awake with thoughts about the coming deed. He wakes his boy-attendant, Lucius, envying the deep untroubled sleep of the boy compared to his own sleeplessness. While the boy is getting him a taper (candle), he expresses aloud the thoughts that have been keeping him awake. The key to his dilemma lies in the first words that he says :

> It must be by his death, and for my part
> I know no personal cause to spurn at him.

In metaphoric speech, Brutus rationalizes his own convictions. (The adder metaphor and the self-made man metaphor are explained in the notes.) Caesar is his friend and he has no reason yet to think him tyrant. Yet the potential is there and, since Caesar brings no conscience to bear on power, there is reason to fear he will abuse it. Therefore, for the general good he, Brutus, must acquiesce to his death.

Act II Scene 2 : Caesar enters, talking about the fearful night has passed. Calpurnia has called out in terror in her sleep. He orders the servant to tell the priests to make a sacrifice and to send him the results of the augury. Then Calpurnia enters and engages with Caesar in what is almost a parallel argument of that of Brutus and Portia. In this case, Calpurnia expresses her fears for Caesar and urges him to stay home. She cites the strange phenomena of the night which the conspirators had reported earlier. Caesar says words to the effect, "Who can prevent what the gods intend?" but he intends to go to the Capitol because whatever is forewarned is for everybody, not for Caesar alone. Calpurnia counters with the point that the gods give omens only for the death of the mighty. "When beggars die, there are not comets seen." To this Caesar answers is what has become a well-known phrase :

> Cowards die many times before their death;
> The valiant never taste of death but once.

Death is a necessary evil, says Caesar, and he thinks it foolish to fear it. At this point the servant comes to report the results of the augury. The priests could find no heart in the sacrificed beast. This being a bad omen, Caesar is asked not to stir from his house. Caesar again turns this to his own thinking; this is a test of his courage. Caesar is more dangerous than danger itself and he will "go forth". Calpurnia on bended knee finally prevails upon him to stay at home; Mark Antony will make the excuses for him.

Act II, Scene 3 : Artemidorus, the soothsayer, now reads a paper naming the conspirators and warning Caesar to shun these men lest he dies at their hand. He is standing in the way of Caesar's progress to the Senate so that he may hand it to him to read.

Act II, Scene 4 : Portia enters with Lucious (the boy-attendant). She sends him to the Capitol to note Brutus, whether he is sick or not and to see what Caesar does and whether he is surrounded by those with requests. She hears what she thinks is a noise, "a bustling rumour". At this the soothsayer enters and Portia questions him as to where he has come from, what time it is, whether Caesar has gone to the Capitol. He says, Caesar has left and that he (the soothsayer) is taking his stand to see him pass. She asks him if he has a suit to Caesar and if he knows whether any harm is intended to him. The soothsayer expresses his fears for Caesar and then says he will take himself off to a broader place of passage to await Caesar. Portia then hurries Lucius on to see Brutus and assure him she is merry. Lucius is to hurry back with Brutus's message.

Act III, Scene 1 : Caesar enters and the soothsayer. Caesar exchanges remarks with the soothsayer to the effect that the Ides of March are come and to which the soothsayer counters that they are not gone yet. The conspirators press Caesar with petitions. Artemidorus tries to get Caesar to read his note (of warning) first. But Caesar spurns him : what concerns Caesar he will deal with last. Cassius counsels all of them to urge their petitions in the Capitol, not on the street, evidently steering the assassination out of the public square. Cassius and the conspirators exchange comment on what is happening so far and Cassius urges quick action because he fears their purpose has been discovered.

It is Metellus Cimber's suit which Caesar stops abruptly with a long speech. He will not listen to fawning the flattery. Metellus's brother is banished and nothing will change this. In angry derogatory words Caesar spurns him and states that Caesar is not wrong. Metellus pleads with the others to intercede for him. The others do and even Brutus pleads, but

Caesar makes a long statement on his own constancy; in the heavens the northern star is the one fixed star; in the world of men Caesar is the one fixed and constant temperament. He will not yield to entreaties in this case.

This is the singal for the assassination. As they yield or plead and Caesar rebuffs, Casca strikes the first blow with "Speak, hands, for me." The others follow. As Brutus strikes, Caesar, gathering his toga about his gashed and bloody body speaks the bitter, most often quoted line — "Et tu, Brute ? Then fall Caesar," and then falls in death. The conspirators quickly shout out words of the deed and then disperse to various parts of Rome to proclaim the deed as a blow struck for liberty. Brutus assures those around him that only the conspirators will stand to take the responsibility of the assassination. Brutus explains that ambition's debt is paid. He also sees this as a fateful deed. He foresees his and the other's death but how soon death will come is left to fate. Now he bids all of them smear their swords in Caesar's blood and march to the market place proclaiming "peace, freedom and liberty." Cassius and Brutus foresee that this act (assassination) will be "played" over and over by future generations (in plays as well as in other states) and they will be called Rome's liberators. The conspirators march off, Brutus and Cassius soon to follow, as a servant enters.

Act III, Scene 2: This scene opens at the Forum where Brutus is at the pulpit ready to the plebeians (the crowd, the people). He tells Cassius to go to another street, take part of the crowd and there address them. The plebeians divide up with the agreement to meet later and compare notes on the two speakers. Brutus then delivers his oration. It is a quiet, sober, reasonable speech in which he tells the people that he was a friend of Caesar and loved him but took a hand in the assassination because he felt Caesar was ambitious and would have enslaved free Romans. He did what he did for a free Rome and he has offended only those who would be bondsmen and not Romans. As he is talking, Antony comes in with Caesar's body and Brutus tells the crowd that Antony, in Caesar's death, will receive the benefit of his dying, as shall the people, saying :

> As I slew my best lover for the good of Rome,
> I have the same dagger for myself, when it shall
> Please my country to need my death.

The crowd is with him and shouts many praises at him. As Brutus breaks into their cheers, they silence each other to listen. He asks them to allow him to leave, and they remain to listen to Antony who has been given permission to give an eulogy of Caesar. The crowd echoes his last words "Stay, ho, and let us hear Mark Antony." Antony goes up to the pulpit and his first words are inaudible to the shouting crowd. They hear the word "Brutus" and immediately bristle at any unkind reference to him. They remark on the tyranny of Caesar and show that they have been put into a mood favourable to be conspirators. This is the mood Antony has to break into with his speech. The crowd pays him attention because Brutus has asked them to. However, once Antony has them listening to him, he no longer needs the permission of Brutus for his audience. He now commands the audience in his own way.

Act III, Scene 3 : This scene shows the unbridled frenzy which Antony had churned up in the crowd. Cinna the poet enters and the mob gets hold of him. They ply him with a number of personal questions and he must answer at once : who he is, what he is, where does he live, etc. After close questioning and as close answering the final question is his name. He answers, "Cinna". They shout for his death as one of the conspirators. He answerers that he is Cinna the poet, not that Cinna who is among the conspirators. But his protests are to no avail; the blood of the crowd boils and they will not listen to reason. His name is Cinna, that is enough. They drag him off for a lynching and carry their fury elsewhere in Rome, calling out the conspirators' names, calling for their houses to be burned.

Act IV, Scene 1 : Seated together in conference are Antony, Octavius and Lepidus. They are compiling lists of those who shall die and, as enemies, they include both the brother of Lepidus and the nephew of Antony. The three intend to look for ways to cut down on some of the legacies stipulated in Caesar's will and, to further this plan, Lepidus goes off to Caesar's house to get the will. When he has gone, Antony speaks disparagingly of Lepidus as a "slight" man, who is not fit to share the "three-fold world". Octavius retorts that Antony had, however, just taken Lepidus's advice on the proscription lists. Antony claims that his worldly experience guides him to use Lepidus as though he were their beast of burden, one who will be dismissed when his usefulness to them is over. Octavius says that Lepidus is, after all, tried and true, but Antony compares Lepidus to a good horse to be fed and rewarded and treated as a property. Impatiently, Antony jumps to a topic of a greater concern to him : Brutus and Cassius are gathering their forces; the time is ripe now for Octavius and Antony to make their alliances and to make plans on how to counter the enemy. Octavius agrees with Antony for he considers their present position one of great danger.

Act IV, Scene 2 : The scene is the camp of Brutus's army near Sardis in Asia Minor. As drums sound Brutus appears, accompanied by his friend, Lucilius. His servant, the boy Lucius, tells Brutus that Cassius is on his way to Brutus's camp and points out that Cassius's servant, Pindarus, is already present. Brutus, in greeting Pindarus, says that his master (Cassius) has been responsible for some actions that Brutus could wish "undone". Pindarus affirms his confidence in his master. Being asked by Brutus, Lucilius says that Cassius received him courteously but with more restraint than of old. Brutus concludes from this that Cassius is a "hot friend cooling", that is, that Cassius no longer feels a friend's affection for Brutus. As Lucilius tells Brutus that Cassius's army will encamp in Sardis by night fall, Cassius himself enters.

Act IV, Scene 3 : A continuation of the scene immediately preceding, this scene, inside Brutus's tent, commences with Cassius's complaint. Specifically, Cassius is upset because his letters in defence of Lucius Pella, accused of taking bribes, have been disregarded. Brutus believes that Cassius demanded himself in intervening on behalf of a bribe-taker, but Cassius contends that in the troubled times they are now enduring, it is inadvisable to censure every little offence. Brutus goads Cassius to fury by saying that Cassius himself is known to have "an itching palm," that is, to take graft; only Cassius's high office has allowed him to escape punishment for it. Brutus reminds Cassius that they killed Caesar in the interests of justice and that therefore they, above all men, must act with perfect righteousness. Cassius, furious at being criticized, says to his friend that he has no right to "hedge me in," that is, no right to correct or reprove him. Brutus enrages him yet further by waving him off as a frivolous, trivial person saying, "Away, slight man." Cassius, almost hysterical with rage, threatens Brutus : "I may do that I shall be sorry for," but Brutus is coldly unconcerned and broaches yet another criticism : that when Brutus sent to Cassius for money with which to pay his troops, his request was denied. Cassius insists that Brutus's messenger misunderstood : he cries that he is "hated by one he loves," meaning that he has lost Brutus's friendship and, after his dramatic offer of his dagger so that Brutus may kill him, he is spent. Brutus is softened, and the friends begin to be reconciled.

Cassius asks his friend to forgive him his outbursts of bad temper, calling them an inherited trait which he cannot control. Brutus answers him soothingly. A poet now comes in to entertain them but Brutus, clearly not amused by the rhyming satirical thrusts at the quarrel just ended, dismisses him with irritation. The two friends continue their conversation over a bowl of wine. Brutus admits to many sorrows. When Cassius urges Brutus to try to bear them stoically, Brutus unburdens himself : his wife, Portia, distraught with anxiety, has killed herself.

Act V, Scene 1 : At the Plains of Philippi, Octavius tells Antony that the enemy is launching an attack at them here contrary to what Antony said they would do. Antony says, "I know them." He claims the enemy is making these manoeuvres to make them believe the enemy has courage. A messenger comes in to tell them Brutus's army is at hand. Antony tells Octavius to take the left flank. Octavius will not be told by Antony where to dispose his troops. He says, "Upon the right hand I. Keep thou the left." When Antony protests that Octavius is crossing him in this Octavius merely says, "I do not cross you; but I will do so."

Act V, Scene 2 : This is a brief scene in which Brutus sends Messala to bring the legions on their other flank down to a concerted full attack since he sees "cold demeanour" or lack of vigous on the part of Octavius's soldiers on the right wing.

Act, V, Scene 3 : In another part of the field of battle, Cassius appears bewailing his soldiers' courage. He had found his own ensign retreating and he slew him, taking the standard from him to rally the men. Titinius, who is with him, reports the hasty action of Brutus in ordering full attack on Octavius's wing. This was evidently a trap and Brutus fell for it by ordering the full attack too soon. Pindarus appears and cries for Cassius to retreat further since Antony is in his tents. Cassius sees his tents on fire and sends Titinius to ride to the field to find out where the armies are positioned and to come hastily back and report to him. Pindarus he sends to the nearby hill to report the progress of Titinius. Then he sighs that this is his birthday and time has run out for him. He presages his own end on the day of his birth. Just then Pindarus reports alarmingly that Titinius has been surrounded and that he is forced to dismount and is taken prisoner. Cassius bewails his friend's capture, berating himself for living long enough to witness it. He calls Pindarus, reminds him of the promise he made Pindarus swear when Cassius saved his life; that he would do whatsoever he asked of Pindarus whenever he should ask it. He says that he will make Pindarus a freeman and that he is to fulfil his oath. He orders him to hold his (Cassius's) sword while Cassius runs upon it. As this is done, Cassius, in his dying breath says, "Caesar, thou art reveng'd, even with the sword that kill'd thee." Pindarus, left alone, regrets the deed that he was forced to do, and says that he will now flee Rome and Romans forever.

Act V, Scene IV : In the field, Brutus and his men enter. Brutus exhorts his men to "hold up your heads." He exits. Cato proclaims his name and defies the enemy with drawn sword, Lucilius does likewise but pretends he is Brutus, saying, "I am Brutus, Marcus Brutus I." This is evidently a ruse to spare Brutus who would be sought as the chief prize by the enemy. As he calls out he sees Cato slain and he rushes into the fight. The soldiers ask him to yield since they are ordered not to kill Brutus but to capture him alive. Lucilius is taken before Antony. The soldier calls out "Brutus is taken, Brutus is ta'en." When Antony asks where is he, Lucilius discloses that Brutus is safe and that no enemy will take him alive. Antony explains to the soldiers that they have taken a good prize but not Brutus. However, he would rather have such men as Lucilius as his friends than as his enemies. He sends the soldiers to scout the combat and report to Octavius the doings of the day.

Act V, Scene V : Brutus and a group of friends come in. As they talk of who is taken or slain, Brutus, resigned to what will be, says "Slaying is the word" and then in turn approaches each of the friends, whispering to each. From their replies, it is evident Brutus is asking each to kill him (hold the sword while he runs on it). Each refuses in turn. To Volumnius he says, before he makes his request, that the ghost of Caesar has appeared to him twice already and he knows therefore that his hour has come. On this basis he asks Volumnius to hold the sword for him, but he refuses. Volumnius says that it is not an office for a friend. Then Brutus turns to Strato, who has been asleep all this while, and says farewell to him. He rejoices that all the friends he has made have been true to him. The alarum sounds to fly, the enemy is near and they all exit. Brutus pleads with Strato to stay with him and do the deed which he had asked of others. Strato agrees and shakes his hand first as they say farewell. Before he dies, Brutus addresses Caesar's ghost :

> Caesar now be still.
> I kill'd not thee with half so good a will.

He kills himself on the sword Strato holds for him.

*

PART II

NOTES

Act I — Scene I

1. *Hence* : go away from here.

3. Mechanical : being artisans.

Ought not walk : ought not to walk.

4. *A labouring day* : a working day. 'Labouring' is here used not as a participle but as a verbal noun.

The sign : *viz.*, the tools or working clothes of their profession. Since it was not a holiday they should not have been without them.

5. *Thou* : an expression used as a mark of contempt by a master for his servant.

8. *What dost thou ... on?* : what did they mean by being in the streets with their best holiday clothes on when it was not a holiday?

10. *In respect of* : in comparison with.

11. *cobbler* : The pun is on (1) 'shoe-mender', (2) 'bungler', 'botcher'.

12. *directly* : straightforwardly, without quibbling.

14. *soles* : a quibble on *soul* and *sole*. of *Merchant* of Venice, Act IV, Scene I, ii, 123.

"Not on thy *sole,* but on thy *soul,* harsh Jew."

15. *What trade ... trade?* : Many editors give this speech to Marullus on the grounds that Flavius is the more conciliatory of the two.

naughty : worthless, good-for-nothing.

16. *be not out with me* : be not angry with me.

16-17. *if you be out ... mend you* : The quibble is continued —

(1) If you are out (*i.e.*, angry with me), I can mend (correct) you.
(2) If you are out at the heels, I can mend your shoes (*i.e.*, I am

a cobbler by profession and can mend your shoes when they are rotten).

18. *Mend me ... saucy fellow?* : the tribune does not understand that the cobbler is referring to mending his shoes, he thinks he is behaving impudently towards him.

19. *cobble you* : mend your shoes. This makes clear to Marullus the cobbler's trade which is still in doubt for him owing to the punning in lines 10 -17.

21. *awl* : tool for piercing leather.

21-23. *Truly, sir ... old shoe* : The cobbler is continuing his punning with the play on 'awl' and 'all', and also on 'meddle' meaning 'to interfere' and 'to have sexual relations'.

24. *recover* : a pun on (1) re-sole *i.e.* to cover again, (2) 'restore to health'.

25. *neat's leather* : cattle hide.

As proper men . . . neat's leather : a proverbial expression meaning 'as fine men as ever walked in shoes'.

26. *handiwork* : workmanship.

27. *Wherefore art not* : wherefore art thou not. The omission of the pronoun thus shows the speaker's impatience.

30. *to see Caesar* : with the introduction of Caesar's name the fooling comes to an end, and the play begins in all seriousness.

31. *triumph* : This was a procession celebrating a military victory. Caesar defeated Gnaeus and Sextus, the sons of Pompey the Great, at Munda in Spain on 17 March, 45 B C; and his triumph took place at the beginning of October the same year.

32. *What conquest . . . home*? : Referring to Caesar Marullus asks if Caesar has added new territories to Roman Empire, if not, he was not entitled to a triumph.

33. *tributaries* : conquered peoples forced to pay tax.

34. *grace* : pay honour to.

captive bonds : fetters.

35. *blocks* : conveys the sense of stupidity.

stones : unfeeling nature.

senseless : without feelings.

The whole line suggests that the citizens lacked feeling and were stupid to rejoice at Caesar's success over his countrymen.

37. *Pompey* : Pompey (106-48 B.C.) was, like Caesar, an immensely popular general. He was one of the First Triumvirate with Caesar and Crassus. He cemented the alliance by marriage with Caesar's daughter, Julia. But Caesar made himself immensely more powerful and wealthy by his campaigning in Europe. Pompey stayed in Rome and proved a rather ineffective ruler. So fearful were the Senate of Caesar's power that they forbade him to return to Rome unless he renounced his office of Consul. He agreed as long as Pompey did the same. Pompey refused. Caesar entered Rome and became Dictator three months later. Pompey fled Rome and was finally murdered. *Julius Caesar* opens just after Caesar has wiped out a final pocket of resistance headed by Pompey's sons.

42. *pass the streets* : pass through the streets.

45. *Tiber* : the river on which the city of Rome stands. In Latin, the river is spoken of as a male, but Shakespeare treats it as a female river; hence 'her'.

46. *replication* : echo, reverberation.

47. *concave shores* : hollowed-out or overhanging banks (which create an echo).

48. *cull out a holiday* : pick out a working day and turn it into a holiday. The verb was probably suggested by association with 'flowers' in line 50, which idea Shakespeare took from Plutarch's remark 'there were some that cast flowers . . . as they commonly use to do unto any man when he hath obtained victory' (*Caesar*, p. 52).

51. *Pompey's blood* : Pompey's kindred, *i.e.*, his sons. The blood that has been shed is implied as well.

52. *intermit* : prevent.

55. *light* : fall.

57. *sort* : rank or station.

59.60. *till the . . . shores of all* : so that the river level even at its lowest ebb may rise to the highest banks.

61. *basest mettle* : lowly spirit (with word-play on metal) mettle, Lead is the basest metal, inert but malleable.

63. *Capitol* : The Capitol was the walled part of Ancient Rome.

64. *Disrobe the images* : pull decorations off the statues.

65. *ceremonies* : symbols of rule.

67. *the feast of Lupercal* : was originally a farming festival held on 15 February to ward wolves off the newborn lambs and kids in the flocks. Later it was adopted by the city of Rome to ward off evil spirits. Young men, dressed only in a girdle of goat skins, 'beat the bounds' of the city. Goat skin was chosen because billy goats are sexually potent and able to fight off the wolves. Just as the billy goats brought fertility to the flocks, so barren women believed the flick of a goat skin flail would enable them to have children.

68. *images* : statues.

69. *Caesar's trophies* : signs of victory on the part of Caesar; the reference is to the scarfs and chaplets with which the statues of Caesar were decorated for the occasion.

70. *the vulgar* : the common people.

73. *pitch* : a term in falcorny meaning the highest flight of the hawk.

72-73. *These growing feathers . . . pitch* : the new honours conferred on Caesar are compared to the feathers of the hawk. Flavius sees their actions as stripping Caesar of some of his power, even as a falcon with plucked wings would have a lower 'pitch', which is the height soared to before diving.

74. *above the view of men* : beyond human sights — like the gods.

Act I — Scene II

Antony for the course : As a priest of Lupercus, Antony, who was at this time consul with Caesar, took part in the Lupercalia race in which it was customary for Roman nobles and magistrates to take part. The runners ran naked through the streets striking in sport those whom they met with leathern thongs, which were strips of skins of goats sacrificed at the feast of Lupercalia.

3. *directly* : immediately, so that you may not be missed by him when he runs.

4. *course* : race.

6-9. *Forget not . . . curse* : Plutarch makes no mention of Calpurnia's sterility; but states the general Roman belief : "And many noblewomen and gentlewomen also go out of purpose to stand in their way, and do put forth their hands to be stricken with the ferula; persuading themselves that, being with child, they shall have good delivery, and also, being barren, that it will make them to conceive with child.''

11. *Set on* : proceed.

ceremony : pay scrupulous attention to all the details of the ceremony. Note the superstitious character of Caesar.

15. *press* : crowd.

17. *Caesar is turn'd to hear* : Caesar is deaf in one ear. In his arrogance he speaks of himself in the third person.

18. *Beware the Ides of March* : The 'ides' means the half-way point in the month; in March, the 15th. There was a certain soothsayer that had given Caesar warning long time afore, to take heed of the day of the Ides of March . . . for on that day he should be in great danger (Plutarch's *Caesar,* pp. 87-88).

Sonnet : formal, stately music played on wooden cornetts.

25. *the order of the course* : how the race goes.

28. *not gamesome* : not fond of sports or games.

29. *quick spirit* : lively temperament.

30-31. *I have not . . . wont to have* : Plutarch mentions an estrangement between Brutus and Cassius which arose from Caesar's granting to Brutus the praetorship, for which Cassius was the rival claimant. Shakespeare makes Brutus's private worries the reason for his apparent coolness.

33. *gentleness* : well-bred courtesy.

34. *show* : manifestation.

wont : accustomed.

35. *too strange a hand* : The metaphor is from horsemanship.

strange : hostile, estranged.

36. *Be not deceiv'd* : do not misunderstand me.

36-8. *if I have veil'd . . . upon myself* : if my face has been clouded, I myself am the man on whom my frowns have been turned.

38 *merely* : solely, entirely.

39. *passions of some difference* : This is the crux of Brutus's

dilemma : the tension between his affection for Caesar and his own political ideas.

40. *Conceptions* : thoughts.

41. *soil* : discredit.

44. *construe* : interpret.

Nor construe . . . neglect : do not make anything more of my neglect of you.

47. *passion* : feelings.

48. *By means whereof* : on account of which.

49. *worthy cogitations* : important thoughts.

53. *just* : true.

55. *turn* : reflect.

57. *shadow* : reflection, image.

58. *of the best respect* : held in the highest esteem.

59. *immortal Caesar* : Cassius's first mention of Caesar, as an immortal exalted high above those of the highest repute in Rome, is bitterly ironical.

60. *this age's yoke* : tyranny.

61. *had his eyes* : There are two possible meanings here :

(1) 'were using his eyes properly' (to see Caesar's tyranny),

(2) 'had the speaker's eyes' (saw Caesar as the speaker did).

63. *seek into myself* : search my heart for something which I know I do not possess.

65. *Therefore* : so far as that is concerned.

68. *modestly* : without any exaggeration.

70. *jealous on* : suspicious of.

71. *a common laughter* : someone who tries to amuse everybody.

did use : were accustomed.

72. *stale* : devalue.

72-73. *To state . . . protester* : to devalue my affection to every new acquaintance who makes a declaration of friendship for me, by using commonplace oaths. There is perhaps the sense of 'tavern oaths' in the use of 'ordinary'.

75. *after scandal them* : later defame him.

76. *profess myself* : declare friendship.
in banqueting : under the influence of wine.

77. *all the rout* : the whole common herd.
Hold me : consider me.

84. *If it be aught* : put honour and honour in front of me.
towards the general good : tending to the welfare of the Roman people.

86. indifferently : with supreme unconcern.

87. *let the gods so speed* : so help me heaven.

90. *outward favour* : external appearance.

91. *Well, honour is the subject of my story* : Cassius seizes upon Brutus's use of the word 'honour' and takes it to mean 'reputation', 'status in the city'.

94. *as lief* : rather.

95. *such as thing as I myself* : Caesar, a man, like himself.

100. *chafing with her shores* : reging at them for their restraint.

104. *accoutred* : dressed.

106. *buffet it* : beat it back with arms.

107. *lusty* : stout.

108. *hearts of controversy* : with courage that opposed and contended with violence of the stream, and also with one another.

109. *arrive* : land at.

111. *AEneas, our great ancestor* : According to Virgil's *Aeneid, II.* 721ff., AEneas was a Trojan Prince, the son of Anchises and Approdite. When the city of Troy was burnt by the Greeks, AEneas carried away his father Anchises on his shoulders and saved him from the fire. Tradition has it that AEneas settled in Rome and was the first ancestor of the Romans.

116. *bend his body* : bow.

118. *a fever* : This is based on Plutarch's account of Caesar's health: 'he was lean, white, and soft skinned, and often subject to the falling sickness (which took him the first time, as it is reported, in Corduba, a city of Spain)' (*Caesar,* p. 37).

121. *His coward lips . . . fly* : his lips became pale from fever and exhaustion. Warburton points that there is an allusion to a

coward flying from his colours or deserting the standard of his regiment in a crisis.

122. *bend* : look, glance.

123. *his* : its.

125. *books* : writing tablets.

126. *Titinius* : Plutarch mentions Titinius as "one of cassius's chiefest friends", as he is shown to be in IV. ii. and V. iii.

127. *amaze* : stupefy.

128. *temper* : constitution, temperament.

129. *get the start of* : outpace, outstrip, a metaphor from racing.

130. *bear the palm* : carry the victory's trophy.

133. *the narrow world* : the world which to others appeared so majestic seemed to Caesar in his far-reaching ambition as too small.

134. *Colossus* : a huge statue of a god, said to have bestrode the harbour entrance at Rhodes.

135. *peep about* : sneak about, without the courage to walk fearlessly.

136. *dishonourable graves* : "Caesar's supremacy has closed every career of honourable ambition. There is nothing for us to seek except our own graves; and even those will be dishonourable, for they will be the graves of freemen" (Kittredge).

137. *are masters of their fates* : can overrule their destinies.

138. *our stars* : A reference is to the basic assumption, on which the science of astronomy was built, that a man's constitution and conduct are determined by the relative positions of the planets at his birth.

139. *underlings* : inferiors; subordinates holding a mean position.

140. *what should be* : what can there be.

141. *be sounded more* : be more resounding in fame.

144. Weigh them : count their letters or syllables.

conjure with 'em : use the names as words of power to summon up spirit.

145. *start* : raise up.

147. *Upon what meat* : Cassius is searching for something which will explain Caesar's phenomenal greatness. *Meat* is used figuratively.

148. *Age* : Not only the Romans as individuals are of no account but the very age in which they lived or their generation has been disgraced.

149. *the breed* : the art of breeding

bloods : men of spirit.

150. *great flood* : The reference is here to the great flood described in classical mythology as having taken place in the time of Deucalion. It was caused by Jupiter in consequence of men's impiety. Deucalion and his wife Pyrrha escaped to the tip of Mt. Parnassus and by the advice of the oracle, repaired the loss of mankind by throwing behind them the bones of their grandmother. Cassius, true to his race, speaks of the classical deluge.

151. *fam'd with* : celebrated for.

153. *walks* : While 'wide' appears to justify the Folio reading 'walkes', it can also mean 'extensive, extending over a large space or region'.

154. *Now is it Rome indeed* : Rome is to-day quite a large and spacious city as it used to be of old.

Room : space.

Room enough : enough of space which might be occupied by others only if these were worth the name of men. Note the pun on 'Rome' and 'room'. It was a favourite device of Shakespeare to introduce light puns in the midst of the most serious passages; the light humour only intensifies the seriousness of the significance.

155. *one only man* : that is, Caesar; while men of importance like Brutus and Cassius are not counted as men beside the personality of Caesar.

157. *a Brutus once* : Lucius Junius Brutus played a leading part in the expulsion of the Tarquins from Rome and he and Tarquinius Collatinus became the first consuls. Plutarch tells us that Marcus Brutus claimed descent from this Brutus.

brook'd : endured, tolerated.

158. *eternal* : here used to express extreme abhorrence, probably by confusion with 'infernal'; or perhaps the connotation is 'eternally dammed'.

to keep his state : to maintain his court.

160. *nothing jealous* : not at all doubtful.

161. *aim* : conjecture.
work : persuade.

163. *present* : moment.

164. *so with . . . entreat you* : if I may ask you as a friend.

165. *mov'd* : urged.

168. *meet* : suitable, fitting, appropriate.
high things : important affairs.

169. *chew upon* : ponder, consider.

172. *these* : such.

175. *show/Of fire* : demonstration of faith. Metaphor from flint.
Train : attendents.

177. *pluck Casca by the sleeve* : This is an anachronism; togas had no sleeves.

179. *worthy note* : worthy of notice.

183. *Cicero* : Cicero (106-43 B.C.) was the leading Roman orator of his day. His writings were intensely studied in Elizabethan schools. His style was held up as the ideal model for all students. His essays, letters and imaginary conversations between well-known historical figures popularised and simplified the ideas of the Greek philosophers, presenting them in a style that was pleasurable and easy to read. Through him, the ideas of the Ancient World became familiar to the people of Renaissance Europe in Shakespeare's time.

184. *ferret* : A ferret's eyes are red. Cicero's eyes are bloodshot in his fiery resentment.

186. *conference* : debate, argument.
cross'd : opposed.

190. *Sleek-headed* : in Plutarch, Caesar says : "As for those fat men, and smooth-combed heads, I never reckon of them; but these pale-visaged and carrion-bone people, I feare them most."

191. *has a lean . . . look* : has a slender and haggard look.

192. *He thinks too much* : *i.e.*, Cassius thinks too much over the state of affairs in Rome which he will try to set aright and hence naturally Caesar fears him.

194. *well given* : well-disposed, friendly.

196. *my name* : I who am renowned throughout the world as Caesar.

199. *looks . . . men* : can pierce through the thoughts of men.

200-01. *He loves . . . Antony* : According to Plutarch, Antony, 'himself passed away the time in hearing of foolish plays' (*Antonius*, p. 183).

201. *he hears no music* : There lies behind this idea the Platonic belief that the man in whose nature the elements are harmoniously blended loves music naturally; on the contrary

> "The man that hath no music in himself,
> Nor is not moved with concord of sweet sounds,
> Is fit for treasons, stratagems, and spoils."
>
> (*The Merchant of Venice*, V. i. 83-5)

202. *sort* : manner.

203-4. *As if . . . any thing* : "as if he scorned himself for being weak enough to give way to so childish an emotion" (Deighton).

206. *Whiles* : so long as.

209. *always I am Caesar* : Plutarch tells how Cornelius Balbus prevented Caesar from rising before the senate : "What, do you not remember that you are Caesar, and will you not let them reverence you, and do their duties?" In this line "The real man Caesar disappears for himself under the greatness of the Caesar myth. He forgets himself as he actually is and knows only the vast legendary power named Caesar" (Dowden).

210. *this ear is deaf* : Plutarch says nothing of this deafness. This physical deafness is a 'symbol of that obstinacy which is deaf to all warnings; it does not wish to hear'.

214. *sad:* serious, perhaps even sullen.

217. *there was a crown offered him* : Plutarch gives two accounts of Antony's offering Caesar the crown in his *Caesar* (p. 83) and in *Antonius* (pp. 186-7); it is the latter that Shakespeare follows the more closely in Casca's narration in this scene. Crown, in Plutarch, was "laurel crown . . . having a royal band or diadem wreathed about it".

218. *put it by* : thrust it aside.

225. *marry* : by the Virgin Mary (an oath).

226. *gentler than others* : less violently than on the previous occasion (hence more reluctantly).

honest : worthy (said sarcastically).

230. *gentle Casca* : Contrast 1.292, "What a blunt fellow is this grown to be?" And indeed Casca's bluntness is his most striking quality in this dialogue, though one may contrast with it his apparent obsequiousness in Caesar's presence at the beginning of the scene.

236. *fain* : willingly.

238. *to lay his fingers off it* : to take away his fingers from it. Casca's meaning is unmistakable. Caesar was half-inclined to accept the crown and half-reluctant. Such infirmity of purpose is contrary to what one knows about the historical Caesar.

240. *still* : each time.

The rabblement : *rabblement* is contemptuous expression for 'rabble' or mob.

241. *chopt* : roughened by manual labour, chapped.

240-41 *The rabblement. . . hands.* Paul Satpfer, French critic, points out that 'if Caesar had been bold enough to set the crown upon his head, the same rabble that applauded his respect for law would have been equally ready to applaud his violation of it.'

245. *swounded* : fainted.

248. *soft* : slowly.

what, did Caesar swound? : Not that Cassius is ever anxious to find out indications of human weakness in Caesar.

249. *the market-place* : The Roman Forum where public business was transacted and public affairs discussed.

251. *like; he* : The Folio text has no stop between these two words and consequently implies that Brutus is uncertain that Caesar is epileptic. This is untenable in view of the fact that the two men were close friends, and that Caesar's illness was common knowledge in Rome.

like : likely.

the falling sickness : epilepsy, so called because a person afflicted with it falls down in a fit. In Rome the malady was regarded to be of an ominous nature. Public assemblies were dissolved if any one present had an epileptic fit. A critic, in Caesar's fit of epilepsy, sees those "portentous things that point with fatal finger to the Ides of March and the costly blood that is then to be shed".

252-53. *No, Caesar . . . falling-sickness* : Cassius deliberately misunderstands Brutus's term, and takes it to mean that they have fallen under Casca's sway — that is, that they are bondmen.

255. *the tag-rag people* : the rabble.

262. *pluck'd . . . doublet* : After Caesar had offended the senate, Plutarch reports that 'Caesar . . . departed home to his house, and tearing open his doublet collar, making his neck bare, he cried aloud to his friends that his throat was ready to offer to any man that would come and cut it' (*Caesar,* p.81).

doublet : Elizabethan jacket. Shakespeare writes as if the Romans dressed like the Elizabethans.

pluck'd me ope : opened.

263. *And* : if.

a man of any occupation : This could mean either (1) 'a tradesman' (to whom the offer was made), or (2) 'a man of action'.

264. *at a word* : at his word.

268. *to think it was his infirmity* : to attribute it to his disease, *i.e.,* the falling-sickness.

271-72. *Caesar had stabb'd their mothers* : A bawdy joke is probably intended here.

272. *they . . . less* : If Caesar had killed their mothers they would have been just as ready to forgive him, on account of their regard for him, as they did now.

273. *sad* : serious.

276. *he spoke Greek* : Cicero was a Greek scholar and had studied the language at Athens. He was also very fond of Greek and Greek literature. "Cecero's recorded witticisms were many of them made in Greek; and on such an occasion he would no doubt have had a Greek quotation ready" (Wright).

278-79 *and I tell . . . face again* : nothing will persuade me to tell you, for I could not do so without telling a lie. And if I lied I shall feel ashamed.

281. *it was Greek to me* : it was unintelligible to me. This is a lie, for Casca did know Greek.

281-3. *I could tell . . . to silence* : In Plutarch the laurel crown offered by Antony 'was afterwards put upon the head of one of Caesar's statues or images, the which one of the Tribunes plucked off .... Howbeit Caesar did turn them out of their offices for it' *(Antonius, p. 187; also Caesar, pp. 83-4).*

put to silence : deprived of their office of tribuneship.

286. *am promised forth* : have promised to dine elsewhere.

287. *dine* : lunch.

288. *hold* : does not change.

292. *blunt* : abrupt, unpolished in manner.

294-5. *So is...enterprise,* : Cassius deliberately mistakes Brutus's meaning and takes 'mettle' to mean 'courage'.

296. *However* : in spite of the fact that.

tardy form : slow outward appearance.

297. *rudeness* : rough manner.

rudeness....wit : "the roughness of manner is but something which gives additional zest, piquancy to his caustic wit."

298. *stomach* : inclination.

disgest : digest.

304. *think of the world* : think over the state of things in which we live, the world : condition of affairs. World might also mean Rome, then the meaning would be, think what you owe to Rome, and what your duty to her is.

306. *honourable mettle* : noble personality.

306-7. *wrought . . . dispos'd* : may be turned from its present nature. The metaphor comes from alchemy and is based on the 'mettle/ metal' quibble.

'Noble' metals (like gold) could not be 'wrought'.

307. *meet* : appropriate.

309. *seduc'd?* : led astray.

310. *bear me hard* : has a grudge against me, bears me ill-will.

311-12. *If I were...humour me* : Warburton explains the lines — "If I were Brutus and Brutus Cassius, he should not cajole me as I do him'. Verity speaks to the same effect —'Cassius sees that his words have had some effect in stirring Brutus against Caesar; he knows that Caesar is the friend of Brutus; and he wonders that Brutus should suffer himself to be influenced against his friend. Cassius regards things from a personal standpoint; personal friendship or enmity is a sufficient motive with him, whereas Brutus would not allow personal feelings either for or against Caesar to affect him, if he thought that the good of Rome required of him some service.''

313. *in several hands* : in different kinds of handwriting.

his : Brutus.

315. *tending to . . . opinion* : concerning the great respect.

316. *obscurely* : indirectly.

317. *glanced at* : alluded to.

318. *seat him sure* : seat himself firmly.

319. *worse days endure* : have to put up with even greater tyranny in the future; or possibly, as Macmillan suggests, ''because, as was generally recognized, the failure of a plot against a tyrant made his rule more tyrannical.''

305-317 *Well, Brutus . . . glanced at.* : 'This speech of Cassius puts him in a lower light than the rest of the play, almost among villains like Iago or Richard III.' MacCallum points out : ''Probably Cassius is making the worst of his own case and is indulging that vein of self-mockery and scorn that Caesar observed in him.''

Act I — Scene III

1. *brought* : did you accompany?

3. *all the sway of earth* : the whole realm of earth shakes like something unsteady.

5. *scolding* : rough; boisterous.

6. *riv'd* : split.

knotty oaks : gnarled and therefore very tough oaks.

7. *ambitious ocean* : The ocean is ambitious in the sense that it is emulating the cloud in the sky, *i.e.*, trying to rise as high as the clouds.

8. *exalted with* : ranked as high as.

10. *tempest dropping fire* : "not an ordinary tempest showering down rain, slit etc. but one showering down fire" (Deighton).

11. *a civil strife in heaven* : "a strife in which the different powers and forces of heaven were at variance with each other, as the different powers and forces of a nation are at variance in civil war."

12. *saucy* : insolent; impudent.

14. *any thing more wonderful* : Craik suggests, "anything more that was awe-inspiring"; but more probably, "anything that was more awe-inspiring', since Cicero does not seem discomposed by the storm that Casca describes.

15. common slave : Dr. Macmillan comments : The wonderful character of the portent was increased by the fact that it was manifested by an ordinary slave, not a mysterious stranger, but a man whom Cicero himself happened to know by sight.

18. *not sensible of fire* : not sensitive to the fire.

19. *I ha' . . . sword* : drawn no doubt in self-defence, which he was still holding in his hand.

21. *glaz'd* : "gazed fixedly, stared".

surly : with a grim or sullen countenance.

22. *annoying* : harming

23. *drawn upon a heap* : crowded together.

26. *bird of night* : the screech-owl, like a raven a bird of ill omen.

27. *Even at noon-day* : the appearance of the owl in broad daylight would be regarded as specially ominous.

market-place : the Forum.

28. *prodigies* : wondrous sights (regarded as omens of the future).

29. *conjointly meet* : happen together. The sense is that if a single 'prodigy' had been seen nothing much might have been thought of. So many happening together must indicate something terrible.

30. *These are . . . natural* : such and such are their reasons; they are merely natural phenomena.

31. *portentous* : ominous.

32. *climate* : region,

33. *strange-disposed* : abnormally upset.

34. *construe* : interpret.

after their fashion : in their own way.

35. *Clean from* : entirely contrary to.

purpose : meaning.

43. *honest men* : men of honour, *viz.*, those who are opposed to tyranny. They are pleased because such a stormy and wild night is a sign to them that the gods are with them.

44. *menance* : threaten.

48. *this unbraced* : with doublet undone.

49. *thunder-stone* : thunderbolt.

50. *cross* : forked, zig-zag.

52. *Even in the aim* : at the very spot at which it was aimed.

53. *tempt* : try, *i.e.*, take liberties with.

54. *part* : proper action.

56. *astonish* : stun, dismay.

57. *dull* : *obtuse,* stupid.

58. *want* : lack.

60. *put on* : manifest.

in wonder : into a state of wonder.

61. *To see* : at seeing.

strange . . . heavens : which can no longer tolerate the present state of things.

64. *from quality and kind* : depart from their true natures.

65. *Why old . . . children* : This line has been explained in two ways: (1) according to proverb lore : these three classes of people have the power of prophecy, (2) that there are so many portents that fools, dotards, and children are able to interpret them. In view of the context, the latter is the more plausible.

fools : natural fools, born idiots.

calculate : prophecy.

66. *ordinance* : usual behaviour as ordained by nature.

67. *pre-formed faculties* : ''faculties intended by original design for certain, special ends'' (Wright).

69. *infus'd . . . spirits* : "deprived them of their natural dispositions and substituted for them others strangely at variance; all designed to awaken inquiry and compel thought."

71. *monstrous* : unnatural, abnormal state of affairs.

75. *the lion in the Capitol* : It is not known if lion were kept in the Capitol, but they were kept in the Tower of London, which may well have represented the Capitol to Shakespeare and his audience.

Hunter paraphrases the lines as follows : "He is like a man that fulminates and flashes, and causes spirits of the dead to arise from their graves, and makes his voice to resound in the Capitol, as if he were a lion roaring."

77. *prodigious* : "portentous in the power which he has engrossed in himself and which indicates some evil about to befall the State" (Deighton).

78. *eruptions* : freaks of nature.

81. *thews* : muscles.

82. *woe the while* ! : alas for the present time.

83. *with* : by.

84. *yoke* : bondage, slavery.

sufferance : long suffering.

88. *save here in Italy* : this exclusion was to conciliate the prejudice of the Roman people against the title of king.

Caesar before the date of his assassination was preparing for a campaign in the East to conquer Parthia, which it was said in the Syballine books would never be conquered save by a king. It was to overcome this difficulty that the senate was prepared to bestow on Caesar the modified title of King.

89. *I know . . . dagger then* : The mere suggestion of a king of Rome rouses all the republican spirit of Cassius. He says submission to Caesar as king of Rome is out of question. Rather than submit to him he will sheath his dagger in his own breast, and thus commit suicide.

91. *Therein* : in the ability to commit suicide.

95. *Can be . . . spirit* : can imprison the resolute spirit.

97. *dismiss itself* : free itself by suicide.

98. *know all the world besides* : let everyone else know.

102. *cancel* : a legal term, meaning to annul a deed or bond.

104. *Poor man*! : ah, you thoughtless, spiritless Casca !

105. *But that he sees* : if he does not see.

106. *hinds* : deer. There is a play on the word 'hinds' which also means 'serfs'.

108. *trash* : it is used here in the original sense of "clippings of trees or (yet more exactly) the bits of broken sticks found under trees in a wood and collected for firewood" (Skeat).

109. *offal* : refuse, wood chips.

rubbish : litter (such as results from the decay or repair of buildings).

110. *matter* : material.

110-11. *to illuminate...Caesar* : 'Rome has voluntarily immolated herself for Caesar's glorification.' The image before the speaker's mind is that of the city on fire. Perhaps an unconscious reference to a later Caesar, Nero, who fiddled and enjoyed the beautiful effects of the conflagration when Rome burned.

111. *vile* : valueless.

O grief : Cassius fears that he has overshot himself and he may be denounced for treason by Casca.

113. *bondman* : slave.

114. *My answer . . . made* : I shall be made to account for my speech.

I am arm'd : for he can fall back on suicide.

117. *fleering* : sneering.

my hand : here is my hand on it.

118. *be factious for redress* : make a group of conspirators set things right.

119-20. *And I . . . furthest* : I will not lag behind any one who may go farthest in his efforts to redress these grievances.

123. *undergo* : undertake.

124. *Of...consequence* : the result of which though honourable would be dangerous.

125. *by this* : by this time.

stay : wait.

126. *Pompey's porch* : The portico of the theatre built by Pompey in 55 B.C. Plutarch makes this the scene of Caesar's assassination, which Shakespeare places in the Capitol.

128. *complexion of the element* : the visible aspect of the skies. Both of these terms are alchemical in origin.

129. *In favour's like* : in appearance is like. The wildness of the elements seems in Cassius's eyes to justify the violence of the deed they were contemplating.

131. *stand close* : keep concealed and make no noise.

132. *gait* : footsteps.

134. *Metellus Cimber* : Thus in Plutacrh's *Julius Caesar;* in the *Brutus* he is called Tullius Cimber. His proper name was L. *Tillius Cimber.* He had been a friend of Caesar, but joined the conspiracy against him.

135-6. *incorporate to* : bound up with, united with.

137. *I am glad on 't* : glad to hear that Casca has joined the conspiracy.

142. *Be you content* : set your mind at rest.

143. *praetor's chair* : the chair of the Chief Roman magistrate.

144. *Where . . . it* : where only Brutus may find it.

146. *old Brutus* : his ancestor, Junius Brutus.

145-6. *set this . . . Brutus's statue* : The practice of affixing scrolls to statues was an Elizabethan one.

148. *Decius Brutus* : His real name was Decimus. Shakespeare uses North's form of the name.

150. *hie* : hasten.

151. *bestow* : distribute.

152. *repair* : return.

156. *the next encounter* : which occurs in the following scene.

yield him ours : joins our faction.

159. *alchemy* : study of chemistry as a magical science, seeking to turn base metal into gold.

His countenance . . . alchemy : Casca sees Brutus's support in terms of alchemical practice, the aim of which was to turn base metals into gold. It is a finely appropriate image for one of the central ideas of the play, especially as alchemy had never succeeded in working the miracle.

162. *conceited* : The pun is on (1) 'understood', (2) 'expressed in metaphorical language'.

Act II — Scene I

2. *the progress of the stars* : the position which the stars have arrived at in their movement across the sky.

5. *When . . . What* : Both words were often used as exclamations of impatience.

7. *taper* : candle.

11. *spurn at* : kick against.

12. *general* : common good (general cause, as opposed to personal).

13. *there's the question* : the point at issue.

14. *bright day . . . adder* : 'The coronation of Caesar will hatch the adder, and give Caesar sting : as the bright day makes a dangerous snake from a harmless egg.'

15. *craves* : demands.

wary walking : one must walk cautiously.

crown him? — that : Brutus turns over and over the idea of Caesar's coronation in his mind and pauses to consider its full significance.

17. *do danger* : work mischief.

18-19. *Th' abuse . . . power* : greatness is abused when intoxicated with power it results in drying up human feelings which prompt people to kind action.

Remorse : pity or compassion.

20-21. *When his affections . . . reason* : when he acted under the influence of his emotions rather than his judgment.

21. *a common proof* : a matter of common knowledge.

22. *lowliness* : being respectful and pleasant to everybody.

That lowliness . . . ladder : that the affection of humility is the means by which the ambitious man rises.

24. *upmost round* : highest rung.

26. *base degrees* : This refers to both the lower steps of the ladder and, by transference, the means employed in the early stages of his career; the pun is on 'base'.

28. *prevent* : anticipate him; that is, he must never wear the crown.

28-9. *since the quarrel...thing he is* : Since the accusation has no validity considering what Caesar is at this moment.

bear no colour for : is not convincing.

30. *Fashion it thus* : let us put the case in this way.

augmented : when he has become king.

31. *these and these extremities* : such and such extremes of severity, or tyranny.

33. *as his kind* : after the manner of his species.

34. *in his shell* : "before his power for mischief is developed."

35. *closet* : study.

36. *flint* : flint with which to light the taper.

44. *exhalations* : meteors. The sun was thought to produce meteors by drawing up vapours from the earth.

whizzing : rushing along with a hissing noise.

51. *piece it out* : complete the sense.

52. *under one man's awe* : in awe of one man.

What, Rome ? : He recalls Rome's glorious history, and the flames of those who sacrificed their lives for its sake.

53. *my ancestors* : Junius Brutus, who drove out the Tarquin from Rome.

54. *Tarquin* : The Tarquins were the last kings of Rome, tyrants driven out by Junius Brutus in 509 B.C. The Roman Republic then began.

56. *I make thee promise* : I promise thee. This seems to be the moment at which Brutus makes up his mind that there is no alternative to Caesar's death.

58. *Thy full petition* : Brutus pledges himself to do all that Rome asks of him : speaking, striking, and thus redressing.

59. *fifteen days* : Some editors emend to fourteen. But it is the dawn of the fifteenth day, which Lucius includes in his reckoning.

61. *whet* : instigate.

61-62. *Since Cassius . . . not slept* : These lines suggest a lapse of time between this scene and I. ii. in which Brutus has wrestled with his conscience. The historical time was actually one month; but Shakespeare is telescoping the action for reasons of dramatic pose.

63. *acting* : accomplishment.

64. *the first motion* : the first impulse.

65. *phantasma* : a terrible day-dream; ordinarily the word means an apparition, but to this 'interim' can hardly be likened.

66. *genius and the mortal instruments* : spirit and body.

67-68. *state of . . . kingdom* : The human organism is viewed as corresponding on the personal level with the body politic.

69. *The nature of an insurrection* : somewhat like revolution.

70. *your brother Cassius* : Plutarch notes that Brutus and Cassius 'were allied together. For Cassius had married Junia, Brutus's sister' (*Brutus,* p. 108).

72. *moe* : more.

73. *hats* : Shakespeare was obviously thinking of Elizabethan hats; although the Romans did have various kinds of head-gear.

75. *mark of favour* : distinguishing characteristics.

77. *the faction* : fellow conspirators.

O conspiracy : Brutus shows the better side of his nature which is opposed to secrecy and dissimulation which are invariably found in all conspiracies.

78. *Sham'st thou* : are you ashamed.

79. *evils are most free* : when evil things range most freely.

82. *smiles and affability* : smiles and agreeable manners.

83. *Path* : walk.

thy native semblance on : your true appearance.

84. *Erebus* : in classical mythology, the dark and gloomy route to Hades, the Roman Hell.

85. *prevention* : from being fore-stalled and thwarted.

86. *upon your rest* : in disturbing your sleep.

87. *do we trouble you?* : This is ironical in view of Brutus's mental state prior to the conspirator's entrance.

98. *watchful cares* : worries causing sleeplessness.

100. *Shall I entreat a word?* : May I speak to you a word in private.

104. *fret the clouds* : interlace the clouds as with a fretwork.

fret : cut ornamental patterns into.

107. *growing on* : encroaching on.

108. *Weighing . . . year* : taking into account that the year is still young.

In winter the sun rises to the south of the east, and in summer to north of it. It was now of course March 15, and the winter had not been very long over.

114. *the face of men* : *i.e.,* in the words of Heath : "If that the face of our fellow-citizens which we should never for the future be able to look up to without the most insupportable confusion after having by our treachery defeated an enterprise, on the success of which the preservation of our common liberties and the very existence of the republic absolutely depend... is of weak motives, insufficient to secure our fidelity to our engagements."

115. *sufferance* : suffering, distress.

time's abuse : the present misgovernment.

117. *idle bed* : the bed in which he is idle, a transferred epithet.

118. *high-sighted tyranny* : The reference is to falconry, and Caesar is being viewed as the high-flying bird looking down on the prey. There may also be sense of a tyranny which aims at unlimited power.

range on : continue to wander in search of prey.

119. *by lottery* : fall in obedience to the caprice of a tyrant one by one as chance should decree.

These : motives.

121. *To kindle cowards* : to inspire even the cowards.

122. *melting* : tender.

124. *prick* : spur, incite.

126. *palter* : say one thing and mean another.

127. *honesty to honesty engag'd* : pledges of honour interchanged.

129. *cautelous* : cautious, crafty. "Crafty, wary to a degree approaching treachery."

130. *carrions* : This is a term of contempt; people who are half dead.

133. *even* : uniform, steadfast.

134. *th' insuppressive mettle* : irrepressible nature.

138. *Is guilty . . . bastardy* : guilty of an act that shows it is not pure Roman blood.

several : individual, separate.

141. *sound him* : find out his feelings in this affair.

144. *his silver hairs* : his venerable age. Cicero was at his time 63 years old.

145. *opinion* : reputation.

148. *no whit* : not at all.

150. *break with him* : disclose the matter to him.

158. *a shrewd contriver* : a mischievous plotter.

means : capacity.

159. *improve* : make good use of.

160. *annoy* : harm, injure.

prevent : forestall.

164. *Like wrath . . . afterwards* : we shall be accused of murdering Caesar in a fit of anger, and if we killed his friends also our action will seem malignant and inspired by malice. In other words personal motives will be attributed to us.

Envy : malice.

165. *a limb of Caesar* : a mere dependant, or derivative, of Caesar.

166. *Let's be sacrificers and not butchers* : Brutus points out that in killing Caesar their motives should be as pure as that of a priest who sacrifices a victim at the altar.

167. *spirit of Caesar* : Caesarism, dictatorship.

168. *spirit* : soul.

come by : get possession of.

171. *gentle* : noble.

172. *boldly* : courageously, because there is a sense of duty.

wrathfully : in a spirit of hatred.

173. *carve him* : dress him up.

173. *Let's carve . . . gods,* : let us dress him up as a food acceptable to the god; in other words, let us not murder him in wrath but offer him as a sacrifice to the goddess of liberty.

174. *hew* : cut

Not hew . . . hounds : as a dead body fit to be thrown as food for dogs.

175. *subtle* : crafty.

176. *servants* : emotions, feelings.

175-77. *as subtle masters . . . chide them* : there are some crafty masters who will goad their servants to do some nefarious deeds, and when the deed is done, will chide the doers; so also the hearts of the conspirators will drive their bodily powers to the deed of murder, but when it is done, their hearts will condemn it.

177-78. *This shall . . . envious.* : This will make it evident that our action was necessary, not malicious.

180. *purgers* : healers. The metaphor is taken from a physician who expels impurities from the bodily system to cure his patient.

184. *ingrafted* : deeply-rooted.

186. *all* : all the injury.

187. *take thought* : give way to melancholy.

188. *that were much he should* : would be a great deal for a man like Antony to do. Since Antony was a pleasure-lover Brutus thinks even grieving for Caesar would be difficult for him.

197. *fantasy* : imaginings.

ceremonies : omens, portents.

198. *apparent* : that have been appearing.

200. *augurers* : a group of state officers who decided whether it was lucky or unlucky to undertake business on a particular day. Caesar had been an augurer.

204. *unicorns may be betray'd by trees,* : unicorns are fabulous beasts having one horn. "Unicorns are said to have been taken by one, who running behind a tree, eluded the violent push the animal was making at him, so that his horn spent its force on the trunk and stuck fast, detaining the beast till he was despatched by the hunter" (Steevens).

205. *bears with glasses* : "Bears" adds Steevens, "are reported to have been surprised by means of a mirror, which they would gaze on, affording their pursuers an opportunity of taking the surer aim."

205. *elephants with holes* : elephants are beguiled into pitfalls lightly

covered with hurdles and turf, a bait being placed thereon to tempt them.

206. *toils* : nets

men with flatterers : Even as wild beasts may be betrayed by simple wiles, so may men.

209. *Let me work* : let me manage this.

210. *give his humour the true bent* : turn his disposition in the right direction.

213. *uttermost* : latest.

215. *bear Caesar hard* : feel enmity toward Caesar.

216. *rated* : chided, scolded.

218. *go along by him* : call at his house.

220. *fashion him* : shape him into a conspirator.

224. *merrily* : merry.

225. *Let not...purposes* : let us not by our looks reveal our hidden thoughts.

put on : reveal.

226. *bear it* : carry it off.

226-7. *But bear it . . . constancy* : but, like our Roman actors, carry it off without looking strained and with dignified composure. Actually Roman actors wore masks; Shakespeare is thinking of Elizabethan actors.

230. *honey-heavy dew* : sleep is often compared to dew on account of the softness of its falling on the eyes. ''Honey-heavy'' conveys the idea of soundness and sweetness.

231. *figures* : 'spectres produced by the imagination' (Macmillan).

fantasies : fanciful shapes.

240. *your arms across* : The attitude of one absorbed in melancholy thoughts.

246. *wafture* : waving gesture.

250. *an effect of humour* : a symptom of some momentary mood.

251. *Which...man.* : to which every man at one time or another is liable.

253. *shape* : appearance.

254. *condition* : state of mind.

255. *know you Brutus* : know you for Brutus.

259. *come by* : obtain.

261. *physical* : medically advisable.

262. *unbraced* : with clothes unfastened.

homours : unhealthy moisture.

265. *dare the...night* : "challenge the pestilence vapours that rise from the ground during the night "(Deighton).

266. *tempt* : risk.

rheumy : moist and catarrhal.

unpurged air : air not purified of its dampness by the sun.

268. *sick offence* : trouble which causes sickness.

You have...mind, : the sickness from which you are suffering is not a physical but mental one.

271. *charm* : entreat, conjure.

my once commended beauty : shows a touch of wounded vanity since Portia feels neglected.

commended : praised.

273. *incorporate* : make one body. Shakespeare has in mind the Christian rather than the Roman marriage-service.

275. *heavy* : sorrowful, depressed.

283. *in sort or limitation* : after a fashion or within strict limits.

285-87. *Dwell I...harlot* : This contains an allusion to the fact that in Shakespeare's time, harlots or public women were not allowed to live in the heart of the large cities but only in their suburbs. Hence, says Portia, that if she has no place in the heart of her husband but lives only in its suburbs, ministering to his smaller needs, then she is clearly a harlot and not a true wife.

289. *the ruddy drops* : the drops of red blood.

290. *That visit my sad heart* : According to Elizabethan medical theory, the blood was manufactured by the liver and flowed to the heart where it was purified and pumped round the body. Sadness was believed to drain the heart of blood.

292. *withal* : for all that.

295. *well reputed* : "of high and stainless reputation"

Cato's daughter : Cato is a name for die-hard Republicanism. Cato the Elder, Portia's great great grandfather, was a general and a statesman of exceptional ruthlessness. He opposed all changes because it would destroy the 'simple life' of Ancient Rome. He especially despised the 'easy living' which some Romans brought from Greece. His great grandson, Portia's father, (95-46 B.C.) fought with Pompey against Caesar in the Civil War, where he took his own life rather than be defeated.

297. *Being...husbanded?* : having such a worthy husband.

299. *I have...constancy* : put my powers of resolution to a severe test.

305. *bosom* : the bosom is often spoken of as the receptacle of secrets.

307. *construe* : elucidate, interpret.

308. *charactery of my sad brows* : what is written in my sad brows, *i.e.,* what the furrows of sadness on my brows mean.

311. *Caius Ligarius* : Thus Plutarch. Actually Quintus Ligarius.

313. *Vouchsafe* :deign to accept.

315. *wear a kerchief* : It was a common practice in Elizabethan England for the sick to wear a cloth round the head.

321. *Soul of Rome* : Ligarius is Brutus's great admirer, and thinks that Brutus symbolises all that is best in Rome.

322. *Brave* : noble.

323. *exorcist* : one who conjures up spirits.

325. *things impossible* : obstacles that seem insuperable.

326. *get the better of them* : overcome them.

327. *sickmen* : there is a double meaning in the expression (1) men who are in physical ill-health, (2) men who have been deprived of their liberty.

328. *make sick* : kill.

331. *To whom* : to the dwelling of him to whom.

set on : advance.

332. *new... fir'd* : rekindled (with life and courage).

Act II — Scene II

2-3. *Thrice hath . . . murther Caesar* !" : Plutarch is less specific about Calphurnia's utterance : 'he heard his wife Calpurnia, being fast asleep, weep and sigh and put forth many fumbling lamentable speeches. For she dreamed that Caesar was slain, and that she had him in his arms' (*Caesar*, p. 88).

5. *present* : immediate.

6. *opinions of success* : Caesar wishes for official information as to whether the ides of March would be an auspicious day for him or not. Plutarch suggests that it was only to please his wife that he consulted the priests.

8. *Think you to walk forth* ? : *i.e.*, in spite of the omens and the portents.

10. *Caesar shall forth* : Caesar shall go forth. It is noteworthy that Caesar uses the third person even in talking to his wife.

11. *Ne'er looked . . . back* : never dared to threaten me in the face.

12. *they are vanished* : they will dissolve into nothingness.

13. *stood on ceremonies* : attached importance to omens, or portents.

16. *the watch* : night patrol (watchmen). An anachronism since there was no night guard in Rome till the reign of Augustus.

17. *whelped* : given birth.

18. *yawn'd* : opened.

19. *fight upon the clouds* : a pitched battle is taking place in the sky, not of phantom warriors but real fierce warriors as the dropping of blood and limbs indicates.

20. *right form of war* : in regular battle-order.

21. *drizzled blood* : dropped blood like rain. Note the tragic irony, for it is here that Caesar's blood is soon to be shed.

22. *hurtled* : clattered, clashed.

24. *squeal* : like ghosts, whose voices are like the squealing of rats.

25. *beyond all use* : outside all usual experience.

28. *predictions* : portents (as described by Calphurnia).

29. *Are to . . . Caesar* : these portents are meant for all the people of the world and do not concern Caesar in particular.

31. *blaze forth* : proclaim.

30. *When beggars . . . seen;* : Shakespeare is here referring to "the great comet, which seven nights together was seen very bright after Caesar's death."

32. *die . . . deaths;* : go through all the agonies of death repeatedly before they actually die. This shows Caesar's coolness in the midst of danger.

36. *a necessary end* : an unavoidable end of human life.

37. *when it will come* : when it is the proper time of a man's death.

41. *in shame of* : to put to shame.

44. *Danger* : here personified.

45. *litter'd* : brought forth (used only of animals).

In one day : on the same day.

49. *consum'd in confidence* : destroyed by overconfidence.

56. *for thy humour* : to fall in with your mood, or caprice.

60. *happy time* : favourable time.

67. *Have . . . so far* : Do you think that after I have proved my courage in so many battles I shall now be afraid of the old senators?

Grey beards: a contemptuous term for the senators.

afeard : afraid.

78. *lusty* : stalwart.

pure blood : nothing but blood.

84. *a vision fair and fortunate* : the dream instead of being ominous indicates goods fortune.

85. *in many pipes* : from many sprouts.

88. *Reviving blood* : 'blood which shall renew the strength of Rome.'

89. *tinctures, stains, relics* : Dr. Johnson explained this as an heraldic term meaning a coat of armour, but Malone and Steevens dissent from him and take the word to refer to the custom of dipping handkerchief in the blood of those who were regarded as martyrs. Probably Shakespeare had both meanings in mind. 'Relics' are the memorials of martyrs, supposed to possess virtues. 'Stains' refers to the handkerchief dyed in the blood of martyrs.

89. *cognizance* : a heraldic term meaning a distinguished badge.

96. *it were a mock* : a jest at your own expense.

103. *your proceeding* : variously explained; 'your advancement' (Craik); 'your advantage' (Delius); 'course taken by you' (Schmidt);

your course of conduct, your career' (Wright); Deighton would have the reading 'to your proceeding' meaning my love which proceeds from me to you, the deep affection which I have for you.

104. *And reason . . . liable* : "And if I have acted wrongly in telling you, my excuse is, that my reason where you are concerned is subject to and is overborne by affection" (Craik).

liable : 'subject to' : or, 'accordant with'.

108. *Publius* : Plutarch makes no mention of a conspirator of this name, but Shakespeare may have recalled Publius Silicius who was sentenced to death by the Triumvirate and was fond of Brutus.

113. *ague* : fever.

118. *prepare within* : Presumably, prepare the wine.

124-5. *and so near . . . further* : Actually Trebonius does not stab Caesar; his task is to lure Antony away.

126-7. *Good friends . . . together* : Shakespeare employs the classic symbol of betrayal : the murderers taking wine with the victim before the killing.

128. *That every . . . think upon* : "The winning and honest suavity of Caesar here starts a pang of remorse in Brutus. Drinking wine together was regarded as a sacred pledge of faith. Brutus knows that Caesar is doing it in good faith and it hurts him to think that the others seem to be doing the like and yet are doing a different thing" (Hudson).

earns : grieves.

Act II — Scene III

5. *bent* : directed.

5-6. *If thou . . . immortal* : This is ironical coming at this point in the play; but it does also help to build up a picture of how Caesar was viewed by some Romans.

look about you : take care.

security . . . confidence : overconfidence gives opportunity for action.

7. *lover* : devoted friend.

10. *suitor* : petitioner.

12. *Out of . . . emulation* : without incurring the malice of jealous rivals.

14. *contrive* : conspire.

Act II — Scene IV

2. *get thee gone* : off with you.

6. *constancy* : firmness, self-control. Refer to II.i.299, 'I have made strong proof of my constancy.'

be strong upon my side : fight bravely on my behalf.

7. *set a . . . tongue* ! : 'so that I may not betray the secret which Brutus has revealed to me.'

8. *to keep counsel* ! : 'to be secret about a matter entrusted to me in confidence' (Deighton).

14. *take good note* : observe closely.

went sickly forth : was sick when he went out.

18. *bustling rumour* : "noise of stir and tumult" (Wright).

fray : fight.

20. *Sooth* : in truth.

I hear nothing : Actually Caesar has not yet gone to the Capitol. In her overwrought state Portia imagines ominous sounds.

23. *ninth hours* : nine o'clock.

25. *to take my stand* : to take up a position where I may be able to see him as he passed his way to the Capitol.

27. *suit* : petition.

34. *at the heels* : close behind him.

35. *praetors* : chief justices.

suitors : supplicants.

36. *Will crowd . . . death* : the crowd will kill a weak man like myself.

37. *more void* : more empty, less crowded.

41. *speed* : prosper.

42. *Brutus . . . a suit* : the words are meant for Lucius's ear in case he might have overheard her last words 'The heavens speed thee in thine enterprise.' She had forgotten the boy's presence when she said them, and now to ward off suspicion, she invents a false cause to account for her anxiety.

44. *commend me* : convey my greetings.

45. *merry* : in good spirits.

Act III — Scene I

3. *schedule* : paper, document.

4. *o'er-read* : read throughout, from beginning to end. Decius cleverly puts in a rival petition in order to prevent Caesar from reading the warning of Artemidorous.

8. *What touches...serv'd.* : Those things which concern me personally must be last attended to.

10. *sirrah* : fellow; contemptuous form of 'sir'.
give place : get out of the way.

13. *I wish . . . thrive* : it is obvious that the conspiracy has leaked out to Popilius Lena.

18. *makes to* : advance towards.

19. *sudden* : speedy, prompt.
fear prevention : fear that we shall be forestalled.

22. *constant* : composed, resolute.

24. *Caesar doth not change* : Caesar's expression does not change.

25. *Trebonius knows his time* : he knows the proper time when he should engage Caesar in conversation.

28. *presently* : immediately.
prefer : offer, present.

29. *address'd* : prepared, ready.

32. *Caesar and his senate* : Caesar's arrogance is reflected in the word order he chooses.

33. *puissant* : powerful.

35. *prevent* : forestall. Caesar knows what Metellus is to ask him.

36. *couching* : 'stooping prostrations'.
courtesies : obeisances.

37. *fire the blood* : 'inflame the pride'.

38-39. *And turn . . . children* : change the law of destiny, which was laid down at the beginning of time, into a law which children might think up.

39-40. *Be not . . . to think* : do not be so stupid as *to imagine.*

rebel blood: uncontrollable passions; unreliable disposition.

41. *thaw'd* : melted.

the true quality : proper function.

With : by.

43. *spaniel fawning* : servile creeping about the foot like dogs.

44. *by decree* : by an august order.

46. *like a cur* : like a street dog; therefore with contempt.

51. *repealing* : recalling from exile.

52. *I kiss . . . repeal* : "When Brutus stoops in the guise of a petitioner, we cannot suppose it is merely with treacherous adroitness. Knowing the man we do not feel that this is the last tender farewell."

57. *enfranchisement* : the rights of free Roman citizen.

58. *If I . . . move me* : "If I could pray in order to move others, I might myself be moved by prayers."

60. *constant as the northern star* : unchanging as the pole-star.

61. *true-fix'd* : immovable.

resting : unchanging.

62. *fellow* : equal. *firmament* : sky.

63. *painted* : decorated. *unnumber'd* : innumerable.

65. *hold his place* : maintain its place.

66. *men are flesh and blood* : men are weak creatures.

apprehensive : endowed with intelligence.

69. *holds on his rank* : keeps his position like the pole star.

70. *Unshak'd of motion* : This has been variously explained as 'unshaked by suit or solicitation', 'unshaken in his motion', 'undisturbed by the force that moves others'.

74. *Olympus* : a Greek mountain, home of the gods.

Wilt..Olympus : Will you attempt the impossible? Caesar's choice of words here, and indeed throughout the speech, makes it clear that he is seeing himself as something between a god and a natural force. The effect of the whole speech is to alienate the audience's sympathy from him immediately before the moment he is attacked.

75. *Doth not . . . kneel?* : If Brutus kneels in vain, can you expect to prevail upon me.

bootless : without effect.

76. *Speak hands for me* : let the actions of my hand speak for me.

77. *Et tu, Brute!* : Even you, Brutus.

80. *Common pulpits* : They existed outside in public places both in Tudor London and Ancient Rome. They were places where you could voice controversial views. St. Paul's Cross in the Churchyard of St. Paul's Cathedral was the scene of many politically disruptive sermons, especially from Puritans.

83. *ambition's debt* : that which was due to Caesar's ambition. Brutus is reassuring the frightened assembly; no one else is to be touched.

86. *confounded* : overcome.

mutiny : tumult.

89. *Talk not of standing* : Brutus is confident that, when the deed is explained to the people, they will be satisfied. There is no need for the conspirators to stand fast together to defend themselves, as Metellus has suggested.

93. *your age* : you as an old man.

94. *abide* : pay the penalty for.

96. *amaz'd* : utterly confounded.

98. *Fates, ... pleasures* : death seems imminent, Brutus prepares to meet it.

99. *'tis but the time* : men concern themselves about the time of their death and how to prolong their life.

100. *drawing days out* : extending the span of life.

stand upon : attach importance to.

104. *abridg'd* : shortened.

109. *red weapons* : blood-stained weapons.

111. *wash* : immerse.

112. *In states unborn* : as yet unfounded.

accents yet unknown! : unknown languages. The speaker anticipates Elizabethan times when Caesar's plays were to be staged.

114. *How many...in sport* : how many times (in the future) shall Caesar be killed for entertainment (in plays).

115. *That who...on Pompey's basis* : at the foot of Pompey's statue. *lies along* : lies stretched out.
basis : pedestral.

117. *knot* : party of men joined in conspiracy.

120. *Brutus shall lead* : Cassius thinks that Brutus's prestige may still save the situation. *grace* : do honour to.

122. *Soft* : wait a moment.

A friend of Antony's : In Plutarch it is Antony who invites the conspirators to come down from the Senate House to visit him, and 'sent them his son for a pledge' (*Brutus, p. 127).*

125. *And, being prostrate* : and bids me when thus prostrate or kneeling.

126. *honest* : honourable.

127. *royal* : nobly munificent.

129. *fear'd* : Antony politely places this word with 'Caesar' and thus half aligns himself with the conspirators; its equally skilfully chosen counterpoise is 'love Brutus'.

136. *hazards* : dangers.

this untrod state : this still unknown set of circumstances. *Thorough* : through.

140. *so* : if it should.

141. *satisfied* : convinced.

142. *presently* : at once.

143. *to* : as a.

144. *a mind* : presentiment.

145-6. *my misgivings . . . purpose* : my misgivings always turns out to be uncomfortably close to what actually happens.

148. *so low?* : because you towered once above mankind.

150. *this little measure* : the dimensions of the dead body.
this : pointing to the dead body.

152. *be let blood* : a grim euphemism for "be put to death".
rank : swollen with diseased, and hence to be cured by blood-letting.

157. *bear me hard* : bear me enmity.

158. *purpled* : Antony says Caesar's blood is the colour of royalty.

159. *Fulfil your pleasure* : This is ironic.
Live : if I should live.

160. *apt* : prepared, ready.

161. *so* : so well, so much.
mean of death : way of dying.

163. *The choice...age* : the most outstanding man of time.

168. *bleeding business* : bloody deed.

171. *As fire drives out fire* : A proverb several times used by Shakespeare.
So pity pity : Pity for the general wrong of Rome has driven out pity for Caesar.

172. *To our . . . points* : our swords have lost their sharpness against you; *i.e.,* you are secure against our swords.

174. *Our arms . . . malice* : The only two satisfactory explanations are given by Grant White and Wright (1) ''So our arms, even in the intensity of their hatred to Caesar's tyranny, and our hearts in their brotherly love to all Romans, do receive you in'' (Grant White). (2) ''Strong as if nerved by malice against you, the death grip of enemies being stronger than the most loving embrace'' (Wright).

175. *Of brother's temper* : full of brotherly love.

177-8. *Your voice...dignities* : Cassius is once again far more politically realistic than Brutus, and offers Antony a share in the power which has come to them by their action in exchange for the support. *Voice* : vote.
dignities : offices.

181. *deliver* : report to.

183. *I doubt...wisdom* : This is ironic.

184. *render* : give.

188. *my valiant Casca* : This is irony; contrast it with Antony's real opinion at V.i. 43-4.

191. *My credit...ground* : Antony quibbles on (1) his physical position in standing in Caesar's blood, (2) his reputation as Caesar's friend.

192. *conceit* : think of, judge.

196. *dearer* : more keenly, more bitterly.

199. *Most noble* : Do these words apply ironically to foes in the previous line, or reverently to Caesar whose body lies before him, or disgustedly to himself for coming in terms with Caesar's enemies? From the tenor of the rest of the speech, it seems most natural to apply them to Caesar.

corse : corpse.

202. *to close* : to arrive at an agreement.

204. *bay'd* : trapped, brought to bay, like a hunted animal.

hart : deer. For the rest of the speech Antony plays on the words hart and heart, common pun in Elizabethan literature.

206. *thy spoil* : the split blood of your flesh

sigh'd in thy spoil : "stained by their havoc of thee and red with thy blood."

lethe : the river of forgetfulness, which (according to Furness) Shakespeare has confused with Cocytus, the river of blood. According to Deighton, the whole expression means 'dyed in that stream of blood which has brought him oblivion of all earthly things". Some commentators suppose that Shakespeare may have taken the derivation from Latin letum, death, though he elsewhere uses the word in correct sense for oblivion.

209. *strucken by many princes* : the hart or deer was so noble that many princes had joined in its hunting.

213. *cold modesty* : dispassionate and moderate tribute.

215. *compact* : agreement.

216. *prick'd* : marked down by a prick, or tick.

221. *Upon this hope* : on condition that you shall, as I hope, etc.

224. *good regard* : sound considerations.

227. *suitor* : beg. This is of course the sole object of his interview, but he introduces it cleverly in a casual manner.

230. *order of his funeral* : the ceremonies arranged for his funeral.

236-7. *I will . . . Caesar's death* : "The infatuation is almost incredible, and it springs not only from generosity to Antony and Caesar, but from the false assumption of the justice of his cause, and the Quixotic exaltation, the assumption brings with it" (Mac Callum).

Antony has played his hand with consummate skill; the grim game is entirely beyond Brutus's comprehension.

Our Caesar's death : as Kittredge says, the phrase "suggests, in an indescribable way, the feeling with which Brutus regards his dead friend. In his opinion, all the conspirators in striking at Caesar did so regretfully, and purely for public reasons."

238. *protest* : proclaim.

241. *true* : fitting, proper.

242. *advantage* : benefit (by showing our generosity).

243. *fall* : happen.

254. *thou . . . earth* : it is rather to Caesar's spirit that the words are addressed.

256. *ruins* : all that is left.

257. *tide of times* : the course of ages.

260. *dumb mouths* : This is a frequent phrase of Shakespeare's for wounds, particularly those which can 'accuse'.

262. *A curse . . . of men* : If the reading is correct, the obvious meaning is that there will be civil war, and the limbs of combatants and non-combatants, will suffer through being maimed and mangled.

263. *Domestic fury* : households shall be divided against themselves.

civil strife : Romans shall fight against Romans.

364. *cumber* : trouble or load down.

268. *quartered* : hacked to pieces.

269. *custom of fell deeds* : the becoming accustomed to cruelty.

270. *ranging* : roving in search of prey.

fell : savage.

271. *Ate* : the fanatical goddess of revenge and mischief, banished by the gods to live among men.

hot from hell : straight from hell.

272. *confines* : regions.

273. *Cry havoc* : Blackstone states that in military operation of old times, 'havoc' was the word used by the generals, by which declarations were made that no quarter should be given. The cry means 'kill and spare none'.

let slip : let go; set free from the leash in which they were held.

The metaphor is from coursing. Hounds are kept back by a leash until the hare has had a fair start, and then are allowed to slip out of the leash.

dogs of war : In Henry IV we have —

> "At his heels
> Leash'd in like hounds, should famine, sword and fire
> Crouch for employment."

274. *shall smell above the earth* : the stench of the foul deed shall rise above the bodies of men rioting above the ground.

275. *carrion men* : men who are nearly corpses.

groaning for burial : because there would not be enough place left to bury the slain. It should be noted that burial was not customary with the Romans of Caesar's time.

Octavius Caesar : a distant relation of the dictator; his ability recommended itself to Julius who treated him as a son and heir.

282. *big* : swollen with grief.

283. *Passion* : sorrow. *catching* : contagious.

286. *seven leagues* : about twenty-one miles. *lies* : lodges.

287. *chanced* : happened.

289. *No Rome of safety* : no safe room or place. Pun on the words 'Rome' and 'room'.

290. *Hie* : hasten.

292. *try* : test.

294. *The cruel issue* : the outcome of the cruelty.

295. *the which* : the result of my experiment.

297. *Lend me your hand* : that is, to carry out Caesar's body. According to Plutarch Caesar's body was left in the Senate House when the conspirators went out to address the people.

Act III — Scene II

Plebeians : ordinary people, workers.

1. *will be satisfied* : we must have a satisfactory explanation.

2. *part* : divide.

7. *public reason* : This could mean (1) 'reasons concerning the public good', (2) 'reasons given in public'.

10. *severally* : separately.

13. *lovers* : dear friends.

15. *have respect to mine honour* : bear in mind that I am honourable.

16. *Censure* : judge.

17. *your senses* : your reason, understanding — as when we talk of people being "in their senses". Brutus appeals to the reason of the crowd, Antony to their passions.

32. *rude* : ignorant, barbarous.

Roman : a free man. It is implied that Caesar's dictatorship was inconsistent with the Roman conception of individual freedom.

38-9. *The question . . . Capitol* : the consideration that made his death necessary are recorded in the archives of the Capitol.

As Macmillan points out, there can hardly have been time for a debate in the Senate. Perhaps, Shakespeare, though he does not use it in his play, has in mind another speech that Plutarch says Brutus made in the Capitol when he and other conspirators took refuge there immediately after the assassination.

39-41. *his glory . . . enforce'd* : his greatness, which was an honourable attribute, not being devalued, nor his crimes unduly stressed.

44. *place* : office, opinion.

46. *lover* : friend.

51. *ancestors* : Lucius Junius Brutus, I.ii. 157.

52. *Let him be Caesar* : This is intended to seem bitterly ironical to the audience. Brutus had slain his friend to prevent him from becoming "Caesar" and destroying the Republic.

53. *better parts* : better qualities.

54. *Shall . . . Brutus* : shall reach their culmination in Brutus.

59. *Do grace . . . his speech* : pay respect to Caesar's body, and give a respectful hearing to Antony's speech.

tending : relating.

65. *public chair* : Plutarch's 'chair or pulpits for orations'.

67. *beholding to* : obliged to.

For Brutus' sake : in Brutus's name.

75. *lend me your ears* : listen to me.

78. *interred* : buried.

82. *answer'd* : atoned for it.

91. *general coffers* : chests of money for the public good.

94. *Ambition...stuff*: an ambitious man ought to be made of a harder heart than to weep so easily.

97. *on the Lupercal* : on the day of the Lupercalia.

107. *bear with me* : have patience with me.

108. *My heart* : "all that is dear to me and with it all my courage."

110. *much reason in his sayings* : But is there? Rather, Antony has been playing with emotions.

113. *I fear...his place* : a common Elizabethan saying.

116. *dear abide it* : dearly pay the penalty for it.

122. *And none...reverence* : Johnson interprets the passage thus :

"The meanest man is now too high to do reverence to Caesar." Wrights puts it somewhat differently. 'And there is none to do him reverence so poor (as himself).'

123-24. *to stir . . . rage* : although Antony seemingly deprecates them, he is all the while suggesting to the mob to mutiny against the conspirators.

mutiny : disorder, riot.

131. *closet* : private room.

his will : According to Plutarch, the will was read in the Senate before Antony's speech.

135. *napkins* : handerchiefs. The line refers to the practice of preserving cloths dipped in the blood of martyrs as sacred relics; and the next line to another kind of relic

139. *issue* : children.

143. *meet* : fitting, proper.

151. *stay* : wait.

152. *o'ershot myself* : gone too far.

154. *Whose daggers . . . Caesar* : said with bitter irony.

"Here, I think, for the first time Antony used these words (honourable man) with a distinct sheer; and then fairly hurls the next line in the face of the crowd" (Furness). Note how cleverly has Antony roused the populace against the conspirators, while at the same time he seems to shield them.

164. *from the hearse* : away from the coffin.

170. *Bear back* : move back.

172. *mantle* : cloak.

175. *overcame the Nervii* : a fierce tribe in Gaul who mounted a surprise ambush (57 B.C.) against Caesar, but were repulsed and slaughtered; this, Caesar's most brilliant military achievement, caused great rejoicing in Rome. But Antony was not present at the battle but the mention of this victory is a telling stroke.

117. *envious* : malicious, spiteful.

181. *As ruthing . . . or no* : as though it eagerly rushed forth to learn for certain whether it was Brutus who had struck cruelly. The metaphor is taken from knocking at the door so that the person inside rushes out to see who knocked.

183. *Caesar's angel* : as near to Caesar as his guardian angel.

185. *most unkindest* : This could mean "most cruel", or "most unnatural", double superlative for emphasis.

187. *Ingratitude . . . vanish'd him* : it was Brutus's ingratitude which overcame Caesar rather than the daggers of the conspirators. Brutus owed almost everything to Caesar.

189. *muffling up* : covering up.

190. *base* : pedestal.

191. *ran blood* : The implication is that Even Pompey, Caesar's former enemy, could not forbear to show sympathy. However, Plutarch took the blood as a token "that the image took just revenge of Pompey's enemy, being thrown down on the ground at his feet, and yielding up his ghost there". And Elizabethan audience would also, no doubt, see in this passage an allusion to a current superstition that the corpse of a murdered man bled in the presence of the murderer.

193. *all of us fell down* : "as when a kingdom falls with a king".

194. *flourish'd* : Dover Wison suggests two meanings (1) "brandish a sword in triumph", (2) "swagger".

196. *dint* : stroke, or impression.

gracious : holy

198. *vesture* : mantle, clothing.

199. *marr'd* : mangled. *with* : by.

Here is himself : Shakespeare provides a powerful and moving climax with the uncovering of Caesar's mangled body by Antony.

206. *About* : to work !

212. *sudden flood* : sudden outburst.

215. *private griefs* : personal grievances.

217. *reasons* : Brutus has, of course, already given these reasons, but the crowd are by now in no condition to remember them. Antony himself was not present when Brutus made his speech.

220. *a plain blunt man* : the words are at variance with the actual fact, but "there is an element of truth in the orator's attitude, and consequently a strain of sincerity in the utterance "(Hunter).

222. *public leave to speak* : permission to speak publicly.

223-5. *neither wit . . . men's blood* : "A complete list of the qualities of a good orator: (1) intellectual cleverness (wit); (2) fluency (words); (3) auctoritas, the weight that comes from character or standing (worth); (4) gesture and bearing; (5) skilful elocution, good delivery (utterance); and finally (6) the power of speech to stir men's blood, without which all other accomplishments avail but little" (Kittredge).

225. *right on* : straightforwardly; without art.

230. *ruffle up* : stir up to anger.

232. *to rise and mutiny* : "Note the last words. Though Antony feels entitled to indulge in this farrcing and enjoy it thoroughly, he does not forget the serious business. He keeps recurring more and more distinctly to the suggestion of mutiny and for mutiny, and for mutiny the citizens are now more than fully primed" (Mac Callum).

238. *deserv'd your loves* : deserved the love of all.

244. *drachmas* : silver coins; difficult to assess their value.

246. *royal* : noble munificent.

250. *arbours* : lawns, orchards and cultivated gardens.

250-1. *Orchards, On this side Tiber* : Caesar's gardens actually lay on the other side of the river.

252. *common pleasures* : public parks.

256. *holy place* : where the most sacred temples are situated.

260. *pluck down* : tear loose.

261. *windows*: shutters

268. *upon a wish* : just when I want him.

merry : in good humour.

273-4. *some notice . . . mov'd them* : some notice of how I had moved the people.

Act III — Scene III

1. *to-night* : last night.

2. *things...fantasy* : the things that have happened weigh ominously on my imagination.

9. *directly* : plainly.

12. *you were best* : it were best for you to do so.

18. *Your will...for that* : You'll get a bang for that.

28. *Tear him to pieces* : "The blackest action committed by the people, in all Shakespeare's Roman plays, is the murder of the poet Cinna in the midst of the tumult" (Furness).

30. *Tear him for his bad verses* : "Were it not that the fate of the poet, Cinna is related by Plutarch, one would like to consider the whole incident as a characteristic invention by Shakespeare. The scornful exclamation, "Tear him for his bad verses", is manifestly English in its humour" (Kreyssing).

33-34. *pluck but his name out of his heart* : This is grotesquely related to Brutus's attempt to destroy the implications of Caesar's spirit or name by killing his body.

turn him going : send him packing.

Act IV — Scene I

1. *These many etc.* : the triumvirate are preparing the list of proscription containing the names of those whom they wish to condemn to death or exile.

prick'd : marked.

2. *Your brother...die* : Lepidus's brother, Lucius Aemilius Paullus, had held the highest offices, including the consulate in 50 B.C. On the assassination of Caesar he joined the republican party,

and was one of those, who, in June, 43 B.C., declared Lepidus a public enemy for having joined Antony. When the Triumvirate was formed a few months later his name was put at the head of the proscription list by Lepidus; he escaped, probably with Lepidus's connivance, and joined Brutus. Although pardoned after the Battle of Philippi, he refused to return to Rome, and died abroad.

4. *Upon condition* : on condition that.

Publius : Antony had no nephew Publius, but his uncle, Lucius Caesar, as Plutarch mentions, was among those who were proscribed by the Triumvirs. Whether by mistake or design, Shakespeare brings a nephew into the story, and, by showing Antony's readiness to damn him as a precautionary measure to further the suppression of the conspiracy, brings about a contrast with Brutus's refusal to take the precaution of killing Antony himself, which was essential for the success of the conspiracy.

6. *with a spot I damn him* : with a mark I condemn him to death.

9. *cut off...egacies* : pay our expenses in money from Caesar's will.

12. *slight unmeritable man* : a man, insignificant and unworthy of consideration.

13. *meet* : fitting.

14. *three-fold world divided* : This was the Roman world — Europe, Asia, Africa. Antony was to govern Gaul, Lepidus Spain, Octavius Africa, Sardinia and Sicily.

stand : be left.

16. *voice* : opinion, vote.

17. *black sentence* : death sentence.

proscription : death penalty; 300 out of 900 senators were executed and 2,000 equites or 'aristocrats'.

20. *divers* : various.

To ease...loads : to lighten for ourselves some of the burden of reproach or disgrace that we may encounter, *i.e.*, by causing Lepidus to share, or laying on him, the blame of some of their unpopular acts.

21. *as the ass bears gold* : An Elizabethan proverb : 'An ass is but an ass though laden with gold'.

22. *business* : heavy work.

To groan...business : shall labour hard to carry the load of slander due to the conscription.

23. *led or driven* : having no independence of his own, he is guided by us.

26. *empty* : unburdened, idle.

to shake his ears : to wander at will like an ass shaking its long ears. A proverb.

27. *in commons* : on the public pasture-lands, or commons, with which most villages were provided, and on to which the villagers could turn their beasts to graze.

30. *appoint* : assign.

store : a supply. *provender* : food.

32. *To wind* : to turn, or wheel.

33. *His corporal . . . spirit* : his physical movements controlled by my mind.

34. *in some taste* : in some measure.

35. *A barren-spirited fellow* : a man incapable of devising anything for himself.

36. *objects* : "wonders, curiosities".

arts, and imitations : suggest things and ideas that are artificial and second hand.

38. *stal'd* : made common or cheap.

which . . . fashion : the metaphor is changed from eating to dress. When things have been made common by others, and gone out of fashion, they begin to be fashionable with him.

39. *as a property* : as a 'mere appendage to help us in the parts we are acting" (Wright).

42. *make head* : raise a force.

44. *made* : made certain.

stretched : used to their fullest extent.

45. *presently* : at once, forthwith.

46-7. *How covert...answered* : how hidden threats may best be brought to light, and open dangers most safely met.

48. *at the stake* : unable to move, like bears attacked by dogs at bear-baiting.

49. *bay'd* : surrounded.

51. *mischiefs* : injuries, schemes to harm us.

Act IV — Scene II

2. *Give...stand* : Lucilius is here passing on Brutus's order to his subordinates.

5. *master* : Cassius

6. *He greets me well* : he sends his greetings by a good man.

7. *In his...officers* : whether from a change in his feelings for me, or through the actions of bad subordinates.

ill : bad.

8. *worthy* : justifiable, considerable.

10. *satisfied* : receive a satisfactory answer.

12. *full of regard and honour* : worthy of all respect and honour.

14. resolv'd : fully informed.

16. *familiar instances* : marks of friendship.

17. *conference* : conversation.

19. *Ever note* : always observe.

21. *enforced ceremony* : strained formality.

22. *tricks* : artifices.

23. *hollow* : insincere.

hot at hand : lively at the start.

24. *Make gallant show* : 'make a brave show of their high spirit, and give promise of great speed and endurance.'

mettle : spirit, courage.

26. *Fall* : let fall. "A high crest was one of the distinguishing beauties of the horse, a mark of mettle . . . and lowering the crest was a sign of inferiority and submission."

crests : ridges of the horse's neck.

jades : horses without spirit or stamina.

27. *sink in the trial* : fail when put to the test.

28. *Sardis* : this town was near Izmir in modern Turkey, about 850 miles from Rome. This was the capital city of the ancient kingdom of Lydia in Asia Minor.

29. *the horse in general* : the cavalry.

31. *gently* : slowly.

38. *wrong I my enemies* : I do not wrong even my enemies, not to speak of wronging my brother.

40. *this sober form* : this calm, grave demeanour.

hides wrongs : conceals grievances.

42. *griefs* : grievances.

I do know you well : Brutus indicates by this that they are old friends and so need not act like enemies.

45. *wrangle* : quarrel.

46. *enlarge your griefs* : state your grievances fully.

48. *their charges* : their troops.

Act IV — Scene III

1. *in this* : the proof which he is going to produce.

2. *noted* : publicly disgraced, slandered.

4. *on his side* : on his behalf.

5. *slighted off* : slightingly disregarded.

8. *nice* : tiny, trivial.

his : its.

That every. . .comment : that every trifling offence should come in for criticism.

10. *condemn'd to have* : accused of having.

itching palm : mercenary streak, itch for money.

11. *mart* : traffic in.

15. *The name...his head* : That the name of Cassius should be associated with this corrupt practice gives it a spurious credit, and so lesser men enjoy the same immunity from punishment as he does by virtue of his high authority.

19. *for justice sake* : This is the first time justice has been instanced as one of the motives for the conspiracy.

20-21. *What villain...justice?* : Who of the conspirators was such a villain as to strike Caesar for any other motive than a desire for justice? This is ironical in that it is addressed to Cassius, for we know his motive to have been anything but disinterested.

And not : except.

23. *robbers* : 'those who were robbing the commonwealth of all that was worth possessing — liberty, good government, justice, etc.' (Deighton).

25. *the mighty...honours* : profit from our noble position. When Essex fell from favour in 1599, Elizabeth I took away his monopoly in the sweet wine trade. It ruined him (Honourable court positions were in themselves worthless, but lucrative because they enabled the holder to sell trade licences at great profit).

26. *trash* : worthless money dishonestly acquired.

27. *be a dog...moon* : the watchdog barks because it believes its shadow, cast by moon, is another dog.

28. *hedge me in* : limit my authority.

31. *Older in practice* : of a longer military experience.

32. *to make conditions* : to manage affairs; or perhaps to make decisions about the place of subordinates in their affairs, with reference to Lucius Pella.

35. *Urge* : drive, harry.

36. *health* : safety, welfare.

tempt : try, provoke.

37. *slight man* : worthless fellow, trifler.

39. *choler* : bad temper.

must I...choler? : Must I give "free course and scope to your quick temper?" (Kettredge).

40. stares : glares.

44. *budge* : flinch.

45. *observe* : pay obsequious respect to.

crouch : bow.

46. *testy humour* : irascible temper.

47. *venom* : poison. *spleen* : spleen was considered to be the seat of choler or melancholy and ill-temper.

digest . . . spleen : the excessive excretion of spleen which acts as an internal poison and gives rise to outbursts of ill-temper must be kept under control at any cost, even if it harms his constitution.

49. *mirth...laughter* : object of mirth and ridicule.

waspish : irritable as a wasp which is apt to sting anybody who is near.

52. *vaunting* : boasting.

54. *to learn of* : to be instructed by.

59. *durst* : dared.

tempted : tried, provoked.

62. *presume* : count.

67. *honesty* : integrity, uprightness.

69. *respect not* : ignore.

72. *coin my heart* : convert my heart into coins.

73. *drachmas* : silver coins.

for : into

74. *hard hands* : hardened by hard toil.

vile trash : base, worthless money.

75. *indiscretion* : irregular and unjust means.

80. *rascal counters* : worthless coins. Counters were round pieces of metal of no value, used only in making calculations.

84. *brought* : carried to you.

riv'd : split.

85. *infirmities* : weaknesses.

91. *Olympus* : Greek mountain, home of the gods.

95. *brav'd* : defied, opposed, challenged.

96. *check'd* : reproved, rebuked.

97. *conn'd by rote* : learned by heart.

98. *cast into my teeth* : reproach me with. A proverbial expression.

101. *Dearer* : more precious.

Pluto's mine : infinite wealth. Cassius runs two names together: Plutus, a fabulously rich man, and Pluto, wealthy king of the underworld.

102. *be'st* : are.

be'st a Roman : 'Cassius appeals to Brutus by that which was his most honourable distincting' (Wright).

It is worth-noting that Cassius in this speech uses the second persons singular in speaking to Brutus, whereas Brutus all along uses the plural, as does in the rest of the dialogue. It is probably an intentional indication of Cassius's extreme emotion for the moment — Wood.

103. *that denied thee gold*: This seems to contradict line 82; but what Cassius is really implying is that although Brutus will have it that he was denied gold, yet Cassius is ready 'to give my heart', etc.

107. *it shall have scope* : you temper shall have free rein.

108. *dishonour shall be humour* : "any indignity you offer shall be regarded as a mere caprice of the moment" (Craik).

109. *yoked with a lamb* : that Brutus and Cassius are ill-mated, though closely associated, is one of the central ideas of the play. Brutus means that he is as gentle as a lamb.

110. *carries anger . . . flint* : "his anger is but a momentary flash".

111. *Who* : which.

much enforced : struck with great force.

shows a hasty spark : suddenly flashes out.

112. *straight* : at once.

114. *blood ill-temper'd* : ill-balanced nature.

117. *What's the matter?* : "Spoken in a tone of conscious sympathy, for Cassius's 'O Brutus !' expresses almost uncontrollable agitation" (Kittredge).

119. *rash humour* : irascible temper.

which my mother gave me : which I inherited from my mother. It is purely Shakespeare's invention. But it is a vivid touch, and is effectively taken up in Brutus's reply.

121. *over-earnest* : too severe; a euphemism for angry.

122. *leave you so* : let the matter drop.

Poet : In Plutarch he is one Marcus Phaonius, who "took upon him to counterfeit a Cynic philosopher, not with wisdom and discretion, but with a certain bedlam and frantic motion".

124. *grudge* : ill-feeling.

126. *stay* : prevent.

130-1, *Love, and...than ye* : 'The verses are a translation of lines uttered by Nestor in the *Illiad,* and in North's *Plutarch* run as follows : "My lords, I pray you hearken both to me,/For I have seen mo year, than suchie three." Shakespeare attributes the couplet to Faonius himself, and, on the strength of this attribution, makes him a poet rather than the pseudo-philosopher of Plutarch.

132. *cynic* : boorish man.

133. *Saucy* : insolent.

135. *I'll know...his time* : "I will bear with his whims when he chooses the right time."

136. *jigging* : rhyming, versifying.

137. *Companion* : fellow-contemptuously used by Shakespeare.

144-45. *Of your . . . evils* : As a Stoic Brutus ought not to have given way to anger over incidental adversities.

place : way.

149. *killing* : being killed. 'I wonder that being so tortured with grief, you did not kill me when I provoked you so.'

150. *touching* : grievous.

Upon what sickness : as a result of sickness.

151-2. *Impatient...grief* : "Impatience and 'absence' concurring wounded the poet's ear; he put up with 'impatient' and hopes his readers will do so" (Capell).

153-4. *for with...came* : for together with the news of her death came tidings of that (*i.e.,* of the strength of Antony and Octavius).

155. *swallow'd fire* : According to Plutarch, she 'took burning coals and cast them in her mouth, and kept her mouth so close that she choked herself.'

163. *taper* : candle.

164. *call in question* : deliberate upon.

Philippi : (pronounced fye-lip-eye) where the Republicans were defeated in 42 B.C. on the coast of Eastern Greece near Thasos; in reality Sardis and Philippi were 260 miles and a sea journey apart.

Bending their movements: directing their movements.

170. *tenor* : purport.

172. *proscription* : death penalty.

bills of outlawry : lists of proscribed persons which were pasted in the Forum declaring certain persons outside the law, and so liable to be put to death by any one.

182. *writ of her* : no news about her?

188. *by strange manner* : in a strange manner.

193. *in art* : theoretically I have as much of this philosophic fortitude as you.

194. *nature* : emotions.

195. *to our work alive* : let us get on with the work that is our present concern.

200. *offence* : harm.

202. *of force* : of necessity, perforce.

204. *forc'd affection* : allegiance out of necessity.

208. *new-added* : reinforced.

212. *Under your pardon* : excuse me; let me please continue my speech. *beside* : besides.

213. *tried the... friends* : "we have fully put our friends to the test, and have obtained from them all the assistance they can possibly give us" (Deighton).

214. *legions* : armies.

cause : plan of fighting.

ripe : matured.

216. *at the height . . . decline* : our fortune being in full high tide must necessarily, by law of nature, begin to ebb. The similitude is rather poetical than practical.

218. *taken at the flood* : taken advantage of at the highest point.

219. *Omitted* : neglected, missed.

217. *a tide in the affairs of men* : In the days of sail power and undredged estuaries, trading ships often had to wait for the right wind and tide. Too long a wait and the cargo might lose its value, especially if it was perishable. Sail at the wrong time and the ship could be wrecked.

220. *bound in shallows* : confined to shallow water. 'They journey through life buffeted by miseries, like a boat continually running aground in shallow water.'

223. *ventures* : merchandise risked in trade. A metaphor.

with your will : as you desire it.

227. *niggard* : supply sparingly, stint.

229. *hence* : go from here.

240. *Poor knave* : poor lad. *o'er-watched* : overtired with keeping awake.

246. *raise* : rouse.

248. *watch your pleasure* : be on the watch for anything you wish to do. Dover Wilson suggests, "keep awake and wait for".

250. *otherwise bethink me* : change my mind.

256. *touch* : play on.

strain : tune.

257. *an't* : if it.

261. *young bloods* : youthful constitutions.

266. *murd'rous slumber* : "Because it is the death of each day's life."

267. *leaden mace* : this is the symbol of authority with the god of sleep. In mythology, Morpheus, the god of sleep, is represented as carrying a wand which Shakespear has changed into a 'mace'.

Layest...boy : The metaphor is of a bailiff of the law touching a man with his official staff in sign of arrest.

270. *If thou dost nod* : if you make the least movement. "The consideration of Brutus to his servant is in marked contrast to the usual harshness of the Roman masters. It rises to a womanly tenderness when without waking the boy he saves him from breaking his instrument." — Houghton.

272. *leaf turn'd down* : an anachronism, since Brutus would be reading from a scroll.

274. *How ill this taper burns* : "looking towards the light of the lamp that waxed very dim, he saw a horrible vision of a man, of a wonderful greatness, and dreadful look, which at the first made him marvellously afraid" (North). It was a common superstition that lights burned dim, or blue, in the presence of a ghost or evil spirit.

276. *monstrous apparition* : fearful figure.

277. *upon* : toward.

Art thou anything : are you any real thing or merely an illusion?

279. *stare* : stand on end.

281. *Thy evil spirit* : "Not content with identifying the ghost, Shakespeare makes Caesar an evil spirit which haunts Brutus, as Brutus was 'Caesar's angel' before he killed him. It was common in Elizabethan tragedy for ghosts to exact vengeance. Shakespeare probably believed in ghosts as most of his contemporaries did, and the ghost is an objective reality, 'not a mere embodiment of Brutus's sense of the egregious mistake he has made in slaying Caesar." — Houghton.

285. *will* : am quite ready to.

286. *Now...vanishest* : "...Does not indicate that the vision is only subjective and therefore overcome by an exertion of Brutus's will, but merely that he tries to persuade himself that it is imaginary... The very next verse shows that he believes he has seen a spirit" (Kittredge).

290. *false* : out of tune.

303. *commend me* : deliver my greeting.

304. *set on* : advance.

betimes : early in the morning.

powers : forces.

Act V — Scene I

4. *proves* : turns out to be.

battles : troops in battle order.

5. *warn* : summon, challenge.

at Philippi here : Historically the meeting at Sardis took place early in 42 B.C., and the Battle of Philippi in the following autumn.

6. *Answering...of them* : "defending themselves against us before being attacked by us."

7. *Tut,...bosoms* : Nonsense, I know their innermost thoughts.

8. *could be content* : "they would like to keep out of our way still."

10. *With fearful bravery* : "with a gallant show of courage carrying with it terror and dismay" — Malone.

face : show of valour.

11. *fasten* : fix the idea.
13. *gallant* : splendid.
14. *bloody . . . battle* : "The signal of battle was set out in Brutus's and Cassius' camp, which was an arming scarlet coat" (North). A red flag was the Roman signal for battle.
16. *battle* : army.
softly : slowly.
19. *exigent* : crisis, emergency.
cross me : thwart me.
20. *I do not cross you...do so.* : I am not merely perversely thwarting you; but I will do as I said.
24. *answer on their charge* : meet them when they attack.
25. *Make forth* : go forward, advance.
33. *The posture of your blows* : what kind of blows you can strike. 'Posture' was a technical term referring to the position of a weapon in either arms drill or war.
34. *Hybla* : 'There were three towns in Sicily of this name and it is uncertain from which of them the far-famed Hyblean honey came' (Deighton).
35. *Not stingless too* : Some editors put a full-stop after 'too'; in that case the sentence means' I do not rob them of all their stings', a sense which appears pointless. Delius would put a sign of interrogation after 'too', and this is a decided improvement. In that case the meaning would be : 'Have I not robbed the bees of their stings too?' That is, though the words of Antony are sweet to the hearing, there are stings in them.
37. *For you...sting* : as the bees give warning that they are going to sting by buzzing, so you talk and chatter before you threaten to strike.
39. *you did not so* : you did not threaten first; *viz.*, you struck without warning.
40. *Hack'd one another* : so many of them struck at Caesar that their daggers clashed against each other in Caesar's body.
41. *show'd you teeth* : grinned.
47. *If Cassius...ru'd* : If Cassius had his way when he advised that Antony too should be slain.

48. *the cause* : the matter in hand. The term is a legal one and this implication is taken up in 'proof' and 'arguing'.

49. *The proof* : the practical test.

52. *goes up again* : goes back into its sheath.

54-5. *or till...traitors* : till you traitors have my murder also to the credit of your swords.

Another Caesar : Octavius, who had succeeded Julius Caesar by his will.

59. *strain* : family.

61. *peevish schoolboy* : silly, stripling. Cassius sneers at Octavius's age, who was at this time only twenty-one.

62. *masker* : amateur actor in a masque, an entertainment often brought on at banquets at court; it was a mixture between play, ballet and opera with sumptuous costumes.

64. *Old Cassius still* : the same spiteful Cassius as of old.

66. *stomachs* : appetite, inclination.

68. *on the hazard* : staked on a throw of the dice.

75. *set/Upon one battle* : risk in one battle.

As Pompey was : at the battle of Pharsalia, Pompey was forced to fight Caesar against his better judgment.

77. *Epicurus* : a Greek philosopher, who maintained that pleasure is the highest good for man. By 'pleasure' he meant the cultivation of the intellect, study, good association of friendly souls in retirement from the world; later Epicureans reduced his noble formula to the sensual idea 'eat, drink and be merry'. Epicurus taught that gods are a superior order of beings who have nothing to do with the happiness and misery of man. According to him, therefore, omen and portents are only illusion of senses.

79. *presage* : give knowledge of the future.

80. *former ensign* : foremost standard.

81. *fell* : alighted.

perch'd : continued to sit.

82. Gorging : feeding greedily, like birds of prey.

83. *consorted us* : accompanied us.

85. *raven crows, and kites* : Birds of ill-omen which proverbially anticipate the death of their prey.

86. *sickly* : dying.

88. *fatal* : foreboding death.

90. *I but...partly* : I only partly believe it.

92. *constantly* : firmly, resolutely.

93. *Even so, Lucilius* : Presumably Brutus has been giving instructions to Lucilius while Cassius speaks to Messala.

94. *The gods today stand friendly* : May the gods stand friendly!

95. *Lovers* : dear friends.

96. *rests still uncertain* : always remain uncertain.

97. *Let's reason...befall* : let us consider what is to be done if the worst happens. A proverbial expression.

101. *Even by the rule . . . himself*: "Brutus says that he had decided not to commit suicide like Cato but to await whatever Heaven should send him....What Brutus really says was that when he was still young he wrote a discourse blaming Cato for suicide, but now he has changed his mind" (Houghton).

102. *Cato* : Cato the younger.

105. *to prevent . . . of life* : to anticipate the term of life, the natural end of life.

107. *To stay* : to await. "The Stoic philosophy which Brutus followed counselled resignation to the wills of gods, and therefore did not allow a man to anticipate his death by suicide."

providence : fate, destiny.

some : whatever. Brutus does not believe in the traditional Roman gods, merely some supernatural power.

109. *led in triumph* : as a humiliated captive.

113. *bears...a mind* : too noble a mind to bear such a disgrace.

120. *Forever...Brutus* : "Cassius is too profoundly moved to find words of his own. He can only repeat wistfully the words that have fallen from Brutus" (Hunter).

123. *lead on* : go forward with your troops.

O, that a man : suspense is intolerable to Brutus.

126. *And then the end is known* : with the ending of the day the result of the battle will also be known.

Act V — Scene II

1. *bills* : written order. "...little bills...in which he wrote the word of the battle" (North).
2. *the other side* : the other wing, commanded by Cassius.
3. *set on* : attack.
4. *cold...wing* : low spirits in the troops led by Octavius.
5. *come down* : from the high ground on which part of the army was still drawn up.

   push : assault.

Act V — Scene III

1. *villains* : Cassius's own men.
3. *ensign* : standard-bearer.
4. *it* : the standard.
5. *the word* : the signal for attack.
6. *on* : over.
7. *Took it too eagerly* : 'followed his advantage too eagerly'.

   fell to spoil : started rifling the bodies of those they had defeated (instead of coming to the help of Cassius).
11. *far off* : further off.
15. *hide* : dig, in order to make the horse run fast.
19. *even with* : as quick as.

    with a thought : as quick as thought.
21. *thick* : dim.

    Regard : watch.
22. *not's* : observest.
25. *his compass* : its full circuit.
29. *make to him on the spur* : advance towards him at full gallop.
31. *light* : alight.
32. *ta'en* : captured.
36. *in Parthia* : a campaign in the Iran/Iraq area, eleven years before. *swore thee* : made thee swear.
42. *search* : probe, penetrate.
43. *hits* : hilt. *Cf.* Plutarch. "But then, casting his cloak over his

head, and holding out his bare neck unto Pindarus, he gave him his head to be stricken off.''

46. *Even with...thee* : Shakespeare seizes with unerring intuition every picturesque or dramatic detail in Plutarch. *Cf.* the latter. 'Of all the chances that happen unto men upon the earth, that which came to Cassius above all other is most to be wondered at; for he, being over in battle, slew himself with the same sword with which he strake Caesar'' (North).

51. *change* : exchange of fortune.

60. *O setting sun* : the expression is inconsistent with line 122 where we are told it is three o'clock. Mark Hunter, however, observes : ''As the conspiracy at its stormy beginning was set with a dramatic background of actual tempest, so its decay and death is dramatically symbolized by setting sun and growing darkness.''

65. *Mistrust...success* : Fear of the outcome of my mission is responsible for this action.

67. *Melancholy's child* : Melancholy people imagine non-existent evils.

68. *apt* : 'susceptible, ready to receive impressions' (Wright).

69. *The things...not?* : imaginary ills.

71. *But kill'st . . . thee* : Like the brood of adder, which, according to popular belief, kill their mother, Error, too kills the mind in which it is born and which may, therefore, be called its mother. Here Error is personified.

82. *this wreath of victory* : Titinius was crowned with 'a garland of triumph' so that when he came hastening towards Cassius's troops they might note at once that the enemy had been defeated by Brutus and therefore might take courage.

84. *misconstrued* : misinterpreted.

85. *hold thee* : receive; ''but enough of this'' (Furness).

88. *regarded* : honoured, respected.

89. *A Roman's part* : what a Roman should do, *viz.*, self-destruction so as not to fall alive into the power of the enemy after defeat,

By your leave, gods : 'In accordance with the Platonic view, Titinius implies that he cannot voluntarily depart from life without the permission of the gods'' (Macmillan).

94-6. *O Julius Caesar . . . entrails* : This is one of the most significant passages in the play. These lines can serve as a motto to the play, and furnish some explanation why the play was called "Julius Caesar".

In : into. *proper* : own.

97. *where* : whether.

99-101. *The last...thy fellow* : "After he had lamented the death of Cassius, calling him the last of all the Romans, being impossible that Rome should ever breed against so noble and valiant a man as he, he caused his body to be buried, and sent it unto the city of Thasos" (North).

103. *I shall find time* : "he puts off the debt of tears until another time, that his personal anguish may not endanger the public cause" (Gervinus).

104. *Thasos* : the island off the coast at Philippi

106. *discomfort us* : dishearten our troop.

108. *Labeo and Flavius* : Plutarch identifies these characters among the friends of Brutus who were slain in battle before his eyes, of whom 'the one was his lieutenant and the other captain of the pioneers of his camp' (*Brutus,* p. 169).

battles : forces.

110. *second fight* : Historically the second fight took place twenty days later.

Act V — Scene IV

2. *What bastard doth not?* : who is of such base blood that he does not?

7. *son of Marcus Cato* : Son of Cato of Utica, and hence Brutus's brother-in-law.

9. *down* : struck down.

11. *mayst be* : may thou be.

12. *Only I yield to die* : I surrender simply in order to die.

13-14. *There is...death.* 'There is so much inducement that you will surely kill me at once, and in doing so with great honour.' *straight* : immediately.

21. *I dare...Brutus* : Lucilius says : "Antonius, I dare assure thee,

that no enemy hath taken nor shall take Marcus Brutus alive, and I beseech God keep him from that fortune; wheresoever he be found, alive or dead, he will be found like himself."

30. *where* : whether.

32. *is chanc'd* : has turned out.

Act V — Scene V

1. *poor remains* : pitiful survivors.

2. *show'd the torch-light* : Statilius, having got through enemy lines to Brutus's camp, was to show a torch if not many were dead, then return; he showed a torch but did not return.

4. *Slaying is the word*: slaying is our watchword; *viz.* what we have to do is to kill ourselves.

5. *a deed in fashion* : The reference is to Cassius's suicide at V. iii.

13. *that noble vessel* : Brutus. 'The comparison of a human being with a vessel is biblical, and from the Bible Shakespeare probably too had' (Hunter).

full of grief: so much of grief.

15. *list* : listen. *several* : separate.

17. *The ghost of Caesar* : If there could be any doubt of the identity of the apparition in IV. iii, these words would settle them.

23. *beat us to the pit* : driven us before them (like hunted animals) into a pit—with the implication of a grave.

30. *there...here* : we must not tarry here.

38. *vile conquest* : Brutus thus dies still believing that Caesar's death was necessary; and that the victory by Antony and Octavius means the end of Rome's freedom, and is therefore 'vile'.

39. *at once* : without further ado.

42. *this hour* : the hour of his death. This is in accord with Brutus's Stoic belief that death is not a calamity.

45. *of a good respect* : of good reputation.

46. *smatch* : smack, taste,

50. *Caesar, now be still* : because avenged by the death of Brutus : "Antony's prophecy, that Caesar's spirit shall come forth ranging for revenge, is fulfilled. Brutus recognized its power at the death of Cassius, and his last words bear witness to his belief

that by his death alone will that perturbed spirit find rest'' (Furness).

52-4. *What man...Messala* : 'Messala, that had been Brutus's great friend, became afterwards Octavius Caesar's friend...' (*Brutus*, p. 172).

55. *can but make a fire of him* : can only burn his body, not capture him alive.

56. *overcame* : conquered.

59. *Lucilius's saying* : See V. iv. 21-2.

60. *entertain* : take into my service.

63. *prefer* : recommend.

67. *latest service* : rendered the last service.

71-72. *general...good to all* : he alone thought honestly for others and for the whole community.

made one of them : joined their party.

73. *gentle* : noble and magnanimous.

the elements : Fire, air, water and earth are the elements of which all things, including the human body, were supposed to be composed. All had to be in perfect balance for physical and spiritual health.

75. This was a man : ''Of another it would be said that he was a poet, a philosopher; of Brutus the only true description was that he was a man'' (Moulton).

76. *use* : treat.

respect : estimation, regard.

77. *burial* : Brutus was cremated and not buried. Verity points out : ''Octavius is to be the new Caesar, inheritor of all that Julius had created, representative of that 'Caesarism' which the conspirators had wholly failed to kill, rather had strengthened when they struck down the mortal frame of the Dictator. It is fitting that 'Caesarism' should, through Octavious, have the last word'' (Verity).

bones : dead body.

79. *order'd honourably* : treated with all honour.

81. *part* : share

PART III

PASSAGES FOR EXPLANATION WITH REFERENCE TO CONTEXT

Act I — Scene I

(1) Wherefore rejoice ?........things. (Lines 35-38)

These lines are spoken by Marullus, the Roman Tribune, in the opening scene of *Julius Caesar.* Addressing the crowd, Marullus is persuading the citizens to go home. In his opinion Caesar does not deserve such a reception by the public. Caesar is coming to Rome after defeating the sons of the great Pompey, and Pompey was the great hero of the Romans. Caesar is coming after winning victory in a civil war. This victory has not brought any gain to the Romans. Had Caesar conquered some other land, he would have brought to Rome huge quantities of plundered booty and large number of slaves tied as prisoners to his victorious chariot. But Caesar has not increased the boundaries of the Roman empire in this war. Nor has he brought any benefit to the Roman public.

Therefore, Marullus says, the Romans have no occasion to rejoice. Their rejoicings are senseless, pointless. The unthinking, unfeeling Romans are like blocks of wood and stone.

(2) Many a time .... concave (Lines 40-50)

These lines have been taken from *Julius Caesar,* written by William Shakespeare. Flavius and Marullus, the two tribunes, are trying to turn the commoners against Caesar reminding them of Pompey's victories, and triumphs accorded to him on several occasions.

The common citizens of Rome have gathered in the streets to receive Caesar with honour. Caesar has defeated Pompey and his sons, all Romans.

This has given great offence to the supporters of Pompey and, therefore, they are opposed to the 'triumph'. Flavius and Marullus are the supporters of Pompey. So they are driving away the citizens who are rejoicing Caesar's victory. Marullus tells them that Caesar is not bringing any new conquest to Rome. He has defeated Pompey and his sons who are Romans themselves. Marullus says that the Roman citizens are hard-hearted. They have forgotten Pompey whom they used to accord triumphs. Many times, the people of Rome have climbed the walls of houses and forts, high towers and windows, even the tops of chimneys, with their children in their arms to see Pompey, passing through the streets of Rome. Seeing Pompey's chariot they have shouted together, making even the river Tiber tremble under its bank. When Roman people shouted there were repeated echoes of the shouts and the river trembled. Marullus means to say that the people have certainly lost their senses. Therefore they have forgotten Pompey whom they used to give honour, and are now ready to welcome the man who has defeated him.

Shakespeare in these lines has given a beautiful description of the gathering. These lines also give the reader the idea that the play is going to begin with Caesar against the spirit of Pompey.

(3) Be gone!......this ingratitude (Lines 55-58)

These are the concluding lines of Marullus's speech addressed to the Roman crowd in the opening scene of *Julius Caesar,* a Roman play written by Shakespeare.

Marullus has already reminded the people in the crowd of their past admiration for great Pompey. As Caesar is much inferior to Pompey, Marullus tells the people in the crowd that they should not at all welcome Caesar. He asks them to go home. He also reminds them that by forgetting the great Pompey, the Romans have committed a crime,— the crime of ingratitude. Therefore, the Romans must repent for it. It is sure that the gods will send a plague to Rome as a punishment for the Romans' ingratitude towards Pompey. The Romans must go home and kneel down and pray to the gods to forgive them for their crime of forgetfulness so that they may not be punished.

(4) Go, go, good countrymen......exalted shores of all (Lines 59-63)

In these lines taken from Shakespeare's *Julius Caesar* we find Flavius asking the citizens of Rome to atone for their ingratitude to Pompey.

A crowd of Romans have gathered in the streets of Rome to welcome Caesar with honour as he has defeated Pompey, Flavius and Marullus. The two tribunes are supporters of Pompey, and naturally, therefore, they are opposed to the triumph to be accorded to Caesar. So they are driving away the citizens. Flavius in these lines asks the people of artisan class to express their sorrow for their ingratitude to Pompey whom they once honoured. These people are going to pay great respects to Julius Caesar who has defeated Pompey. So, Flavius says they should repent. He asks them to gather all the poor people of artisan class together and take them to the bank of the Tiber. The people should weep and shed tears into the river, so that the water rises from its lowest level and touches the highest point of the shore.

The people hearing this speech of Flavius go away. This shows that the citizens of Rome are not stable in mind.

(5) These growing..........servile fearfulness (Lines 77-80)

These lines have been taken from William Shakespeare's play "Julius Caesar". Flavius and Marullus managed to chastise the crowd which assembled in the street of Rome to welcome Caesar back Rome. Both are not happy with Caesar.

In the lines given for explanation, Flavius refers to the new honours conferred on Caesar by his flatterers. They have decked the streets of Rome with his images. Flavius asks Marullus to remove the decorations of Caesar. Caesar is then compared to a falcon. A falcon flies at a great height before swooping down on its prey. Similarly Caesar has been offered undeserved honour. He is winging in the air. If the feathers were plucked from the falcon, it will cease to fly at the great height. Similarly the new honours done to Caesar must be withdrawn. He can be thus kept within limits. If the falcon has profuse feathers it flies above the view of man. Similarly if Caesar is offered unlimited honours, his ambition will soar high. He will elevate himself to the position of God. He will look down upon the ordinary men. The Romans will remain under him in object slavery. He will be looked with awe. Hence Flavius proposes to strike at the root of Caesar's ambition.

The metaphor is apt. The metaphor is from falconry. Armour comments : " Shakespeare is keen on illustrating his meaning from metaphors drawn from sport. He knew that they would be readily grasped and fully appreciated by the sport-loving Elizabethans."

Act I — Scene II

(6) For our elders say........sterile curse (Lines 6-8)

These lines have been taken from *Julius Caesar* written by William Shakespeare. In these lines Julius Caesar asks Antony to touch his wife Calpurnia during the holy race so that her barrenness may be removed.

Julius Caesar entertains imperial dreams. Naturally he desires a son. At the annual festival of Lupercal priests used to run a holy race. They touched all barren women who stood in their paths. This ceremony was supposed to be held for the removal of barrenness. Caesar, therefore, asks Antony, who is one of the priests, to touch Calpurnia. Caesar insists that Antony should not forget this. He explains that their elders say that if the childless women are touched in the course of this sacred race, they will be cured of barrenness.

These lines clearly show that Caesar was inherently superstitious.

(7) Vex'd I am.......to my behaviours (Lines 39-42)

These lines have been taken from *Julius Caesar* written by William Shakespeare. Here we find an expression of Brutus's gloomy nature.

Cassius's heart is full of malice against Caesar, and he is trying to poison the mind of Brutus against him. He finds that Brutus is already wearing a gloomy appearance. Not knowing the true cause of his gloominess Cassius says that Brutus has become unfriendly to him. Hearing this Brutus tells him he should not misunderstand him. He keeps his troubles to himself. He says that he has, of late, been troubled by some conflicting emotions. These emotions concern Brutus only, and have not been communicated to others. That is why, perhaps, he looks gloomy and indifferent to his friends.

This shows that Brutus has been agitated over Caesar's autocratic ambitions and has been secretly thinking what to do. His love for Caesar and love for Rome are in conflict. He has, in fact, a quarrel not with his friends but with himself. Here the self-introspective character of Brutus is suggested.

(8) I have heard........had his eyes (Lines 58-62)

These lines have been taken from *Julius Caesar* written by William Shakespeare. These words are spoken to Brutus by Cassius, a born politician. Cassius has a personal malice against Caesar and wants to poison Brutus's mind against him.

With an intention to probe Brutus's real feeling about Caesar Cassius tells him that Brutus does not realize his own worth. Cassius says that he has heard many respectable men of Rome speak highly of Brutus. All except Caesar say that their age is suffering under tyranny. They wish if Brutus knew how noble and great he is. They also wish Brutus to relieve them of this age's yoke.

(9) Therefore, good......yet know not of (Lines 66-70)

These lines are spoken by Cassius and are addressed to Brutus in Act I, Scene 2, of the Roman play, *Julius Caesar.* Like a typical idealist-philosopher, Brutus does not know that he is held in very high esteem by the people of Rome. Cassius is indulging in subtle flattery here and he is assuring that he will help Brutus in understanding his own greatness. Cassius had pointed out earlier that no one can see himself except in a mirror. Brutus too cannot see his own worth. Cassius, therefore, promises to act as a mirror to Brutus. In other words, he has very cleverly prepared the mind of Brutus for accepting flattery. Of course, Brutus was really popular and what Cassius said was not all flattery. But Cassius has succeeded in making Brutus's mind prepared to join the conspiracy against Caesar.

(10) If you know..........me dangerous (Lines 74-78)

These lines are spoken by Cassius and addressed to Brutus in Act I, Scene 2, of *Julius Caesar,* a Roman play written by William Shakespeare. Cassius had earlier pointed out that Brutus could see himself only in a mirror. Cassius had also offered to act as a mirror to Brutus and to show him by reflection all the greatness that is present in Brutus's personality. Continuing Cassius is here asking Brutus to have faith in him and not to consider him a dangerous person. By way of assurance, Cassius claims here that he is not a hypocrite. He is not in the habit of flattering people to their face and of condemning them behind their back. He also does not claim to be friendly with the low, common people. In other words, Cassius is trying to convince Brutus of his true affection and friendship. He suggests that Brutus should not think of Cassius as a treacherous friend who is flattering Brutus to his face and who would speak ill of him behind his back.

(11) What is it...........indifferently (Lines 84-87)

This statement of Brutus is from *Julius Caesar.* Cassius asks Brutus a question: "Can you see your own face?" He goes on to regret that Brutus cannot see his hidden worthiness. While Cassius is speaking, there is heard from the distance, where the race is being held, a great shout from the crowd. Brutus is startled. Cassius remarks that Brutus does not want to see Caesar made king.

Brutus asks him what it is that Cassius has intended to impart to him. He also assures him that if it is anything that concerns the public welfare, he will contemplate both death and honour quite impartially. He will think honour to be cheaply purchased even by the loss of life. That price will never make him falter or hesitate at clutching such a price.

Here Brutus is pompous in his statement. These lines also examine the honesty of Brutus.

(12) Well, honour........as I myself (Lines 92-96)

These lines are taken from Act I, Scene 2 of Shakespeare's Roman play, *Julius Caesar.* After Brutus says that he prefers honour to death while acting for the general good, Cassius tells Brutus that he too is speaking on the subject of honour. Cassius states that he does not know that Brutus thinks of this life. But Cassius wants to lead a life of honour and prestige. He lives in a Republic and he is convinced that all Romans living in the Republic of Rome are honourable men of equal stature. Cassius suggests that Julius Caesar is in no respect superior to Cassius, or Brutus, or any other Roman. Cassius, therefore, hates the situation prevailing in Rome, in which Cassius is to live as a subordinate to Caesar. Cassius strongly declares that he will prefer to die rather than live, dishonourably under a person who is not at all superior to him.

(13) I, as Aeneas...............tired Caesar (Lines 112-115)

This long line is an extract from William Shakespeare's play "Julius Caesar". An animated conversation is going on between Cassius and Brutus. Brutus has offered his services to Cassius for the welfare of Romans. Cassius then switches on to the weaknesses in Caesar's body. Once Caesar had challenged Cassius to swim across the Tiber.

Before he could reach the destination, Caesar sought the help of Cassius. Cassius then carried Caesar on his shoulder and rescued him. Cassius compares himself to Aeneas. Aeneas was a celebrated Trojan hero. He carried his father on his shoulder and thus rescued him from the fire which destroyed Troy. Similarly Cassius carried Caesar on his shoulder and saved his life. Caesar was tired of swimming.

This story about Aeneas is told by Virgil. Aeneas was a Trojan prince, the son of Anchises and Aphrodite. Tradition had it that Aeneas settled in Rome and was the first ancestor of the Romans. Anchises was king of Dardanus on Mt. Ida. Shakespeare had already this simile in Henry VI; v.ii.61. Shakespeare also belittles Caesar as a swimmer. It is perhaps a part of his scheme to show Caesar lower in comparison with Brutus and others. It is also to be noted that line has twelve syllables.

(14) And this man is now.........but nod on him (Lines 115-118)

These lines have been taken from *Julius Caesar* written by William Shakespeare. Here Cassius is speaking about the honour Caesar has received without deserving it.

According to Cassius Caesar is not greater than him in any respect. Cassius claims to be stronger than Caesar. He gives an example. Once Caesar and Cassius were swimming in the river Tiber. Caesar was on the verge of being drowned. Cassius saved the life of helpless Caesar that time. But this Caesar Cassius says, has been given divine honours even in his life-time, and Cassius is a miserable creature who must bow down if Caesar recognizes him by careless nod.

This statement in which Cassius makes a comparison between Caesar and himself expresses presence of envy and jealousy in Cassius's attitude to Caesar.

(15) Ye gods..............bear the Palm alone (Lines 128-31)

These lines are taken from Shakespeares' *Julius Caesar,* Cassius is trying to excite Brutus's special aversion by emphasizing Caesar's weakness.

Cassius says that Caesar does not deserve the prizes of supremacy. He is a man of weak disposition. Cassius is truly surprised to see that a man of such a weak temperament as Caesar should be assigned the prize of victory in the Roman empire, and enjoy supremacy alone.

Here Shakespeare has used a metaphor taken from Olympic games, in which reward of victory was given only to one man.

(16) Why, man..............graves (Lines 133-136)

This line is taken from William Shakespeare's ''Julius Caesar''. While Cassius and Brutus are talking with each other, a second general shout is heard from the festivity of Lupercal. Brutus thinks a new honour is being bestowed upon Caesar.

In the line given for explanation, Cassius compares Caesar to the famous statue of Colossus at Rhodes. In the first line, Caesar is placed in reference to the world. He is so mighty, of such consequence, that he stands on this earth with legs apart. The world is characterised as "narrow" because he is so mighty in it. He is like a Colossus. This was a famous bronze statue which stood astride at the entrance at the harbour of Rhodes. It was said that ships with sails on could easily pass between its legs. Then comes the second comparison, of other men in relation to Caesar. The other men are petty. They are so small as to walk about under his huge legs, not even shoulder high to the superman, Caesar. Being so tiny, their vision is described with a minimizing verb: they do not scan horizons or search the skies, but "peep about". Ultimately they find nothing but grave. Even those graves will be dishonourable, for they will not be the graves of freemen.

Comparison in these lines is stark, vivid, dramatic and even jolting to the mind and senses, as it is meant to be. Thus Shakespeare has created in the reader's mind and perceptions Cassius's state of mind, dissatisfaction and disgust. The last line is an instance of transferred epithet.

(17) Men at some...........are underlings (Lines 137-139)

These lines are taken from Act I, Scene 2 of the Roman play, *Julius Caesar,* composed by Shakespeare. Brutus and Cassius are talking on the streets of Rome when they hear the people cheering Caesar. The envious Cassius compares Caesar to a mighty Colossus, and the contemporary Romans to pigmies. He is continuing the idea and explaining the situation further by suggesting that the Romans have become fatalist and that is why they are accepting Caesar and his tyranny without protest or rebellion. The Romans surely feel that Caesar's rise in power is due to the favourable disposition of the stars. But Cassius says that this is not so. Certain opportunities come in the lives of all men when even fate will favour them. But the Romans of his age are all persons of inferior calibre. They are by nature underlings, that is to say, men who are easy to govern. If, therefore, Caesar has grown so great, the Romans should not blame fate or the stars. It is the inferiority complex of Romans themselves which is responsible for having made Caesar into a Colossus.

(18) Why should.............as 'Caesar' (Lines 142-146)

These lines are spoken by Cassius to Brutus in Act I, Scene 2 of *Julius Caesar,* a Roman play written by Shakespeare. In order to flatter Brutus

Cassius is here comparing the two words "Brutus" and "Caesar". The name Brutus is as good as Caesar. It sounds equally good and can be used with as much ease as the name Caesar. Moreover, in Rome, the name of Brutus inspires people as much as does the name of Caesar. In other words, Brutus is as popular as Caesar, and Brutus's name too can act like magic upon the people. Then why should Caesar become such a great man and such a darling of the Romans?

(19) Age, thou art .... talk'd of Rome (Lines 150-154)

These lines have been taken from *Julius Caesar* written by Shakespeare. These words are spoken to Brutus by Cassius.

Cassius is trying to convince the idealist philosopher, Brutus and win him to his side. He says that Brutus is in no way inferior to Caesar. Yet Caesar is going to enjoy supremacy. This the Roman citizens should not tolerate. He has worked himself into a passion and says that never in history since the great flood has there been a time with only one man to rule. It is really a disgrace to this age, that it should allow one man, that is Julius Caesar, to become so great. It seems that Rome has become devoid of the race of ancient heroes, and man of spirits.

Very cleverly Cassius is trying to excite a passion of hatred in Brutus against Caesar.

Shakespeare here alludes to the universal deluge of classical mythology in which Deucalion and his wife Pyrrha alone escaped. Some people are of the opinion that Shakespeare had in mind Noah's flood which was better known to Shakespeare's audience.

(20) Oh, you and I have heard.....easily as a king (Lines 158-161)

These lines have been taken from *Julius Caesar* written by William Shakespeare. In these lines Cassius invites Brutus to set himself as a rival to Caesar.

In these lines Cassius excites Brutus's passion by a reference to the traditional devotion of Brutus's family to the cause of liberty. He reminds him of Junius Brutus who was instrumental in expelling the Tarquins from the throne of Rome and setting up a republic. He says that they have heard from their parents that once upon a time there was in Rome a Brutus who would rather allow an absolute devil to rule over Rome than a mere king.

Very contemptuously Cassius refers to Caesar and means to say that Brutus should take upon himself the task of preventing Caesar from rising to the absolute power.

(21) The angry spot...........some senators (Lines 183-88)

These lines are taken from Act I, Scene 2 of the Roman play, *Julius Caesar* composed by Shakespeare. While Brutus and Cassius are talking, Caesar's procession returns. Brutus is in these lines describing how Caesar looks as also others in the procession. Caesar's face is flushed and Brutus interprets it as being the red colour of anger. Caesar looks angry and the others in the procession appear so timid that they look like children who have been scolded by their leader, Caesar. Calpurnia's cheek is quite pale. Then there is Cicero, the great orator. Brutus has seen him many times speaking in the Senate. When other senators oppose Cicero in the debate Cicero gets angry and his eyes become fiery red. Brutus sees in Cicero's eyes the same red colour.

From all this Brutus comes to the conclusion that something has happened which Caesar does not like and that is why he looks so angry and also that Caesar has scolded others in the procession.

(22) Let me have men.............dangerous (Lines 189-192)

These lines have been taken from William Shakespeare's play *Julius Caesar*. *Caesar* catches a glimpse of Cassius from a distance and sketches him in these immortal lines before Antony.

Cassius is a man of spare build and has the look of a hungry man. He studies seriously. He is given to meditation. He does not know the soothing effect of sleep. Such men as Cassius are most dangerous and should be avoided like prison. On the other hand, Caesar wants to see around him men with smooth-combed hair and having glossy and unwrinkled faces. He wants a man who sleeps profoundly at night without being troubled by study and cares. For such men enjoying perfect health are quite peace-loving types of humanity who never think ill of others.

Caesar reveals his shrewdness and fatuousness in these lines. There is even a sort of irony in his dogmatically stated aversion to "lean and hungry men" being a counter-point as it is to Cassius earlier remark "Upon what meat doth this our Caesar feed."

(23) He reads.................smile at anything (Lines 200-206)

These lines have been taken from *Julius Caesar* written by William Shakespeare. In these lines we find an analysis of Cassius's character by Julius Caesar.

Caesar thinks that a man like Cassius is very dangerous. But Antonio says that he (Cassius) is one of the noble Romans, and should not be feared. At this Caesar says that Cassius reads and broods too much. He is a shrewd observer of human nature and events, and he can correctly read human nature and motives. Cassius does not play and is not, unlike Antony, a sportsman. He does not love music and seldom smiles. Even if he smiles, his smile is dry as if he scorns himself for being weak enough and childish to give way to emotion. He is very serious.

Caesar says that such men are dangerous and are to be feared. These lines are significant so far as the estimate of Cassius is concerned.

(24) Such men as...............I am Caesar (Lines 208-10)

These lines are taken from Act I, Scene 2 of the Roman play, *Julius Caesar,* written by Shakespeare. Caesar has given his own assessment of the personality of Cassius to Antony. In these lines Caesar is making the concluding remarks about Cassius. Summing up all the defects of Cassius's character, Caesar says that Cassius is extremely envious by temperament. That is why, he cannot bear the sight of any one superior to himself. When Cassius comes across someone like Caesar who is his superior, his heart grows restless and he is filled with the poison of envy. This is the reason why Cassius is dangerous, because the poison of envy may make him do something terrible.

But at this point Caesar remembers that he is Julius Caesar and too great for Cassius. So, in a tone filled with self-assurance and conceit, Caesar says that he himself is not afraid of Cassius. He is merely reminding Antony that men like Cassius are to be generally feared.

(25) And still as he refused................down at it (Lines 245-50)

These lines are spoken by Casca to Brutus and Cassius in Act I, Scene 2 of the Roman play, *Julius Caesar,* written by William Shakespeare. Casca is here giving a description of what happened when Caesar was offered a crown by Antony.

Caesar refused to accept the crown three times. On the third occasion the mob of low class Romans shouted, clapped their hands loudly and threw their dirty bad-smelling caps in the air. There was so much foul smell coming from the breathing of the mob and from their clothes that Julius Caesar was choked.

He fell upon the ground senseless. Caeser is here expressing his own contempt for the low-class mob which plays such an important role in the play, *Julius Caesar.*

(26) No, Caesar hath it not.........falling sickness (Lines 257-258)

These lines have been taken from *Julius Caesar* written by William Shakespeare. Casca describes here how the crown was offered to Julius Caesar. While describing Casca informs them that Caesar had fainted down and was foaming at mouth.

Brutus, hearing this says that it is quite likely, because Caesar suffers from falling sickness. Brutus refers to epileptic fit from which Caesar suffers. But Cassius is quick to catch this phrase and uses it against Caesar. He immediately retorts that it is not Caesar who suffers from falling sickness but the Romans who allow themselves to fall to the position of underlings.

Cassius here wants to excite Brutus and other friends of his against Caesar by pointing out a drawback in their character. Cassius seems to possess a deep sense of hatred against Caesar and wants to harm him.

(27) Nay, an I tell.................Greek to me (Lines 284-87)

These lines are taken from Act I, Scene 2 of the Roman play, *Julius Caesar,* written by Shakespeare. When Julius Ceasar fainted after refusing the crown the third time, Cicero made some comments in Greek. Being asked by Cassius as to what did Cicero say, Casca is giving in these lines his own comments. Casca does not know Greek and, therefore, he would not pretend that he understood what Cicero said. Again, Casca bluntly says that if he gives a false report about what Cicero said, he would be so much ashamed that he would never show his face to Cassius. The only thing that Casca says is that some people in the crowd understood Cicero's words and they smiled at one another and shook their heads. But Casca confesses that Cicero's words were wholly unintelligible to him.

(28) So is he now......better appetite (Lines 301-06)

These lines are taken from Act, I, Scene 2 of *Julius Caesar,* a Roman play, written by Shakespeare. After the departure of Casca, Brutus comments that Casca used to be quick-witted and sharp in his school-days, though now he looks dull. But in these lines Cassius assures Brutus that even at present Casca is sharp and intelligent. He is also bold and quite capable of performing any daring act. Casca, in Cassius's opinion, is the fittest man for taking the first step in the murder of Caesar. The dullness of appearance and bluntness of speech are only a pose. Casca does not want others to know that he is very intelligent and sharp. He, therefore, speaks rudely like a rustic. This rough and crude manner of Casca talking, his normal words may not impress. But his rough and blunt words always impress the hearers and they accept his words quite readily. So, Casca's crude manner and rough words are a clever device used by him to make his own words more impressive.

(29) Well, Brutus.........seduc'd? (Lines 311-316)

These lines have been taken from *Julius Caesar* written by William Shakespeare. These lines reveal to us a thorough picture of Cassius's mind. Cassius has spoken to Brutus against Caesar in order to win him to his side. Brutus is already vexed by conflicts going on inside him. So he goes away promising to meet him some other time. After Brutus goes away Cassius speaks these words.

This soliloquy shows that Cassius admires the noble nature of Brutus. But after all Brutus is a human being, and very few man can remain firm in their principles. Cassius feels that Brutus, too, will not stick to his philosophy. He has noticed that Brutus is half-willing to raise his army against Julius Caesar. Cassius has flattered and poisoned his mind. He suggests that good natured people may fall in evil company, and their name may be tainted. So they should keep company with men of their own type.

This soliloquy of Cassius shows that Cassius is really a shrewd observer and knows the ins and outs of human mind and nature. Cassius is always unerring and touches the weakest aspect of human nature. Therefore, he flatters Brutus to win him to his side.

(30) Caesar doth........humour me (Lines 317-319)

These lines have been taken from *Julius Caesar* written by William Shakespeare. These words are spoken by Cassius in his soliloquy.

Cassius is happy that he has been partially successful in inciting Brutus against Julius Caesar. His words have had some effect on the mind of Brutus. But he fails to appreciate Brutus's attitude. He knows that Caesar does not have a high opinion about Cassius; but he loves Brutus. It is really surprising that Brutus has allowed himself to be influenced against his friend. Cassius is sure that had he been in place of Brutus, he would not have allowed anybody to influence him against his friends.

These lines throw light on Cassius's character. He has his own way of looking at things and is not affected by others. Therefore, he dislikes Caesar's change of attitude.

Act I — Scene III

(32) Either............destruction (Lines 11-13)

These lines have been taken from Shakespeare's *Julius Caesar*. We have Casca's own interpretation of the storm.

The conspirators are going to meet for deciding the course of action. t is a stormy night and almost everyone finds a meaning into the storm, according to his own understanding. Casca thinks that the storm indicates that gods have declared a civil war amongst themselves. And if it is not so, they have become angry with human beings for their impertinent actions and are sending storms to punish them.

These lines show that Casca is a god-fearing man and so he interprets the storm from his own angle of vision.

(33) When these..........they point upon (Lines 28-32)

These lines are spoken by Casca to Cicero in Act I, Scene 3 of *Julius Caesar*, the Roman play, written by Shakespeare. Earlier Casca had given an account of all the unnatural things that took place in Rome.

Now, in these lines Casca states that one or two of such ominous things could be called accidents. But there are too many terrible omens and taken together, they prove that there is something very much wrong. When such it is a sure indication that something very terrible is going to happen in the near future.

(34) "Why, you shall find.........monstrous state (Lines 68-71)

These lines have been taken from *Julius Caesar*, written by William Shakespeare. In these lines Cassius is explaining to Casca the inner meaning of the thunder and lightning and other supernatural incidents.

Casca tells Cassius that powerful gods have sent these abnormal forces as messengers to confound us. It is natural for man to fear. Why should, then, Cassius be so much anxious and worried about all this? Cassius tells Casca in reply that he is dull and does not understand the real meaning of all this. On a careful consideration of such fires and other supernatural incidents he can easily find that gods have filled them with power to give man warning against some horrible state of things.

Very cleverly Cassius here refers to Julius Caesar's growing power and ambition and consequent death of Roman republicanism.

(35) Now, could I,..........eruptions are (Lines 72-78)

These lines are spoken by Cassius to Casca in Act I, Scene III of *Julius Caesar,* a Roman play by Shakespeare. Cassius has been walking in the streets of Rome during the storm and he is now explaining why he was not afraid of the terrible omens. Casca feels that the unnatural happenings are the expression of the anger of the gods who want to punish the sinful Romans. But Cassius gives another twist to the situation. There is in Rome at the moment a man who is as terrible as the unnatural happenings. That man is not named here, but Cassius means Caesar. According to Cassius Caesar is behaving like a tyrannical dictator. He speaks in a voice like thunder, he takes vengeance swiftly like lightning, he roars like a lion and he even opens graves to bring dishonour upon dead men. Caesar is not at all superior to either Casca, or Cassius in his personal qualities. But Caesar has become terrible just as the unnatural storms and other happenings have become. In other words, Caesar is as much *a freak of nature* as the unnatural happenings are.

(36) Let it be who..........us womanish. (Lines 80-84)

These lines are taken from Act I, Scene 3 of the Roman play, *Julius Caesar,* written by William Shakespeare. Here Cassius is speaking to Casca and is explaining why the Romans are not rebelling against Caesar. In their bodily construction the contemporary Romans are manly and vigorous like their forefathers. But it appears that they have inherited the spirit of their mothers. The fact that Romans are behaving like cattle and are willingly accepting the tyranny of Caesar without any murmur, proves that the Romans have become effeminate and womanish in spirit. They are no longer manly.

(37) Therein, ye gods..........dismiss itself (Lines 91-97)

These lines have been taken from *Julius Caesar,* written by William Shakespeare. Here Cassius is cleverly trying to win Casca to his side.

When Casca says that the senators are willing to make Julius Caesar the king of Rome, Cassius tells him that he will choose to commit suicide to save himself from slavery. He says that God has given even the weakest man the power to avoid dishonour by self-inflicted death. This weapon of suicide in the hand of a weak man is strong enough to baffle the power of a tyrant because a tyrant can imprison only the body of a man and not the spirit. Stone walls, well-fortified prisons and chains of iron, and airless underground cells cannot check the human souls. A man tired of this world under a tyrant can easily get rid of all sufferings by killing himself.

This speech of Cassius shows a lofty idealism in the character of Cassius. Here he shows himself to be a true lover of his country and not a hater of Julius Caesar.

(38) And why should......make a mighty fire (Lines 103-106)

These lines have been taken from *Julius Caesar* written by William Shakespeare. In these lines Cassius is exciting hatred against Julius Caesar in the mind of Casca. Cassius wants to win Casca to his side. Therefore he says that Julius Caesar is an insignificant trash and yet the Roman people who are weak think Caesar to be strong and powerful.

When Casca says that he can also commit suicide in order to rid himself of slavery Cassius says that there is no reason why Julius Caesar should be a tyrant. Roman people are very unfortunate. They are as weak and meek as sheep. Caesar has realized this. That is why he behaves like a wolf. Romans are just like deer. Therefore, Caesar behaves like a lion.

In these lines Cassius seems to say that the people of Rome have become weak and demoralized and this has given opportunity to Caesar to exert his power and influence. Cassius does not want to tolerate this and is bent upon nipping Caesar's ambition in the bud. These lines also show Cassius's cleverness and maturity as a politician. In course of his talk with Casca Cassius states how powerful an instrument suicide is which can liberate a man from the prisons of tyrants. Continuing the idea Cassius says that when a man is tired of his life, he can put an end to it in a moment. This power of life to end itself is known to everyone. Similarly, he knows that the bond of tyranny he is suffering under Caesar can be ended in a moment by him at his own sweet will.

(39) Those that..........a thing as Caesar (Lines 107-11)

These lines are taken from Act I, Scene 3, of the Roman play, *Julius Caesar,* written by William Shakespeare. Cassius is explaining as to how the gutless, foolish Romans are making Caesar greater by having lost their ownself-respect and Republican individuality. If one wants to build a fire in a hurry, one will have to light the fire with straws and leaves. The Romans are like a heap of dry rubbish, a pile of straw and garbage. They are made of base matter which will burn quickly. Caesar, like a clever man, is burning this base heap of rubbish. In other words, the Romans are allowing themselves to be used for making Caesar great. The Romans are burning their own self-respect and honour and the personality of Caesar shines all the more in this borrowed light.

(40) For now ...... most terrible (Lines 126-30)

There lines are taken from Act I, Scene 3 of the Roman play *Julius Caesar,* written by William Shakespeare. Cassius has informed Casca that many noble-minded Romans are waiting in the portico of the theatre built by Pompey. Thereafter Cassius comments on the stormy night. No one dares to go out in the streets on such a fearful night. But the foul weather is quite appropriate for their conspiracy. The clouds have rained blood, and the conspirators are going to shed the blood of Caesar. Like the unnatural fire seen in the stormy, rainy night, the murderers are going to ignite the fires of Civil war which will plunge Rome in the most terrible blood-bath. Cassius is, ironically enough, making a prophecy of what their conspiracy will lead to

(41) O, he sits ...... to worthiness (Lines 157-60)

These lines are taken from Act I, Scene 3 of *Julius Caesar,* a Roman play written by William Shakespeare. When Cassius informs Casca that Brutus has been three-fourths won over by the conspirators, Casca is very happy. Casca is, in these lines, explaining the value of Brutus's support to their cause. Brutus is highly respected by the Romans and his association with the conspirators would give them respectability. The killing of Caesar was going to be a black deed and an act like a base metal, as for example, lead or zinc or iron. But Brutus's support was like the science of alchemy through which a base metal can be changed into gold. Similarly, the killing of Caesar will be thought to be a noble deed when the Romans find Brutus to be in favour of the killing. If the conspirators by themselves kill Caesar, they will be declared to be murderers. But Brutus's support will make it a noble deed. J.H. Walter sees in this an ironic forecast of their lack of success.

Act II — Scene I

(42) It must be by his death....walking. (Lines 10-15)

These lines have been taken from *Julius Caesar* written by William Shakespeare.

Brutus is thinking aloud in his orchard. A conflict is going on inside his mind. He has no personal grudge in his heart against Julius Caesar. He knows that Caesar is above reproach. But he is worried about the future of Rome which he loves more than Julius Caesar. He thinks that there is possibility of Caesar being crowned. If Caesar is recognized as a king his nature will change. A snake comes out in the broad day light, in the warmth of the sun. So a man must walk cautiously on a sunny day against the danger of a snake. Similarly Caesar may rise high and become as dangerous as a snake and show his tyrannical power when he will get the sunshine of royalty. Therefore, the Roman people must be careful against Caesar when he becomes a king.

This soliloquy of Brutus shows that Brutus is a great patriot. He wants to kill Caesar whom he loves, for the sake of his country.

(43) But 't is a......his back (Lines 21-25)

These lines have been taken from William Shakespeare's play *Julius Caesar*. In these lines Brutus sets forth the reason why Caesar should be murdered. In the preceding lines he has confessed that he does not remember any occasion when Caesar has been ruled by his feelings rather than by reasons. But now he admits that the past is no guarantee for the future.

It is a matter of common experience that all ambitious men show good feelings at the beginning. They pretend humility and goodness to all, so that under cover of these they rise to power and position. When their ends are secured, they cast off humility and appear in their true character. In this respect the ambitious men are like the climber of a ladder. A man reaches the highest rung of the ladder across the lower ones and from that highest rung of the ladder looks to the clouds. He scorns the ladder which has elevated him so high. Similarly, when an ambitious man reaches the height of his ambitions by pretended humility, he casts off the humility which helped him to rise and aims at something still higher.

(44) And since......in the shell (Lines 28-34)

These lines have been taken from William Shakespeare's *Julius Caesar*. In these lines we find Brutus justifying the reason why Caesar should be murdered although his character and conduct at present do not justify his murder.

Brutus arrives at the conclusion that Caesar is ambitious and he hides his real nature under the cover of the humanity. He thinks that Caesar may be regarded as a serpent's egg which, when hatched, grows into venomous snake. When Caesar is crowned, he may feel excessively powerful and may be a danger to the Roman republicanism. In order to prevent such a possibility Julius Caesar should be killed.

This argument of Brutus shows his lack of practical wisdom and also his lack of human psychology. He does not know that each individual has a nature of his own. This lack of knowledge leads him to commit a blunder unconsciously.

(45) O conspiracy, ...monstrous visage (Lines 77-81)

These lines are taken from Act II, Scene 1 of *Julius Caesar,* a Roman play written by William Shakespeare. In the night of 14th March, the conspirators, led by Cassius came to Brutus's house for final preparation and talks regarding Caesar's murder, which was to take place on 15th March, the Ides of March. Lucius informs Brutus that the faces of all the visitors are muffled and that he cannot identify any of them. Brutus is both surprised and pained by this. Being an upright and honourable man, he cannot understand why the noble Romans should hide their faces. But he remembers that it is a conspiracy and he speaks these lines addressing the spirit of conspiracy, as it were. The dark forces of evil roam during the night. And yet conspiracy is ashamed to move freely in the darkness. Is it not ironical? Brutus continues to ask another question. What would conspiracy do then in bright day-light? Would it conceal itself in some dark underground cavern? Where would it seek for such a dark place? Where it could hide its shameful face and terrible intention to kill Caesar?

(46) Seek none......from prevention, (Lines 81-85)

These lines are taken from Act II, Scene 1 of *Julius Caesar,* a Roman play, written by Shakespeare. When the conspirators go to Brutus's house at night, with their faces muffled, Brutus realises that they all are engaged in a black, sinful act. He, therefore, advises them not to show their sinful intentions reflected on their face, or else, even the darkest regions of Hell will not be dark enough to hide their sinful faces. Brutus suggests that the best thing for the conspirators to do would be to wear expressions of smiles and affability on their faces. They should not allow their faces to be the index of their mind. Thus alone can the conspirators walk out in the bright day-light and commit their heinous crime with an open countenance. In short, Brutus suggests that conspiracy can succeed only when it is hypocritical.

(47) No, not an oath......by lottery (Lines 114-119)

These lines have been taken from *Julius Caesar* written by William Shakespeare. In these lines Brutus is making a spirited reply to the suggestion made by Cassius that conspirators should swear their resolution.

Brutus does not agree with this suggestion. He says that it is only a weak man who takes oath for the pursuit of his aim. A strong and sincere man has the spirit to right the wrong and he never takes an oath. Brutus says that if the conspirators have sincerity of purpose, they need not take an oath. The faces of the Romans reflect the troubles they are suffering from. Corrupt practices seen all round and inward suffering of the patriots should be sufficient to inspire them to action. If these things do not inspire them, it is futile to take oaths. They should give up their attempts and go back to their inactive beds. Let tyranny (in the shape of Caesar) move about freely so that each one of them may have their ruin as his turn comes.

These lines reveal that Brutus has a noble mind and wants to kill Caesar inspired by a vision of suffering of the people of Rome that may be caused by the growing power of Julius Caesar.

(48) But if these........us to redress. (Lines 119-124)

These lines are taken from Act II, Scene 1 of the Roman play, *Julius Caesar,* written by William Shakespeare. Brutus rejects the proposal for swearing an oath and lists many things that are enough to unite them in their resolve to kill Caesar. In fact, these are enough to instil courage even in the heart of cowards. These are enough to change even the soft and tender hearts of women into hard steel. These causes are, therefore, enough to act like a spur to drive their resolution and make them strong enough to take revenge against Caesar and thus put an end to his tyranny.

(49) What other bond......fall for it? (Lines 124-128)

These lines are taken from Act II, Scene 1 of the Roman play, *Julius Caesar,* written by William Shakespeare. Brutus is of opinion that oaths are not required to unite the conspirators who have the power to keep a secret since they have given their solemn promise to eliminate the tyrant Caesar. The resolution of the Romans will not falter from their aim. Since their aim is an honest one and they are pursuing it with honesty, they do not need an oath to bind them. He is sure that the purity of their aim and the honesty of their purpose is enough to make them do or die. The Romans do not need to swear an oath.

(50) Swear priests......as men doubt (Lines 129-132)

These lines are spoken by Brutus to the conspirators, while rejecting the proposal to swear an oath, in Act II, Scene 1, of *Julius Caesar,* a Roman play written by Shakespeare. Brutus gives here a list of those who take oaths and points out why they do so. Priests who cheat innocent people in the name of God are in the habit of taking oaths. Cowards and cunning people too swear oaths. Old, weak people and those who are too weak to struggle against the oppressions of tyrants take oaths. All the people of the above categories are forced to swear oaths because nobody will believe them if they do not swear an oath. Then there are those who fight for an unjust cause and these people swear an oath to convince others that their cause is a just one. But Brutus and the other noble Romans who have resolved to eliminate tyranny and dictatorship do not belong to any of these categories, and so there is no need for them to swear an oath.

(51) When every drop of blood......pass'd from him (Lines 136-140)

These lines are taken from William Shakespears's *Julius Caesar.* Brutus expresses his strong protest against the proposal of swearing their resolution.

Brutus says that their honourable mission and their courage do not need an oath. It is known to everybody that when a noble man of Rome breaks even a single particle of his oath, each drop of blood in his veins, is guilty of an act showing that he is not a true-born Roman. Therefore, it is not necessary to take any formal oath. Only words will be enough.

This shows Brutus's sincerity of purpose and nobility of mind. He does not want any disgrace brought upon the good name of the Romans, by breaking off of an oath taken by the conspirators.

(52) Let us be sacrificers.....must bleed for it (Lines 166-171)

These lines have been taken from William Shakespeare's *Julius Caesar*. These words are spoken by Brutus when suggestion is made by Cassius that Antony should also be killed simultaneously with Caesar.

Brutus says that they are going to fight a principle and not against a person. They want to crush Caesarism and not Caesar himself. He wishes they could crush that spirit without shedding even a drop of Caesar's blood. But that is not possible. Brutus feels that they are compelled to murder Caesar for their cause. Brutus says that they should act like sacrificers and not like butchers. Butchers kill animals and cut them into pieces. Antony is, according to Brutus, only a limb of Caesar. So he does not want that they should also kill Antony which will amount to cutting Caesar's limbs, after cutting his head.

These lines reveal that Brutus is a good man. But his arguments are far from realities. He fails to recognize the real nature of man.

(53) Never fear that.....most flattered (Lines 202-208)

These lines have been taken from *Julius Caesar,* written by William Shakespeare. These lines, spoken by Decius, throw light on the character of Julius Caesar. Caesar is great but he is easily flattered, which is, after all a human nature.

The conspirators are planning to murder Julius Caesar the next day, at the Capitol. Cassius expresses his fear that Julius Caesar may not come to the Capitol that day. He has recently grown superstitious and may be convinced by the fortune tellers. At this Decius, who knows a weakness of Caesar's character says that nobody should worry about that. He will be able to bring Caesar to the Capitol. He knows that Caesar loves flattery. Caesar loves to hear the story about how the powerful animals are caught by their feelings. Caesar is delighted to hear how unicorns are caught by being made to dash against trees, how bears are deceived with looking glasses, and how elephants are dragged to fall into pits, how the lions are overpowered by foils, and how men are ruined by flattery. When people tell Julius Caesar that he hates flattery, he admits it. But even at that moment he feels most flattered. Decius is certain, therefore, that he will be able to bring him to the Capitol with flattery.

Here we come to learn that Julius Caesar is great, but after all he is a human being and is not free from human frailty. He is also subject to flattery. Decius is seen here as a master of the art of flattery.

(54) No, my Brutus.......ought to know of (Lines 267-270)

These lines have been taken from *Julius Caesar* written by Shakespeare. In these lines we see Portia's love and respect for her husband Brutus.

Portia, noticing Brutus in a restless condition, wants to know the real cause of his anxiety. Brutus sets aside this matter only by saying that he is sick. But Portia is not going to be convinced. She tells her husband that a man does not expose his sick body to the damp air of morning. Brutus is wise enough to know this fact, and yet he has gone out. This means that Brutus is not suffering physically. She says that certainly Brutus is worried and she wants to know the cause of his anxiety. Portia, being Brutus's wife, has the right to know the cause and she must know what is worrying Brutus. As his wife she has also a duty to share his anxiety.

These lines reveal that Brutus does not want to let the cause of his anxiety be known to his wife. But she is devoted and dutiful and in a bold and dignified manner she wants to know everything about her husband's worries.

(55) Within the bond of marriage......not his wife (Lines 280-287)

These lines have been taken from *Julius Caesar* written by William Shakespeare. In these lines Portia tells her husband that she has a right to know the cause of his anxiety by virtue of being his wife.

When asked why he looks worried, Brutus tells his wife that he is sick and that is all. But Portia has noticed that something is torturing his mind. As a devoted wife she wants to share her husband's sorrow. She tells her husband that she is his wife not in a limited sense. Nowhere in their marriage bond it is mentioned that Portia will have not right to share her husband's sorrow. By marriage they are united into one. But Brutus's behaviour shows as if Portia is meant only to share food with him, comfort him in his bed and delight in his company and not to share his sorrow and suffering. She is not ready to compromise with such a position. She does not want to remain only a mistress in the suburbs of his pleasures. She is his wife and must see into the depths of his heart. Portia does not want to be treated only as a mistress but his wife. Therefore, she must know everything that relates to her husband.

In this spirited and dignified speech Portia reveals her character as an ideal woman. Shakespeare has depicted here the noble relation between husband and wife.

(56) I grant I am a woman......secrets (Lines 294-302)

These lines have been taken from *Julius Caesar,* written by Shakespeare. In these spirited words Portia wants to know the secrets of Brutus's mind.

Brutus's mind is full of conflicts and he looks very much worried. When his wife Portia wants to know the cause of his anxiety he simply tells her that he is sick. But Portia says that Brutus must be suffering from some worries. Brutus in course of his talk has already admitted that Portia is very dear to him. Now Portia says that she has every right to share her husband's sorrow. She tells her husband that he must not think that she does not have the patience to keep much superior to all other women. The daughter of Cato (a great philosopher of Rome) and wife of Brutus, Portia must be above the normal level of women. She has already given ample proof of her power of endurance. She has wounded herself in her thigh to make sure that she can bear any secrecy. She is quite sure that if she can patiently bear the pain of that wound she must have the patience of keeping her husband's secrets. She assures her husband that she will not divulge the secrets confided in her.

Here we find Portia's devotion to her husband. She thinks she has a firmness. But we see that though she can endure the physical wound, the acute mental suspense of the fate of the conspirators is too heavy for her and ultimately it brings about her ruin. She is not as strong a woman as she claims to be.

Act II — Scene II

(57) When beggars die......of princes. (Lines 30-31)

These lines have been taken from *Julius Caesar* written by William Shakespeare. Calpurnia, Caesar's wife, is asking Caesar not to go to the Capitol as she has had some unpleasant dreams. Julius Caesar, in reply, says that the abnormal phenomena of nature do not concern only himself but all other Romans. So there is no reason why so much importance should be attached to these events.

Calpurnia then argues that the death of a beggar does not affect the world at all. But the death of a great man, or a prince, is an uncommon event and it may bring about changes in the world. So his death is foreshadowed by unusual events in nature.

Thus Calpurnia means to say that Julius Caesar is a great personality and abnormal events of the previous night concern him. She, therefore, requests her husband not to go out of house.

This statement is an extract from William Shakespeare's play "*Julius Caesar*", Julius Caesar is told by his wife Calpurnia that she has seen bad dream. She interprets the dream for the impending death of Caesar. Caesar replies stoically. He says that whatever is purposed by God cannot be avoided. Calpurnia adds significantly that the death of a prince is heralded by some supernatural happenings in the sky.

The lines given for explanation express the heroic sentiment of Caesar. He contradicts Calpurnia and says that a coward experiences the agony of death at every step of his life. He shrinks from the experience of danger. A man who fears death at every step is a man who dies many times before his natural death comes. His life is a tale of perpetual fear and apprehension. On the other hand a valiant man like Hamlet faces death with equanimity: "the readiness is all." A valiant man never bothers about death as long as he lives in this world. Caesar wonders why people fear death. Death is the inevitable end of the journey on this earth. Nobody can alter this law of life. Die one must. It will come when it is fated to come. Nobody can escape it. Caesar is not coward to live in perpetual terror of death. He is fully prepared for death. He will rather welcome death when it comes.

This speech of Caesar is the best commentary on his fearlessness. No coward soul is his. He is an alien to fear. As we read this statement of Caesar, we feel the presence of a mind that is neither weak nor vacillating, as some critics depicted him. There is something grand in the heroism that breathes through every line of this speech.

(59) Danger knows......terrible (Lines 44-48)

These lines have been taken from William Shakespeare's *Julius Caesar*. In these boastful words Caesar expresses his defiance of danger. The auguries were not favourable to Caesar. The beast that was sacrificed by the priests did not contain any heart. This is rather an evil omen. But Caesar pays no heed to it.

The lines given for explanation are the continuation of the above-mentioned statement. He thinks that by this omen the gods are reproving Caesar's cowardice. Again, why should he be afraid of danger? He is more dangerous than Danger itself. Danger knows this full well. Caesar considers Danger as a living object. He amplifies this idea. He and Danger are like two lions brought forth on the same day. Caesar is elder and more terrible of the two. It is rather Danger which should fly before the face of Caesar and not Caesar who should be afraid of danger. No, Caesar is the last person to stay at home for fear of any danger.

This kind of pride is the very top of weakness. All the evil omens are in vain. His pompous and inflated speech, intolerable when he is speaking in the third person, seem to challenge the gods and to despise all men but himself. Shakespeare, like a Greek dramatist, meant them to contain his fate and the cause of it.

(60) If Caesar hide.....love is liable (Lines 100-04)

These lines are taken from Act II, Scene 2, of the Roman play *Julius Caesar,* written by William Shakespeare. Decius, in his clever, flattering manner is giving many arguments against Caesar's decision to stay at home to please Calpurnia. In these lines Decius uses the argument that if Caesar stays at home people will say and would not divulge the secret. But here we find her extremely weak and utterly helpless. The tension tells upon her mind and this ultimately brings about her ruin.

Act II — Scene IV

(61) O constancy......keep counsel (Lines 6-9)

These lines have been taken from *Julius Caesar* written by Shakespeare. Here we get Portia's helpless utterance when she finds the mental suspense about the fate of the conspirators extremely unbearable.

She wants that she must have strength to keep the secrets to herself. She knows that mentally she is as wise and strong as a man. But at the same time she confesses that she is a woman and has a tender and weak heart. It is really very difficult for her to bear the secrets.

This utterance of Portia reminds us of her proof of endurance which she once had given her husband. She had said that she was superior to other women and would not divulge the secret. But here we find her extremely weak and utterly helpless. The tension tells upon her mind and this, ultimately, brings about her ruin.

Act III — Scene I

(62) These couchings.....spaniel-fawning (Lines 39-43)

These lines have been taken from William Shakespeare's play *Julius*

Caesar. The conspirators draw round Caesar in the Senate House to stab him to death. Following the plan, Metellus Cimber begs the freedom of his brothers from Caesar. He kneels down.

Caesar rejects his appeal immediately. He says that Metellus's humble bowing and courtesies are not to change the heart of Caesar. This may have effect on inferior minds. Caesar cannot change what has been ordained and decreed from the first in the capricious manner of children. He further reminds Metellus not to be fool as to think that Caesar does bear any unreliable disposition. He is a constant man. He cannot melt from the stable quality he ought to have. Metellus's sweet words and obeisance and dog-like flattery will not turn the mind of Caesar, and he will stick to what he has decreed.

This speech of Caesar shows his love of justice. This is nowhere better illustrated than in this dignified speech. Yet we must note the unhappy turn he gives to the expression of his determination by the words 'I spurn thee like a cur out of my way'. His outrageous language further alienated the aristocracy who were the leaders of the conspiracy.

(63) But I am......doth hold his place (Lines 60-65)

These lines have been taken from Shakespeare's *Julius Caesar*. When Metellus Cimber pleads before Caesar for the revokal of the order of banishment of his brother, Caesar rejects it. Then others, like Brutus and Casca, also request Caesar to consider his plea sympathetically.

Caesar then expresses his stern refusal to listen to the prayer of Cassius for the freedom of Publius Cimber. It would be impossible to move him by prayer, if he had the weakness to move others by prayers. In point of constancy, he compares himself to the pole-star which remains fixed up in one and the same place in the sky. Of the innumerable stars in the sky, there is none other which bears comparison with it in point of constancy. Similarly, no power on earth can make Caesar budge an inch from what he has resolved, namely, the banishment of Publius Cimber.

These lines have a strain of bombast and arrogance that is not to be found in the other speeches of Caesar. Dover Wilson opines: "This is to claim super-divinity since even the gods are moved by prayer." Mr. F.S. Boas comments on this speech and says "the death-blows of the conspirators are a tragically ironical retort to such pretensions of superiority to human weakness."

(64) Here wast......the heart of thee. (Lines 204-208)

These lines have been taken from Shakespeare's play *Julius Caesar.* As Antony is talking with the conspirators, his eyes fall on Caesar's dead body; and in these lines he feelingly refers to him.

He points to the place where the dead body lies. He says that in this place Caesar was surrounded and killed by his enemies. He was killed just as a deer is brought to bay by hounds and ultimately killed. The murderers now stand with the stain of the victim's blood upon their hands and cloaks. They are marked with the blood which they have robbed of Caesar and are crimsoned with his death. Antony continues the metaphor. He says that the whole civilized world was a forest to Caesar. Just as a deer roams at large in a forest, so Caesar roamed at large through the world. He then puns on the word 'hart' applied to Caesar. Antony says that Caesar was also the 'heart of the world', that is the source and centre of the world's vitality.

This pun intensifies the meaning or mood of the play. The mind and the ear sort out heart-deer and heart-dear and, in the hearer's emotion, both concepts, the noble, hunted creature and the beloved one, overlay each other so as to emphasise the mourning love which Antony would convey.

(65) How many ages......unknown (Lines 113-115)

These lines have been taken from Shakespeare's *Julius Caesar.* In these lines Cassius congratulates his fellow conspirators because they have brought freedom to the Roman people by killing Julius Caesar.

Julius Caesar has been murdered by the conspirators who are now planning how to justify this act to the people in a convincing manner. First they express their happiness. Cassius says that this act of patriotism (killing Caesar) will be acted on the scenes at many places in many languages.

Shakespeare seems to have had in mind Julius Caesar of history. He believes that as the incident of heroic deed of Caesar's murder is imitated in his own days, so this will.

(66) And Caesar's spirit.....for burial (Lines 270-273)

These lines have been spoken by Antony in his soliloquy. Brutus allows Antony to carry over the dead body of Julius Caesar to the platform and speak from there. After that Brutus and Cassius leave, Antony lets loose his true thoughts. His real thoughts are all bloody. This is where he uses the elocution, "meek and gentle with these butchers". Showing here a quite different attitude than he had last shown them in person. In graphic imagery he prophesies the revenge and destruction in Rome.

These lines quoted for explanation contain the last part of the terrible prophecy that Antony makes over the dead body of Julius Caesar. The spirit of Caesar, which is thirsting for revenge, will come out of the world of the dead. It will be accompanied by Ate, the goddess of mischief, who will come straight from hell. Both will wander about all parts of Rome in search for revenge. Antony imagines Caesar as a monarch even though he is dead. The spirit of Caesar, like a monarch, will shout the war-cry of destruction. In military operations of old times, 'havoc' was the word used by the generals, by which declarations were made that no quarter should be given. The 'cry' means 'kill and spare none'. And the spirit of Caesar will set free the leash of the war-famine, slaughter and fire the stench of the foul murder of Caesar shall rise from the bodies of men rotting above the ground and pollute the whole earth. The people will curse the murderers of Caesar when the dead bodies will not be given burial and will rot in the streets of Rome.

The metaphor 'let slip the dogs of war' is from coursing. Hounds are kept back by a leash until the hare has had a fair start, and then are allowed to slip out of the leash. It should also be noted that burial was not customary with the Romans of Caesar's time. While writing 'burial', Shakespeare had in mind the Christian custom, of his own country.

Act III — Scene II

(67) Not that I loved Caesar......I loved more (Lines 22-23)

These lines have been taken from *Julius Caesar* written by Shakespeare. In these lines Brutus explains why he has killed Julius Caesar.

Brutus is explaining to the mob in his Forum speech why he has taken the decision of murdering Caesar. He says that he loved his friend Caesar and his country Rome. But when he saw his friend getting ambitious which would be fatal to the freedom of his country, he decided to kill his friend. He felt excessive pain when he killed Caesar. But he could not help it. He had to sacrifice his friend on the altar of his motherland.

This speech shows that Brutus is too much of an idealist. His arguments can never convince the general mass. Brutus does not know this fact. Very soon the impression which his speech has made on the audience fades away.

(68) The evil that men do......let it be with Caesar (Lines 80-82)

These lines have been taken from *Julius Caesar* written by Shakespeare. In these lines Antony is trying to create an opportunity to praise Julius Caesar.

Brutus has already delivered his speech explaining the reason why he and his friends have killed Caesar. The people of Rome are almost convinced that Caesar's murder is justified. Antony, a great friend of Caesar, is granted a chance to deliver his funeral speech. In fact, he wants to incite the people against the conspirators. So he very cleverly tells the people of an unfortunate fact that a man's qualities are forgotten soon after his death. Only his faults are remembered. Antony ironically says that he does not want any exception to this custom in the case of Caesar. So Caesar's virtues which may be mentioned in the speech which he is going to deliver, may be buried with his dead body. Antony wants to show that he is going to give a burial also to Caesar's virtues as it were.

These words spoken by Antony are very carefully worded. Antony is very practical and wants to get his immediate purpose served.

(69) O Judgment......come back to me (Lines 109-112)

These lines have been taken from *Julius Caesar* written by William Shakespeare. In these lines we find that Antony, while delivering his funeral speech on the death of Caesar, becomes overwhelmed with excessive emotion of grief and makes a sudden, short and impassioned address by judgment.

Antony has mentioned and described the personal virtues of Caesar to the people of Rome and has noticed a favourable change in their minds. Antony, therefore, wants to know why the Roman people are hesitating to show due honour to the dead body of Caesar whom they loved so much when he was alive. He addresses judgment and says that men are no longer reasonable. They have lost their power of judgment and reason has escaped to the animal world.

We find here that Antony is very clever and possesses a remarkable skill in the art of oratory. He knows when he should pause, and when he should express his overwhelming emotions. That is why, surely, Antony's funeral speech has had a greater and deeper effect on the mind of the Roman people than of Brutus.

(70) But yesterday......such an honourable man (Lines 123-132)

These lines have been taken from *Julius Caesar* written by Shakespeare. In these lines we find Antony indirectly inciting the people of Rome against Brutus, Cassius and other conspirators.

Antony, during his funeral speech on the death of Julius Caesar has mentioned some of the virtues of Caesar's character. He has noticed that his speech has had a favourable impression on the mind of the audience. He wants the people of Rome to show due respect to the dead body of Julius Caesar and also to rise against the conspirators. He reminds the people that before his death Caesar commanded respect from the Roman people. He was mighty enough to stand even against the combined strength of the entire Roman Republic. But after death, his dead body is lying to which no Roman is modest and lowly enough to pay respect. Then he raises his voice and says that he can easily instigate the people of Rome to start mutiny against the conspirators. But he does not want to do so. Inciting the people against the murderers would be doing wrong to honourable men. Antony ironically says that he does not like to wrong the honourable men, like Brutus and Cassius. He will rather wrong the people of Rome, the dead body of Caesar, Rome and himself. Antony, in fact, means that the conspirators are not honourable and they should be punished.

This speech of Antony shows that he is a clever orator. He reads the mind of the people, and knows how to tackle them. He gets success in moulding the citizens more than Brutus because of his oratory.

(71) And they would go.....unto their issue (Lines 137-142)

These lines have been taken form *Julius Caesar* written by Shakespeare. In these lines Antony is trying to excite the curiosity of the Roman people about Caesar's will.

Antony has mentioned some of Caesar's qualities and hearing his speech the people are almost convinced that Caesar was not all ambitious. Sure of this he wants to work the people upto the maximum pitch of excitement. He, therefore, mentions the will, but does not read it at once. He cleverly says that if he reads Caesar's will the people will come to know how much Caesar loved the Roman people. The people of Rome will be mad and so much full of gratitude to Caesar that they will kiss the wound of dead Caesar and soak their handkerchiefs in his sacred blood. They will request for Caesar's hair to preserve it as a mark of memory of rare genius and they will ask their children to preserve it after their deaths.

In this way Antony is working up the curiosity of the Roman people to work them into a frenzy. Antony is a very clever orator and very skilfully he is trying to incite the people of Rome against the conspirators who have wrongfully done Caesar to death.

(72) You are not wood......come out of it (Lines 147-151)

These lines have been taken from *Julius Caesar* written by William Shakespeare. In these lines Antony tells the Roman people how Caesar loved them.

While speaking about the virtues in Caesar's character, Antony refers to the will of Caesar. Antony says that the very will of Caesar is ample proof of the Caesar's love for the people of Rome. Antony is, in fact, interested not so much in reading out Caesar's will to the Roman people as in inciting the Roman people against the conspirators. In order to raise their curiosity to the highest pitch Antony says he had better not read Caesar's will. After all, the Roman people are not made of hard stuff such as wood and stone. They are human beings and capable of feelings and emotions. If they know the contents of Caesar's will, their hearts will be inflamed by the passion of anger and revenge and they will go mad. Hearing this, the people of Rome become more curious about the will, and force Antony into reading it.

In these lines we see how clever Antony is. He feels the very pulse of Roman people. He knows very well that to an ordinary citizen wealth is more important than an abstract ideal. He forces the common citizens to force him to read the will. Antony wants to put emphasis on the fact that Caesar has made in his will the Roman people his legal heirs. This will serve Antony two purposes — first, he will convince the audience that Caesar was not ambitious and knowing that Caesar has left wealth for them, the Roman people will be full of love and gratitude for Caesar. Then they will take revenge upon the murderers.

We see here Antony's marvellous device of rhetoric. While pretending to hide something from the people he lets them know everything about this which he actually wants to do.

(73) Ingratitude.......Caesar fell (Lines 189-193)

These lines have been taken from *Julius Caesar* written by William

Shakespeare. In these lines Antony paints the picture of the conspirators' brutal deed and great Caesar's fall.

Antony knows that of all the conspirators Brutus is the only man who commands some respect from the people of Rome. So he must shake the citizens' faith in Brutus in order to get his purpose served. Therefore, during his funeral speech he emphasizes the point that it is Brutus's ingratitude which has proved more fatal to Caesar than the traitors' daggers. Caesar at first tried to defend himself when the conspirators attacked him. But when he saw Brutus with dagger in hand coming to stab him he pulled up the mantle over him and surrendered himself completely to the mercy of the traitors' daggers. Consequently he fell down at the foot of Pompey's statue, and the place was covered with a pool of blood flowing from the wounds of Caesar.

These words show that Antony wants the Roman people to take revenge upon the conspirators. He very cleverly expresses his emotions in these lines.

(74) But were I Brutus......rise and mutiny (Lines 230-234)

These lines have been taken from *Julius Caesar* written by William Shakespeare. In these lines Antony makes a theatrical outburst to incite the Roman people against the murderers of Caesar to the highest degree. Antony has spoken of Caesar's greatness and his love for the Roman people. He has noticed that he has been able to lead the people to verge of frenzy. He now wants to give a final touch. He says that he is not an orator like Brutus nor does he possess Brutus's wit and intelligence. Had he Brutus's power of oratory he would have been a different Antony, to stir up the people of Rome to mutiny. He would then also make every word of Caesar eloquent, crying for rebellion and revenge. Then even the stones of Rome would rise in rebellion for revenge for the injustice meted out to Caesar.

Here Antony seems to be a real orator. He possesses more efficiency than Brutus. He has been successful in rousing the people against the conspirators.

Act IV — Scene I

(75) This is a slight.......to share it? (Lines 12-15)

These lines have been taken from *Julius Caesar* written by William Shakespeare. Here we have Antony's estimate of Lepidus. Lepidus has sided with Antony and Octaviaus. But Antony wants to use him only as a tool. He does not want to give him the benefit of destroying the conspirators. Antony seems to be very cunning and deceitful. He tells Octavius that Lepidus is an insignificant fellow without possessing any merit and ability. He is fit to be utilized for carrying messages and nothing else. He thinks it ridiculous to give one-third of the Roman empire to such a worthless man.

Here we come across some of the blemishes of Antony's character. He is very clever, greedy and deceitful. Therefore, he makes a very uncharitable estimate of Lepidus.

(76) He shall bear them.....in commons (Lines 21-27)

These lines have been taken from *Julius Caesar* written by William Shakespeare. These words are spoken by Antony about Lepidus, during an important talk between Antony and Octavius.

Antony has a very low opinion about the worth and ability of Lepidus. Octavius expresses his wonder why after all, Antony has included the names proposed by Lepidus in the list of persons to be killed. Antony then compares Lepidus with an ass. He thinks that Lepidus is no better than an ass. They are placing honours on his shoulders in the same way they put burden on the shoulder of an ass. An ass bears the burden of gold to man's destination. But it does not enjoy the wealth. In the same way Lepidus will be used only to carry out the plans made by Octavius and Antony. He will be used as a tool and will not enjoy and benefit.

Antony's comparison of Lepidus to an ass throws light on the weaker side of Antony's character. He has great love for Caesar; but that love seems to spring from his personal interest. He seems to be devoid of any ideal principle. Therefore, he wants that Lepidus should not be allowed to enjoy any part of their combined action.

Act IV — Scene II

(77) When love begins.....sink in the trial (Lines 20-27)

These lines have been taken from *Julius Caesar* written by William Shakespeare. These lines reveal Cassius's real character. He is cunning and selfish and has displeased even Brutus.

Brutus learns from Lucilius that Cassius's reception of him was full of formalities. Then he makes this observation.

He says that when there is absence of real love between friends, their behaviour is artificial and full of ceremony. True love is plain and simple and docs not require show and artificial manners. He says that insincere men are like horses that show great spirit when kept under control. But in real test they fail to prove their worth. Cassius is a man of that type. Now Brutus badly needs his help, but Cassius does not show his generous spirit, which was once present in him.

Idealist Brutus has now come to realize a little of Cassius's real nature. But yet he will go on making the same old mistake of relying too much upon him. Shakespeare has used a metaphor taken from horsemanship which is common in Shakespeare's poetry.

(78) He must be.....as a property (Lines 35-40)

These lines occur in Act IV, Scene I in William Shakespeare's play *Julius Caesar*. These lines contain the uncharitable estimate in which Lepidus is held by Antony. He is to be treated like a horse.

This man has no ideas of his own, no originality. So he must be properly guided. He can do nothing of his own initiative and is to be guided by the masterful Antony and Octavius. He is a base man, incapable of devising anything by himself. He feeds his understanding with curiosities, artifices and imitations — things which become part of his mental stock only when they have been worn out and made cheap by other men. Antony amplifies the epithet "barren-spirited" by saying that Lepidus's ideas are all second-hand and out of date. Antony cannot think of Lepidus without thinking of the fact that he is merely a tool. He has no creative energy in him.

Antony is unkindly towards Lepidus. His proposal to treat Lepidus as a property, only to share the odium of their work and not its rewards, shows his uncharitable nature.

Act IV — Scene III

(79) Remember March......Not for justice? (Lines 17-21)

These lines have been taken from *Julius Caesar* written by William Shakespeare. We see here that Brutus and Cassius have started finding faults with each other. In these lines Brutus justified his comment on Cassius's taking bribe.

Brutus judges man and the world by his own standard. He reminds Cassius of Ides of March, the day they killed Julius Caesar, the greatest man of Rome. He tells Cassius that they killed Caesar only for the sake of justice. None of the conspirators touched his body for his personal cause, because that would have been mean. Julius Caesar supported robbers and greedy men and so he was killed. Brutus wonders how the supporters of justice, who sacrificed such a great man, can be corrupt themselves.

These lines show that difference has cropped up between Brutus and Cassius. We get here an another opportunity to distinguish between the characters of Cassius and Brutus. Cassius seems to be very much worldly, selfish and bereft of any moral principle whereas Brutus is guided completely by his moral principle and lacks practical sense.

(80) I had rather be a dog.....such a Roman (Lines 26-28)

These lines have been taken from *Julius Caesar* written by William Shakespeare. Brutus talks about his moral principles in these lines.

Brutus has come to know that Cassius has taken bribe. Brutus does not like this. He reminds Cassius that they have killed Caesar because he (Caesar) sheltered robbers and greedy people. Therefore it is not proper for an honourable Roman to take bribe. Brutus thinks that he prefers to be a dog who barks at the moon, but he will never be an unscrupulous and greedy Roman. It is clear here that Brutus indirectly says that even a dog is better than Cassius who has taken bribe.

Brutus sticks to his noble principle even in adverse circumstances. But Cassius changes his principles according to time and place. These two opposite characters have met together and the germ of their ruin is dormant in the very combination.

(81) By the gods, you.....waspish (Lines 46-51)

These lines have been taken from *Julius Caesar* written by William Shakespeare. These words are spoken by Brutus when he is in quarrel with Cassius. Brutus has come to know that Cassius has taken bribes which, according to Brutus, is unbecoming of a noble Roman who has murdered Julius Caesar for a noble cause. Moreover Brutus has not received any financial help from Cassius, when in need. He has also received the news of his wife's death. Because of all these reasons, he is in an extremely depressed mood. While talking with choleric Cassius becomes very angry. But he controls his emotions and taunts him. He swears by the name of gods that Cassius will have to swallow his anger in future. His anger will not affect Brutus any longer, however hard and strong it may be. Henceforth whenever Cassius becomes angry and stings like a wasp, Brutus will laugh at him. That is to say, henceforth, Cassius will be only a laughing stock and an object of ridicule to Brutus.

Here we find a great difference between the characters of Cassius and Brutus. Brutus can check his anger but Cassius fails to check it and easily expresses it.

(82) By heaven,.....any indirection (Lines 72-75)

These lines have been taken from William Shakespeare's play *Julius Caesar*. The quarrel between Brutus and Cassius is in the last stage. Brutus says that he had sent a man to Cassius for money but Cassius refused to give money. Brutus says he wanted money because he could not raise money by the vile means adopted by Cassius.

Brutus will rather convert his heart into coins and drop blood in place of a few Roman gold coins. He cannot realise money from people whose hands are hardened by hard toil. He cannot procure money by any dishonesty. If he does so, that money will be worthless to him. He is, therefore, ready to cut open his heart and convert it into gold coins by making circular pieces out of it.

Critics have observed that this lofty rhetorical sentiment expressed by Brutus is inconsistent with what he spoke of himself in lines 19-28. Hunter says : Brutus, though he will not stain his own honour by extorting money from peasants, is perfectly willing to profit by Cassius's "indirection".

(83) Come Antony.....to cast into my teeth (Lines 93-99)

These lines have been taken from *Julius Caesar* written by William Shakespeare. In these lines Cassius expresses his emotions of grief and wants to touch Brutus's heart.

Cassius has taken bribes, and over this issue both Cassius and Brutus have started quarrelling. Idealist Brutus has expressed his anger. Cassius is of choleric temperament. He starts expressing his grief in a theatrical manner thereby trying to touch Brutus's heart. In a fit of excessive emotion he calls Octavius and Antony to come and kill him. He is tired of this world and desires death. He wants that Antony and Octavius should take revenge on Cassius alone. He is now hated by his friend, and brother-in-law, Brutus. Brutus challenges him and waits to keep him under check, as if he were a slave. He thinks himself very unfortunate.

His faults are scrutinized, and written in a note book, taken by heart, and again hurled right in his face. It is better to die than to bear such humiliation.

These words show that Cassius has become very sorry to receive ill-treatment at Brutus's hands. But he is very cunning and seems to be touching Brutus's heart.

(84) Be angry.....in cold again (Lines 107-113)

These lines have been taken from *Julius Caesar* written by William Shakespeare. Brutus has charged Cassius of taking bribes and both Brutus and Cassius are quarrelling over this issue. Suddenly Cassius becomes excessively aggrieved and he expresses his emotions. In his theatrical outbursts he draws out his dagger and offers his heart. Brutus is moved to pity and in these words he consoles Cassius.

Brutus's anger has now disappeared. He says that henceforth he will never cross Cassius. Cassius will have complete freedom to indulge in anger and Brutus will tolerate it. He will take Cassius's anger and insults done to Brutus as a peculiar caprice of Cassius. Brutus here compares himself to a lamb and his anger to the fire of a flint. He says that he (Brutus) will henceforth be as meek as a lamb. A lamb becomes angry and expresses its anger in momentary flashes — that, too, when it is too much irritated. Similarly Brutus's anger will be temporary. When a flint is rubbed again and again it gives out sparks only for a moment and becomes cold immediately. Similarly Brutus will henceforth seldom become angry and when he becomes angry his anger will be cold very soon.

In these lines we find a great difference between Brutus's nature and that of Cassius. Brutus, in fact, should be in worse mood because his wife is dead. But he controls his anger. Cassius is of choleric temperament and becomes angry at a slight provocation.

(85) There is a tide.....now afloat (Lines 217-221)

These lines have been taken from William Shakespeare's play *Julius Caesar*. Brutus is talking with Cassius on the policy of war. Brutus maintains that it would be advisable for them to march to Philippi and meet the enemy there. His reason is that it is the most opportune moment for them to strike.

The course of human action may be compared to tides of sea. Here the figure is of a man the voyager, the sea voyager, who must set sail with the tide or else languish in shallows for ever after. The meaning is that man must seize the opportunity when it presents itself or be content to live in failure ever after, is apparent to the intellect.

The figures of the mariner and the sea voyage give emotional and aesthetic overtones of distance, of the mystery and finality of tides, of the weed-grown shallow waters. This lends a poignance to the meaning, to the feelings of Brutus. This gives the gravity and the seriousness of a prophetic pronouncement.

Act V — Scene I

(86) Antony.....honeyless. (Lines 32-35)

These lines are taken from *Julius Caesar* written by William Shakespeare. Brutus and Antony are now face-to-face. They are engaged in an exchange of hot words, which according to an old fashion, is a prelude to fighting.

Antony has taunted Brutus that he uses good words in his bad strokes. At this Cassius tells Antony that they do not yet know what kind of soldier Antony is and whether he is a good fighter or not. But so far as his words are concerned, surely they are very sweet. It appears that Antony has robbed the bees of Hybla (which is a town in Sicily and famous for honey) and has put it into his speech.

Here Cassius seems to be referring to Antony's art of oratory which turned the mind of the Roman people.

(87) Flatterers......have rul'd. (Lines 45-47)

These lines have been taken from *Julius Caesar* written by William Shakespeare. In these lines Cassius is reminding Brutus of his suggestion to murder Antony at the time of murdering Caesar.

In an exchange of hot words Antony addresses Cassius and Brutus as flatterers. Antony says that these persons, even at the time of murdering Caesar, knelt before him and flattered him. Wounded by this statement, Cassius tells Brutus that he had suggested that Antony should also be killed along with Caesar. But Brutus's lofty idealism prevented him. Brutus had argued that time that Antony was no better than Caesar's limb. Cassius says that had his suggestion been accepted, they would not have had to bear such insults. Cassius feels that Antony has really grown dangerous as he had already expected.

These lines show that Cassius can make a correct estimate of man's character while Brutus fails to do so, because of his lofty idealism which guides his actions.

(88) Now you know.....that do presage. (Lines 77-79)

These lines have been taken from *Julius Caesar* written by William Shakespeare. In these lines Cassius expresses his changed attitude to life and to ominous signs.

Previously Cassius was never a believer in supernatural events. He was a staunch follower of Epicurus, according to whom gods are indifferent to the human world. But now the disappointments, failures and change of fortune have made him believe in the omens. He has seen two eagles following them from Sardis to Philippi and this morning he finds crows and ravens, in place of eagles. He fears that these signs mean that they are going to be defeated and destroyed. He tells Messala that there was a time when he believed in Epicurean philosophy. But now he has changed his attitude. And for his change of mind these supernatural events are partly responsible.

Here Cassius seems torn between hopes and fears. He has now lost all his courage and hope.

(89) Their shadows seem.....give up the ghost. (Lines 87-89)

These lines have been taken from *Julius Caesar* written by William Shakespeare. In these lines Cassius tells Messala that changes of fortune, and failures and disappointments have changed him from an Epicurean to a superstitious man. There was a time when he used to ignore bad omens, but now he cannot do so any more.

He has seen a few ravens, crows and kites in place of two eagles which have followed them from Sardis to Philippi. These ominous birds look upon them as if they are dead bodies. The constant flight of these birds produce shadows covering their heads. These signs have filled Cassius's heart with extreme fear.

Here Cassius seems to have lost his faith in Epicurus, and it is evident here that he has grown superstitious these days.

Act V — Scene I

(90) Even by rule.....us below. (Lines 101-107)

These lines contain Brutus's answer to the enquiry of Cassius as to what he should do in the event of defeat in the battle. Brutus says that whatever else he might do, he would not commit suicide. Suicide is inconsistent with his stoic philosophy. When Cato had committed suicide, Brutus had nothing but unreserved condemnation for him. Somehow or other it seems to Brutus a lease and cowardly act to anticipate the natural duration of life for fear of what might happen in future. Brutus, for himself, is determined to await the time of death appointed by the higher powers which govern the destinies of man on earth.

Marcus Cato was the father-in-law of Brutus, sided with Pompey against Caesar and committed suicide at Utica in order to avoid falling into the hands of Caesar. It is a pity that Brutus does not act on this principle but commits suicide in the end. This contradiction is explained by Ritson thus : Brutus is at first inclined to wait patiently for better times, but is roused by the idea of being 'led in triumph' to which he will never submit.

Act V — Scene III

(91) O setting sun......The sun of Rome is set. (Lines 60-63)

These lines have been taken from *Julius Caesar* written by William Shakespeare. In these lines Titinius expresses his emotions when he looks at the dead body of Cassius, lying in a pool of blood. Titinius compares Cassius with the setting sun. It appears that Cassius dies when it is almost evening. Titinius addresses the setting sun and says that when its day is over, it sinks in its red blood. His day is over and in his absence there will be clouds of danger in the sky of Rome.

This passionate statement of Titinius at the death of Cassius reveals that the time has come when the glory of Rome will completely fade away.

(92) Julius Caesar......proper entails. (Lines 94-96)

These lines have been taken from *Julius Caesar* written by William Shakespeare.

Brutus looks at the dead body of Cassius and makes this utterance. He says that though Julius Caesar is dead, his spirit is still powerful. His spirit follows the conspirators and it has turned the weapons of his enemies into their own bodies.

Realization has now come to Brutus that their fight against Caesarism has proved futile. The dead Caesar is still powerful and the conspirators have been paid in their own coins.

Act V — Scene V

(93) His life......was a man. (Lines 68-75)

This is the high tribute paid by Antony to his enemy Brutus. Brutus was the noblest of the Romans that ever lived in the tide of time. He was always actuated by the purest of motives. The other conspirators rose against Caesar and killed him purely out of their jealousy at Caesar's greatness. Brutus was motivated by the consideration of the general good of Rome and pure republican ardour. He was the most gentle man. Besides, his character was a perfect one. In him all the qualities had developed in the exact proportion, none preponderating over others. He was such a perfect specimen of humanity that Nature will be proud of him and declare to the world — "This was a man, the like of whom is not to be found."

The passage throws light on the character of Brutus. It also throws light on the dual personality of Antony. Hunter truly notes : "It is characteristic of Shakespeare's Antony to abandon himself freely to the generous impulse of the moment. His emotional temperament is lightly fired."

QUESTIONS AND ANSWERS

Q. 1. "The opening scene strikes the key-note of the play." Discuss.

or

Attempt a brief critique of the opening scene of *Julius Caesar*.

Ans. *Julius Caesar,* like *Coriolanus,* opens with the scene of a crowd in commotion. It serves the purpose of the prologue in Greek drama. Theatrically, the opening is very effective : its tidal motion, its noise, its harangues and passionate recriminations, its evocation of past pomp, past holidays, past exclamations, all these make for a richly rhetorical beginning. Operatically dominated by the tribunes' emotional questions, it points to conflict broadly conceived : to Caesar *versus* Pompey, to plebeians *versus* patricians, to holiday and triumphs *versus* murder and mourning, to the single leader and the jostling, many-headed crowd. And it points to conflict in the public and political world, the world that is always dominated by the rhetorical question.

"Is this a holiday?" "What, know you not ...?" "Wherefore rejoice?" "Know you not Pompey?" "Have you not made an universal shout?" "And do you now put on your best attire?" The rhetorical question establishes itself immediately as the dominant figure. For it is the question that voices the opinions and feelings of the questioner and does not really expect an answer; that generates emotion and is a form often of incremental repetition; and that tends, ironically, to lead to more and more answers disguised as questions until finally released in rage, in the violent action of 'Go fetch fire. Pluck down benches. Pluck down forms, windows, anything' (III. ii. 275-276).

The question that obsesses the tribunes is the political one. Isn't Pompey also present in Caesar's triumph? How can one rejoice in what is Pompey's loss rather than Caesar's gain. The identical question will be asked by Antony when Caesar has fallen and Brutus and Cassius have culled out their own holiday. In an exhortion manifestly lacking in questions, and therefore in stark contrast to what has by now been established as a rhetorical norm, is Flavius's concluding apostrophe to

Marullus to help him keep Caesar at 'an ordinary pitch/Who else would soar above the view of men/And keep us all in servile fearfulness.' For eventually even the rhetorical question must compel some men to decisions, must compel them to answer to their own hearts.

The rhetorical question, in a subtler way, leads us to the real motive of the drama. The jealousy of the tribunes who reprove the citizens for their ingratitude to Pompey reveals how there were certain forces against Caesar. It is the defunct spirit of republicanism which has been re-incarnated in Brutus. This spirit of republicanism prepares us for the conspiracy which is hatched in the scenes that follow.

Many have remarked the anachronistic thronging of Roman streets with Elizabethan artisans, tradesmen in a sixteenth century holiday mood, idle creatures on a labouring day. But we are struck by the tribune's concern to ascertain the trade of everyone they encounter, the reiterated question being 'what trade?' "This concern for careful differentiation", observes Allen, "of each individual and his trade is belied, however, by the crowd psychology that obviously predominates, by the loss of individual differentiation among the cruel men of Rome. Unlike those in *Romeo and Juliet,* the puns and jests that accompany the replies are not intrinsically significant. They do not point to a comic matrix for the play, the quibbling is never metaphysical." (M.J.B. Allen, "Toys, Prologues and the Great Amiss" in *Shakespearean Tragedy,* p. 14). But this crowd is vulgar and therefore fickles, thoughtless, and easily manipulated by emotional appeals. Cheering Caesar, it has forgotten the once-loved Pompey; bitterly scolded by Marullus, it goes away, emotionally shaken. These qualities foreshadow the part that the plebeian crowd will plav in events which are to come.

Deighton opines, "The opening scene serves not only the stage purpose of leading us to the events that are to follow but that of showing us the character of the common people and the spirit of the age." A great change had come over the spirit of the political life of Rome. Before Caesar had left for Gaul, "Rome had been the ideal sphere of public life, the arena in which the principles were alone allowed to combat, and from which the banishment of personal aims and passions was the first condition of virtues. But in his absence Rome had degenerated; the mob had become the ruling force, and introduced an element of uncertainty into political life; politics had passed from science into gambling. A new order of public men had arisen, of which Cassius and Antony are types;

personal aims, personal temptations and personal risks are now inextricably interwoven with public action.'' This is the picture of Rome that we find in the first scene of the play.

Q. 2. Describe the conspiracy against Julius Caesar. Comment on Brutus's and Cassius's attitude and role in it.

Ans. In giving an estimate of the character of Brutus, John Palmer remarks, ''there is a fundamental lie in his character.'' This 'fundamental lie' is nowhere so glaringly seen as in Brutus's attitude towards conspiracy in the theory and its execution in practice. Brutus's attitude towards conspiracy reveals itself in the soliloquy in which he indulges just before the conspirators make their entrance into his orchard. It runs thus —

> '' O conspiracy
> Sham'st thou to show thy dangerous brow by night,
> When evils are most free? O then, by day
> Where wilt thou find a cavern dark enough
> To mask thy monstrous visage? Seek none, conspiracy;
> Hide it in smiles and affability:
> For if thou path, they native semblance on,
> Not Erebus itself were dim enough
> To hide thee from prevention.''

(II. i. 78-85)

Conspiracy, according to this view, is a dark and monstrous crime, more fitted for the black night than the broad day-light. It is a hellish thing, and the dim Erebus is the proper place for the conspirators. Thus we find that Brutus has nothing but unreserved hatred for conspiracy; but in practice he becomes a member of the darkest conspiracy in human history. Nay, it is a conspiracy directed against the best of his friends and patrons, who has given him no cause to spurn at him. This might seem contradictory but the soliloquy in which he discusses the necessity of the murder of Caesar gives the key to this contradiction in his character. Brutus regards the murder as an act of justice, a thing calculated for the general good. Caesar, as he is no danger to the State, but this elevation to the rank of a king might transform him into a tyrant: hence he should be despatched.

On the other hand, Cassius's attitude is not so much a political but a personal necessity. Cassius knows that 'Caesar doth bear him hard'. That he is a schemer even Caesar guesses, and consequently is afraid of him :

> "Yond Cassius has a lean and hungry look;
> He thinks too much: such men are dangerous."

and he feels that a secret personal jealousy and ambition burns in him,

> "Such men as he be never at heart's ease
> Whiles they behold a greater than themselves,
> And therefore are they very dangerous."

Of all the conspirators, Cassius was the leading light. It is Cassius who first of all felt the importance of having Brutus in their company. He met Brutus on the day of the Lupercalia and by slow, cautious steps worked on his mind. By slow, clever process he succeeded in bringing home to Brutus's mind that all Romans worth the name looked to him for deliverance from the apprehended evil of autocracy. Brutus was made deeply thoughtful; by a sophistical argument he convinced himself of the make-believe that Caesar, though not a tyrant and autocrat yet, would become one if he were crowned king.

Mr. Wilson Knight has finally summed up these two characters as revealed in this scene :

> "Brutus acts wholly upon principle; Cassius partly upon impulse. Brutus acts only when he has reconciled the contemplation of some action to run before and govern his opinions. Brutus is a philosopher; Cassius is a partisan. Brutus, therefore, deliberates and spares; Cassius precipitates and denounces. Brutus is the noble instructor; Cassius the better politician. Shakespeare, in the first great scene between them, brings out these distinctions of character upon which future events mainly depend."

Q. 3 "Why, man, he doth bestride the narrow world like a Colossus." Give the substance of this speech and comment on it.

Or

Summarise the arguments used by Cassius to win over Brutus to his side. What light do they throw on the character of Cassius and Brutus.

Ans. The procession of Julius Caesar passes by the street of Rome. Cassius and Brutus stand alone on the street. Cassius asks Brutus whether he is going on to see the race. Brutus answers that he will not; that he is not fond of sport and, in fact, lacks Antony's enthusiasm for athletics. Brutus politely tries to take his leave so that Cassius will not miss the race. However, Cassius reproaches Brutus for being cold and distant to him, his friend. Brutus claims to be preoccupied with private troubles.

"Conceptions only proper to myself," and he reassures Cassius that their friendship remains intact. Cassius is relieved. He asks a rhetorical question :

"Can you see your face?"

He goes on to regret that Brutus cannot see his praiseworthy qualities. Cassius adds that many people are unhappy about the state of affairs in Rome. They wish that Brutus ought to take a good look at the situation. Brutus asks Cassius, in effect, what dangerous affair is he trying to lead him into by his flattery. Cassius replies that he is not given to flattery or to currying favour. Brutus suddenly hears the shout of the crowd and is startled. He remarks that he fears the people are making Caesar king. Cassius quickly remarks that Brutus does not want to see Caesar made king. Brutus answers frankly that, although he loves Caesar, he does not want to see him king. He further says that what Cassius has to say concerns the "general good," then he will face even the danger of death. He loves honour greater than death.

Cassius responds that "honour" is the subject of his message. He goes on to tell that he would rather not live at all than "to be/In awe" of a mere man like himself. Once Cassius, fully dressed, on a dare from Caesar swam a race with him and, before the race was over, Cassius had to rescue Caesar from drowning in the Tiber's waves. Cassius resents this weakling's present lofty status and he resents even more the need to pay homage to him. He continues with another detail: how weak and shaking Caesar was when ill with fever. He deplores Caesar's position as a giant while other men scurry at the giant's feet. In Cassius's analysis the cause for Caesar's supremacy is "not in our stars," that is, not in fate, but in "ourselves," meaning in the passivity and weakness of will of men like Brutus and Cassius. He adds meaningfully that once there was "another" Brutus (meaning the grand father of his friend) who would as soon have had the devil rule Rome as have a king in Rome.

Brutus entreats Cassius to say no more. He had considered this matter, expects to think more in it and, in good time, will speak his mind about it. Until that time, Cassius should know that Brutus would rather be a villager than a Roman, should the republic go under.

Cassius dwells exactly on the one theme, the public good. Brutus in turn, is frank about his feelings at the prospect of a king over Rome : "I would not, yet I love him well." In these words Brutus reveals the division in his own mind between Caesar as ambitious public figure and Caesar as his personal, well-loved friend and companion. In contrast, Cassius's complaints are on a personal level. Indeed conversation with Brutus reveals Cassius's typical attention to the personal element : for instance, his readiness to interpret Brutus's moodiness as a cooling of their friendship; his specific objections to Caesar the man as king.

Q. 4. Describe the storm scene and comment briefly on its dramatic significance.

Ans. See Act I, Scene III of the Detailed Summary for the description of the storm scene.

The importance of the scene lies in the fact that it puts the audience in the right frame of mind. It prepares the audience for the events to come. The events which follows are as bloody, fiery and dreadful as is the tempest. Stopford Brooke commenting on the scene, remarks : "We have seen how often Shakespeare uses the common belief that nature mixed himself up with those great human events which striking at the chief men, strike humanity. Nay more, he made nature reflect the passions of men when they reached intensity. He writes as if he believed that a spiritual power in nature was in touch with the deep things in man and in his history. We remember the storm which accompanies the murder of Duncan; the fury of the elements which reflects and heightens the agony of King Lear. And here to develop this thought of his and at the same time to dramatise it he represents at length what each of the characters thinks of the storm. The storm is thus a great revealer of the character."

Cicero is the very model of a Stoic philosopher here, reacting with fatalism and impassivity to the phenomena described. These phenomena have in common their extraordinariness, even freakishness: a lion that roams but does not seek prey; a night owl heard in day; fire that does not burn flesh. The mental reaction of Casca to the storm is that he is essentially a timid and superstitious person. He feels much depressed on such a night and is, therefore, reprimanded by Cassius for the dullness of his spirit. Cassius, the bold, intrepid man, goes a step further and reads in the storm a warning of Caesar's end.

Q. 5. Summarise the scene between Caesar and Calpurnia. Add your comment to it.

Ans. See first para in Summary of Act II, Scene II.

Comment : Caesar has shown; in the scene at the Lupercal and here, that he believes in or tolerates the practice of the customs and belief in the superstitions of the Roman people. Yet now, to suit his mood, Caesar, dominant over all, goes against the angry nature which was most strongly feared by the Romans — not being able to find the heart in the sacrificed carcass. Calpurnia, on the other hand, is too tender and docile before her husband. She cannot assert herself as forcefully as Portia. The dictator treats his wife as a child to be humoured or according to his caprice, but Portia assumes that by the right and virtue of her place she is entitled to share her husband's inmost thoughts.

Q. 6. How does Decius Brutus induce Caesar to go out to the Senate House? What light does this part throw on the character of Caesar and Decius Brutus.

Ans. See second para in Summary of Act II, Scene II. Decius Brutus, when the conspirators were debating their acts, had assured them that he would find the means to persuade Caesar to come to the Senate. In this scene he shows himself apt. He equals Biblical Joseph's skill in interpreting dreams : He re-reads the omens to such advantage and favourable intention that Caesar is easily flattered to a reversal of his decisions.

Caesar shows a strong will but also a capriciousness. He shows that he can be persuaded equally for regard for someone (his wife), by flattery, and by his drive for power. In the final stages of this scene Caesar emerges as the dominant Roman figure, a gracious host, one whose word is awaited, a ruler petitioned, a man who knows other men. But sometimes he seems entirely obtuse and this is mainly when he succumbs to flattery. This is the price of his ego.

Q. 7. Describe the scene of the murder of Julius Caesar. Add your brief comment to it.

Ans. See paras one and two in Summary of Act III.

The final moment of Caesar can be looked on in many ways. If it is historically true that Caesar said; Et-tu-Brute! then fall, Caesar''; It can be interpreted in two ways. First, Brutus may have been considered by Caesar a true and loyal friend and thus the ingratitude. Shown by his wielding a dagger too is too much to bear. However, Caesar was no naive person in power politics, he could not have put great store by the politer qualities of people. Moreover, Caesar was not the one to resign himself to failure (death) because, idealistically, his friend has failed him.

Therefore a second interpretation may be that knowing that Brutus was an unrealistic idealist, he thought Brutus's participation in so practical an act quite out of keeping with the man's style.

Q. 8. Compare the speeches of Brutus and Mark Antony and comment on them. (Act III, Scene ii).

Ans. This is the scene in which Brutus is upstaged by Antony, certainly as a player's part, and definitely in point of effectiveness in their historic roles.

Brutus, speaking first as he thought best to do, makes what he thinks will be the definitive statement on the assassination. He gives a reasonable exposition of the motives for the act. He delivers a sober, quiet statement in simple prose, though not without the balanced and periodic sentences characteristic of Roman rhetoric.

He displays his lack of insight into human characters. Forthright and simple, he nevertheless uses a superficial catch-phrase to rally his defence :

> "Not not I loved Caesar less, but
> that I loved Rome more."

He gives a reason ("his ambition") for his part in assassination. Yet he leaves the motive unexplored in depth. The mob understands it even less, they want to make him Caesar instead. He offers his own life in expiation and this wins him temporary acclaim from the mob. He rallies them in temporary enthusiasm for freedom with his rhetorical questions :

> Who is here so base that would be a bondman?
>
> Who is here so rude that would not be a Roman?
>
> Who is here so vile that will not love his country?

Brutus has blundered in the tone of his speech to the crowd. He fails to understand that public opinion is changeable and fickle. Brutus is so unrealistic that he thinks the crowd will deeply and finally accept his motive : "as he was ambitious, I slew him". It is even more telling dramatic irony that Brutus now introduces Antony, exhorting the crowd for Antony's sake :

> "not....man depart,
> Save I alone, till Antony have spoke."

Foolishly, naively, Brutus thinks he has settled the matter.

On the other hand, Antony had evidently stayed to hear out Brutus. He gathers enough statements from his speech to use with devastating sarcasm in his seemingly innocent funeral oration. It is with the key words used by Brutus that Antony sooths, persuades and then arouses the crowd; praise, permission, honourable and ambition. As Brutus has said (Antony meekly begins), he is speaking by Brutus's permission. He is only speaking in praise of Caesar. Brutus is an honourable man. Brutus has said Caesar was ambitious and for this reason he slew him. It is in the variation on these words and phrases, by tone, gesture and reiteration, that Antony wrings sarcasm. This grows more biting as the speech continues, until Antony feels it safe to turn it into open hostility at the end.

The first part of his speech is spoken as by a humble pleader and it is his humble attitude :

"Here, under leave of Brutus and the rest,"

Coupled with a humble reiteration of respect for the one who gave him permission :

"For Brutus is an honourable man,"

This is just the beginning. Antony is slowly building a favourable image of Caesar that will effectively destroy the only motive for the murder : ambition. He stages his first of three dramatic gestures of emotional appeal. Antony sobs with emotion at the picture of the good and great-hearted Caesar. The crowd's attention is on Antony's own grief and thus he has won over a hostile crowd to sympathy. In the second part of the speech, Antony enlarges on the image of Caesar as a benevolent and magnanimous, though powerful, ruler. He tantalizes the crowd with the mention of the will of Caesar. He then exposes the mutilated corpse to the crowd. He shows this to be a personal killing. In clever, mocking sophistry he holds the crowd to him. He feeds them the hate and fury by degrees, as if with a syringe he were controlling the flow of hate and fury into their veins. What he wills them do, he subtly disclaims for himself the power to do :

"For I have neither wit, nor words, nor worth,"

When Brutus was modest, he was being direct and forthright. Antony, however, is devious, sly, really mocking and cleverly opportunistic:

". . . . But were I Brutus,
And Brutus Antony, there were an Antony
Would ruffle up your spirits."

Thus, by his very disclaimers; he achieves what he falsely claims he cannot.

Antony thus sets in motion by a bit of calculated demagoguery, expressed in stirring verse, and delineated with cleverness, sophistry; sarcasm, cynicism and knowledge of mob psychology, the fury which will bring about his prophecy made earlier over Caesar's body :

> "A curse shall light upon the limbs of men;
> Domestic fury and fierce civil strife
> Shall cumber all the parts of Italy."

Thus the speeches of Brutus and Antony form one of the most complete contrasts in Shakespeare.

Q. 9. Describe the death of Brutus. Consider Antony's summing up of his character : "This was the noblest Roman of them all."

Ans. Brutus and a group of friends come in. As they talk of who is taken or slain, Brutus, resigned to what will be, says "Slaying is the word" and then in turn approaches each of the friends, whispering to each. From their replies, it is evident that Brutus is asking each to kill him (hold the sword while he runs on it). Each refuses in turn. To Volumnius he says, before he makes his request, that the ghost of Caesar has appeared to him twice already and he knows therefore that his hour has come. On this basis he asks Volumnius to hold the sword for him, but he refuses. Volumnius says that it is not an office for a friend. Then Brutus turns to Strato, who has been asleep all this while, and says farewell to him. He rejoices that all the friends he has made have been true to him. The alarum sounds to fly, the enemy is near and they all exit. Brutus pleads with Strato to stay with him and do the deed which he had asked of the others. Strato agrees and shakes his hand first as they say farewell. Before he dies, Brutus addresses Caesar's ghost :

> "Caesar, now be still.
> I kill'd not thee with half so good a will."
> He kills himself on the sword Strato holds for him.

Antony's tribute to Brutus as the "noblest Roman of them all" does justice to himself as well as to Brutus. It is in well-rounded phrases, high sounding and in the vein in which Brutus himself spoke both of his own noble and trusting nature and of others about him. Gone is the viperish rancour with which Antony had thrown accusations at Brutus as a murderer. Now he sees Brutus's motives as loftier than those of the other conspirators.

Secondly, in the words of Schanzer, "It would seem that as in Hamlet Shakespeare wished to represent the Renaissance ideal of the encyclopaedic man, the 'uomo universale', in Brutus he wished to represent the ideal of the harmonious man, whose gentleness, courtesy, and love of music all bear witness to his 'well-tempered' nature. It is to this quality in him that Antony pays his final tribute :

> "His life was gentle; and the elements
> So mix'd in him that Nature might stand up,
> And say to all the world 'This was a man'."

Q. 10. "The character of Cassius serves as a foil to that of Brutus". Discuss.

Or

Contrast the characters of Brutus and Cassius.

Or

"Cassius is evidently intended to bring out the main features of the character of Brutus more distinctly by contrast" (Macmillan). Discuss.

Ans. One can see a parallel, limited to the extent to which the pairs of personalities differ, in Brutus's and Cassius's relationship with that of Don Quixote and Sancho Panza. One instance will define the parallel. The imagination of Don Quixote is inflamed with the chivalric code of righting wrong. He hurls his defiance and himself upon the wind-mills. He thinks them to be the enemy dragon. He must rescue the honour of womanhood and the courage of manhood from them. Sancho pleads with him that these are but wooden blades of a wind-mill. Yet he rushes on full tilt. Sancho covers his eyes from the rude shock his master will get. Thus, when Brutus says he puts honour and trust above all else and declares this to be his code of living, Cassius tells him that honour is the subject of his story. He then goes on to make a bitter lament against Caesar. If Caesar is going to charge head-on against anything, let it not be a harmless mill, honour *per se;* Cassius offers him a real tangible target. He brings Brutus to the reality of Rome and out of the clouds of abstract virtue. But the realistic Cassius is dismayed at the way Brutus plans the conspiracy. For instance, Brutus dismisses Cicero, suggested by Cassius as a candidate for the conspiracy. Later the same Cicero is put to death by the conspirators. Brutus is against the elimination of Antony even though Cassius repeatedly warns him against him. It is Antony who sparks the turning of the populace on the conspirators. It remains till the final confrontation between them. In the parley Brutus again overrides Cassius's plan, which, again, result shows to have been the more realistic. Yet, after they have had their quarrel and reaffirmed friendship, their actions synthesize. Cassius takes the melancholia of guilt and the presage of death from Brutus and when they part, they are increasingly alike in temperament and in feeling. Cassius was formerly Epicurean in his life-attitudes. He has now taken on some of Brutus's Stoic endurance. Brutus was a man of iron reserve. But his quarrel with Cassius and irritability with the poet showed himself capable of emotionality and testiness. They are more significantly alike in that each regards the other as the man most true, most worthwhile in his life. While dying Cassius laments to Brutus :

> "Then, if we lose this battle,
> You are contented to be led in triumph
> Through the streets of Rome."

Brutus, ready to die, is satisfied at least that Cassius (among others) has not betrayed him. Finally, as each dies, the retribution of Caesar upon him is similar, for Caesar's justified vengeance is the last concern of each.

Thus the hard-core realist and the idealist, thought apart, have synthesized as a pair in their philosophy of life and in the searching examination of their own guilt. Gervinus, a critic, opines : "Brutus appears throughout just as humanly noble as Cassius is politically superior, each lacks what is best in the other, and the possession of which would make each perfect."

Q. 11. Compare and contrast Brutus and Antony.

Or

"Brutus is contrasted not only with his friend Cassius but also with his enemy Antony" (Macmillan).

Or

"As a politician Antony is wise and Brutus is a fool. As a man Brutus is noble and Antony ignoble and yet not quite ignoble" (S. Brooke). Bring out clearly the contrast implied in the line.

Ans. The character of Antony is designedly in contrast with that of Brutus. The main point of contrast is very plain. Antony is a dissolute sensualist, while Brutus is an austere moralist. Brutus is narrow-minded. Antony appreciates every kind of beauty, even the beauty of virtue to which he makes no pretence. Brutus, therefore, wrongly supposes that Antony being a lover of sports and pleasure is a person who need not be seriously considered as a possible adversary. On the other hand, Antony rightly appreciates the nobility of Brutus's character.

The contrast between his political skill and the simplicity of Brutus is brought out most plainly in the Forum speeches of the two men.

Consult question No. 10 for the rest of the question.

Q. 12. Examine the twin themes of Caesarism and Republicanism with reference to their existence in *Julius Caesar*.

Ans. The plot for the assassination has ostensibly been formed against tyranny. Cassius starts the train of thought.

> "There was a Brutus once that would have brook'd
> Th'eternal devil to keep his state in Rome
> As easily as a king." (Act I, Scene II).

Brutus then indirectly assents to the implied suggestion here. He announces that Brutus would prefer to become a villager than to remain under Caesar's tyranny. Cassius speaking of his readiness to kill himself, says that by suicide he will shake off "tyranny". Their cry after the assassination is :

"Liberty ! Freedom ! Tyranny is dead !"

Cassius sees the conspirators enshrined through the ages:

> "So oft as that shall be,
> So often shall the knot of us be call'd."

The men that gave their country liberty. In Brutus's speech after the assassination the freedom issue is again vaunted. Brutus exhorts the Roman mob to breathe the new air of freedom released for them. Let us examine the meaning of Caesarism.

The first to sound the note of dissatisfaction with Caesarism was the tribune Flavius. Caesar according to him, was a falcon soaring high up in the sky. It was better his feathers were plucked. Antony is the next one to give us a view of it as a thing that exists :

When Caesar says, "Do this", it is perform'd. Cassius's bitter complaint is about Caesarism. One of his less sarcastic statements of it would indicate that one-man absolute rule is what is meant here :

> "When went there by an age, since the great flood,
> But it was fam'd with more than with one man?" (Act I, Scene II)

He further defines it in persuading Casca to the cause. Brutus has nothing to say against Caesar personally, but one possibility he takes exception to :

> "Crown him? — that; —
> And then, I grant, we put a sting in him
> That at his will he may do danger with."

It would seem that the "Kingship" poses the biggest threat of Caesarism. Previously Casca and Cassius has scouted this threat in Act I, Scene III.

The meaning seems to be that this kingship would hand over to Caesar ultimate tyrannous power, absolute power, though its not having validity in Italy. Yet Brutus thought Caesar dangerous not before, but should he get the crown. It is Caesarism that is being struck at. Caesar himself never questions his own authority but frequently speaks of his invulnerability. It is only once or twice that he shows himself that he is absolute.

> "The cause is in my will : I will not come;
> That is enough to satisfy the senate."
>
> (Act II, Scene ii)

Here is the issue of Caesarism and the cry opposed to it, as Cassius urges the conspirators at the assassination. The last word on deliverance from bondage comes from Brutus from his speech defending the assassination of Caesar. The people seem to make no fine distinctions between freedom and bondage. After the speech of Brutus, the cry was,

> "Let him be Caesar."

It would seem that the meaning of the play is that Caesarism is a threat to the freedom of men and the conspirators have acted as liberators of Rome. The distinction of added power and danger through kingship as opposed to Caesarism remains unexplained.

Shakespeare wrote at a time when Elizabeth ruled as a determined monarch subjecting Parliament to her will, aided by Star Chamber proceedings which hunted treason and tracked it down ruthlessly. It is unlikely that Shakespeare would be so impolitic as to write a play against monarchy or kingship; the monarch herself patronized the Player's company. Nor did Shakespeare write plays as tracts against either Government or any one of the evil practices of man.

Furthermore, we return now to the question of tyranny and the republicanism for which the assassination struck a blow. This idea disappears after the assassination. When Brutus and Cassius confront Antony and Octavius, they quarrel with them peevishly but neither says anything about having struck a righteous blow for freedom. They make no attempt to talk over the other to their thinking. Instead, the whole conflict becomes a personal one with Brutus and Cassius. Both are beset by presages of oncoming doom and death; and when they die, both give credit for their deaths to the vengeance of Caesar's spirit. There is no declaration by either as they die that they have set the cause of freedom in motion and could be satisfied for the cause. Brutus declares some vague generalization on this issue :

> "I shall have glory by this losing day
> More than Octavius and Mark Antony
> By this vile conques shall attain unto."

(Act V, Scene V)

So we see the meaning of Caesarism *versus* republicanism is never resolved for us, but the existence of the two have been defined in the play.

Q. 13. Why is this play called *Julius Caesar,* when Caesar dies in the third act and Brutus has such a consistent place in the drama from the first act to the fifth?

Ans. It is a paradox that this drama, so limpid in style, so symmetrical in plot, and so clear-cut in portraiture, should yet prove puzzle to us. Allusions elsewhere to the great dictator as 'mightiest Julius' and 'broadfronted Caesar' prove that Shakespeare did not underestimate the man. Yet when we open the drama, of which he is the titular hero, we find that he appears in only three scenes, and that he is killed before the play is half over. The plot covers almost three years, from February, 44 B. C., to the battle of Philippi in the later part of 42 B.C., but during only the first month of this period was Caesar alive. Moreover, on the few occasions when he does appear, he is shown in an unfavourable or, at least, an equivocal light.

We see him first on the way to the festival of the Lupercalia. We also see him superstitiously bidding Antony touch Calpurnia in his holy chase as a cure for barrenness. Yet he is arrogantly indifferent to auguries of ill concerning himself. He dismisses as a dreamer the soothsayer, who bids him 'beware the Ides of March.' His speech has the imperious tone of a Sultan, whose lightest word is law. He constantly talks of himself in the third person, as Caesar, 'as of some power above and behind his consciousness ! He is already, it is clear, an uncrowned king. Antony offers him Crown at the Lupercalia, which he reluctantly puts by from fear of popular indignation. According to Casca's mocking account of the episode he could not endure the foul breath of the hooting rabblement, but fell down in the market-place and foamed at mouth. Nor is this falling-sickness his only infirmity. He is deaf of one ear – a serious handicap for a leader of men. He had never the wiry endurance of Cassius. Alarmed by Calpurnia's bad dreams, he has sent to consult the augurs, but without waiting for their report he declares he will go forth. When the answer is unfavourable, he still refuses to be kept at home.

> "No. Caesar shall not. Danger knows full well
> That Caesar is more dangerous than he."

Yet he yields a moment afterwards to Calpurnia's entreaties, and thinks of asking Antony to tell the Senators that he is not well. Yet he changes his mind when Decius re-interprets the dream in his favour. Such vacillation is a ridiculous prelude to the attitude of inflexibility that he adopts at the Capitol. There is a touch of the sublime in his declaration, 'what touches us ourself shall be last serv'd'. But it is the very intoxication of absolutism that claims to be 'constant as the Northern star', or as immovable as Olympus. Finally, the death-blows of the conspirators are a tragically ironical retort to such pretensions of superiority to human weakness.

Are we to conclude that Shakespeare deliberately intended to turn Caesar into a laughing stock for the benefit of the groundlings in the Globe, or that he had radically misconceived his true character? Is Boswell right when he says. 'There cannot be a stronger proof of Shakespeare's deficiency in classical knowledge than the boastful language he has put in the mouth of the most accomplished man of all antiquity, who was not more admirable for his achievements than for the dignified simplicity with which he has recorded them?'

Certainly in Elizabethan times the legendary Caesar dominated people's thoughts as a figure of imposing greatness. There were a number of plays about Caesar and many books, some in translation, appeared on the power and rule of princes. Further, in Elizabethan times, the figure of Caesar as seen in this play would be realised as that of a tragic hero : a great "prince". He was the focus of power, the single figure who represented the might and glory of the state to the populace. Shakespeare, therefore, did also realise Caesar's greatness. The fact is that Caesar is the hero of the play, but not the Caesar whom we see passing across the stage, weak in bodily presence and his will. Whatever his personal limitations, he is a transcendent power in the world, because he focuses in himself the inevitable tendencies of his age.

This is illustrated in the opening scene. The populace is, in fact, weary of a liberty that means nothing to it, and what it wants is an idol — crowned or uncrowned — whom it may worship. It is this need that Caesar satisfies, and while it exists, he is strong with a strength that death multiplies a hundred-fold. The conspirators strike down the man Julius, but they cannot kill 'Caesar'. The 'Spirit of Caesar' survives and the latter half of the play is the exhibition of its complete triumph. The infirmities of the dictator in the flesh are merely the foil to his irresistible might when set free from physical trammels. His picture, as conqueror or statesman, leaves the awe-inspiring spectacle of his spirit, a silent, impalpable force, scattering destruction among his enemies. Before Brutus dies, he admits :

> "O Julius Caesar, thou art mighty yet !
> Thy spirit walks abroad, and turns our swords
> In our own proper entrails."

"Hence, to quarrel with the poet for not entitling the play *Brutus* would be ridiculous in the extreme" (Stanley Wood).

Q. 14. Discuss the appropriateness of the title of *Julius Caesar.*

Ans. See Answer to Question 13.

Q. 15. It has been remarked that the play of *Julius Caesar* has wrongly named and should have been called *Brutus.* Does this objection seem reasonable?

Ans. See Answer to Question 13.

Q. 16. Who is the hero of the play — Caesar or Brutus? Fully discuss the problem.

Or

"Caesar is not the hero of the play (*Julius Caesar*) but Brutus." Discuss.

Ans. See Answer to Question 13.

Q. 17. "The play is a political play and of a kind different from that of any other in his works." Elucidate this remark.

Ans. See Part B.

Q. 18. What were the motives behind the conspiracy against Caesar? Discuss.

Ans. See Answer to Question 12.

Q. 19. 'O Julius Caesar, thou art mighty yet !
Thy spirit walks abroad, and turns our swords
In our own proper entrails.''

Can this be accepted as the key-note of *Julius Caesar*?

Ans. These words of Brutus uttered on the death of Cassius may rightly be taken as striking the key-note of the drama. Add answer to Question 13.

Q. 20. What is meant by 'Dramatic Irony'? Discuss the presence of dramatic irony in ''Julius Caesar''.

Ans. Dramatic Irony is that kind of irony in which the language used by a dramatic character has one meaning for the audience who are in the know of things and another meaning for the persons addressed. This duality of significance is the soul of dramatic irony. It represents a character moving towards a catastrophe of which he is unaware, but the spectators who are in the secret of things are fully aware. Thus when a man on the point of being murdered talks of securing a triumph very soon, while his approaching doom is manifest to the audience and to some characters as well, we get an instance of dramatic irony. Dramatic irony is a special contribution of Greek tragedy. Instances of dramatic irony are abundantly found in *Julius Caesar*. One glaring example of this irony is in Act III, Scene I : ''We have Caesar most blown with arrogance and goading it in the loftiest style when the daggers of the assassin are on the very point of leaping at him.'' He compares himself to the pole star of which there is no fellow in the firmament, and in answer to this come the blows of the conspirators. When he bids the would-be murderer–'Be near me, that I may remember you', it produces a shock in the mind of the audience and later events show how the words of the dictator turn out true in an ironical sense.

The whole of *Julius Caesar* is pervaded by a spirit of irony. We find Brutus most confident in those very things in which he is most in the wrong or acting like a man ''most ignorant of what he is most assured''; as when he says that ''Antony can do no more than Caesar's arm when Caesar's head is off.'' This, to be sure, is not meant ironically by him but it is turned into irony by the fact that it was Antony who became the chief instrument in the downfall of the conspirators by means of his eloquent oration. Another instance of irony occurs just after the murder when the conspirators are exulting over their work and thinking of future stage celebrity —

> "So often shall the knot of us be call'd
> The men that gave their country liberty."

Yet it is here that they were wrong and the subsequent development shows that the cause of the conspirators was fore-doomed. When Brutus says of Antony, "I know that we shall have him well to friend", how sadly was he mistaken ! The crowning example of this irony occurs in a subtle and refined form when the idealist Brutus "overtops and outshines the greatest political genius that the world ever saw." The central idea, the moving purpose of the work, is a piece of dramatic irony in itself.

Q. 21. What is meant by Nemesis? Show how it is fully in operation in the play.

Ans. Broadly speaking, Nemesis is "retribution as it appears in the world of art." The ancient Greek conception of Nemesis is broader than the modern conception. The Greeks believed Nemesis to be a companion goddess to Fate, and as Fate went through the world distributing the good things of life without regard to merit or desert, so Nemesis followed in her steps and without regard to merit delighted in cutting down the prosperity of man. The modern conception of Nemesis places sin in close link with punishment. "Whatever a man soweth that he shall also reap" — this is the principle of Nemesis that is most potent in modern drama.

In *Julius Caesar* we find Nemesis in full operation. Caesar himself reaps the full consequence of his action. He had defeated his rival Pompey and his two sons, and by uprooting the old order of things wanted to establish something like a personal monarchy. He had trampled liberty under foot and wanted to enslave the Romans. His own action rebounds on his head and he is struck down by the conspirators. Immediately before his murder, Shakespeare seems to take special care to underline his arrogant self-confidence, his insulting high-handedness and his vanity as an infallible being. He says that he is afraid of no danger; — danger knows he is more dangerous. He boasts that he is fixed as the Northern star; he arrogantly bursts out to his suppliant and offers to kick him out as a fawning spaniel. It seems that Shakespeare made use of the old Greek belief — 'whom the gods will kill, they first make mad'. *Julius Caesar* is presented as if he were power-mad, and immediately after comes the first stab of the conspirators — the plunging dagger of Casca. Dover Wilson excellently sums up the action of Nemesis in Julius Caesar in these words : 'Shakespeare was following both established dramatic tradition and the historical scholarship of his age when he gave his Caesar that strut, that habit of self-deification which annoys many modern readers'. We may also agree with Kittredge that at the end of his career Caesar 'has become the victim of infatuation and lost that sense of values which alone could maintain him in equilibrium', and that 'Shakespeare legitimately made the most of these to produce the effect of Nemesis'. Caesar in his life-time had become a 'legend' and his blunder at the end of his career was to believe very much in his own 'legend' so as to magnify himself into immortality. There is a full operation of Nemesis in the fact that he falls beside the statue of Pompey whom he had suppressed and through whose fall he had risen to power, and the "statue seems to gleam in complete triumph over the rival who lies bleeding at its feet".

The conspirators too provoke Nemesis by their action. The murder of Caesar was not only a great crime but also a great political blunder. They failed to see that republicanism in Rome was a dead letter and what Rome wanted most was a Caesar. The murder of Caesar is accomplished, and for a time their cause seems to triumph. But the 'spirit of Caesar' rises soon and tears them and their cause all to pieces. They themselves acknowledge their error and fate. Cassius in his death-bed cries out :

> "Caesar, thou art revenged,
> Even with the sword that kill'd thee"
> Brutus too echoes the idea with the words
> "O Julius Caesar, thou art mighty yet !
> Thy spirit walks abroad and turns our swords
> In our own proper entrails."

This fate of the leaders of the conspiracy is a full illustration of the working of Nemesis, that relentless deity in the moral world.